Romans

A Digest of Reformed Comment

Romans

A Digest of Reformed Comment

Romans

A Digest of Reformed Comment

GEOFFREY B. WILSON

MINISTER OF BIRKBY BAPTIST CHURCH
HUDDERSFIELD

THE BANNER OF TRUTH TRUST

THE BANNER OF TRUTH TRUST
3 Murrayfield Road, Edinburgh EH12 6EL
P.O. Box 621, Carlisle, Pennsylvania 17013, USA

★

© Geoffrey B. Wilson 1976
First published 1977
Reprinted 1984
ISBN 0 85151 238 0

★

Printed in Great Britain by
Hazell Watson & Viney Limited,
Member of the BPCC Group,
Aylesbury, Bucks

CONTENTS

CONTENTS

PREFACE

My purpose in this work is to express as concisely as possible the essential message of Romans. In this new edition the text followed is that of the American Standard Version (1901), published by Thomas Nelson Inc., and it is hoped that this, together with the attempt to achieve greater accuracy and simplicity of comment, may increase the book's usefulness.

It is with no sense of formality that I acknowledge my indebtedness to the authors and publishers who have graciously allowed me to quote from their works, and I also wish to record my gratitude to the staff of Dr Williams's Library and New College Library for their courteous assistance.

Huddersfield,   GEOFFREY WILSON
December 1975

INTRODUCTION

Paul's introduction to the Roman Epistle is a consummate blend of authority and tact. Since he was personally unknown to the Christians at Rome he took particular pains to explain his motives in writing to them. It was because he had been hindered from paying them a personal visit that he determined to write this letter. In the wisdom of God, Paul was prevented from going to Rome at the time and in the manner he had planned. The apostle longed to see his fellow-Christians there in order to impart to them 'some spiritual gift', but God had devised something better. Rather than permit Paul to make the desired journey, God inspired him to instruct the Roman Christians in the doctrines of grace by means of this epistle.

Thus the providential frustration of Paul's laudable design led to the permanent enrichment of the whole church of God. This letter has preserved the authoritative and systematic teaching of the apostle to the Gentiles and it still provides the infallible norm by which every presentation of the gospel must be judged. Instead of simply establishing the believers at Rome by oral teaching, a far greater honour was reserved by God for his servant; for every Christian who desires to become firmly grounded in the faith must still sit at the feet of Paul of Tarsus, and receive with all humility that 'gospel of God' which was first committed to him 'by the revelation of Jesus Christ' [Gal 1:12].

CHAPTER ONE

V1: **Paul, a servant of Jesus Christ, called to be an apostle, separated unto the gospel of God,**

Paul, a servant of Jesus Christ, Paul introduces himself to the church at Rome as 'a servant of Jesus Christ'. The word, bond-slave, expresses his complete submission to the lordship of Christ. This relationship is not unique to Paul, but is shared by all true Christians. Therefore he begins by confessing his own interest in the gospel. This shows that there can be no valid exercise of authority where there is no personal experience of Christ's redeeming power. Those who are still the 'servants of sin' cannot work for Christ, however many titles and offices they may temporarily usurp. To all such Christ will say one day, 'I never knew you: depart from me, ye that work iniquity' [*Matt* 7:23]. Rebels must be first subdued by Christ, for only then can they serve him acceptably. The conquest of Christ's grace inevitably precedes Paul's commission for service; compare *Acts* 9:5 with *Acts* 26:16. Further, those who confess 'Jesus is Lord' must also make a credible avowal that they are indeed his servants by their daily obedience to his commandments. Thus, before everything else, Paul is a Christian.

called to be an apostle, Paul now passes to that which distinguishes him from other Christians. He is not only a participant in a common faith, he has been elevated to the apostolate. It is in virtue of that unique authority bestowed upon him by the risen Christ that he addresses the church at Rome.

The word 'apostle' means 'sent one' or 'messenger' but unlike the Twelve Paul had not been a witness of the earthly ministry of the Lord, hence he described himself as 'one born out of due time' [Acts 1:21, 22; 1 Cor 15:8]. And though the former persecutor of God's church was 'the least of the apostles', he admitted no inferiority in regard to the authority of his commission or the scope and effectiveness of his labours [1 Cor 15:9, 10].

The unique function of the apostles as witnesses of the resurrection and as the inspired and authoritative interpreters of the will of the Lord constitutes the sole foundation for all genuine discipleship [1 Cor 3:10, 11; Eph 2:20; Rev 21:14]. Since their office is essentially unrepeatable the only 'apostolic succession' known to the New Testament is continuing fidelity to that sacred deposit of truth which was once for all delivered to the church by them.

By contrast, the defection of Judas supplies impressive proof that an external call is no substitute for regenerating grace [Acts 1:16–26; John 6:70, 71].

separated unto the gospel of God, The immediate and enduring effect of Paul's call to apostleship is his separation to the gospel of God. The once zealous Pharisee (separated one) became totally dedicated to the gospel, when God's eternal purpose reached the beginning of its historical fulfilment on the road to Damascus [Gal 1:15; Phil 3:5, 6; Acts 26:16–18]. This 'good news' proclaimed by Paul is no mere human innovation – it is the gospel of God.

The dominant place that God occupied in Paul's thought and affections is evidenced by the heavenly 'digression' which naturally follows the first mention of the divine name. As God's ambassador he is never happier than when he is speaking of the excellences of his sovereign.

V2: **which he promised afore through his prophets in the holy scriptures,**

The gospel is no novelty, no after-thought on the part of God. Indeed it was foreshadowed in the Old Testament provisions for worship and was 'promised afore through his prophets'. Paul constantly emphasized the fact that the Old Testament revelation reached its supreme climax in the gospel. He was always able to endorse the voice of prophecy without any sense of incongruity. Augustine's celebrated dictum, that the New Testament is concealed in the Old, and that the Old Testament is revealed in the New, well expresses the apostle's thought here.

As antiquity is in itself no guarantee of reliability, this prophetic testimony has been preserved without error 'in the holy scriptures'. Christ himself declared that the 'scripture cannot be broken' [*John* 10:35], and his apostles held to the same exalted conception of the Old Testament. The scriptures are described as 'holy' because they must be received and reverenced for what they are, God's august self-disclosure to sinful man. The prevalent modern view of 'limited inspiration' is recklessly put forward despite the apostolic anathema, for did not Paul passionately aver, 'Yea, let God be found true, but every man a liar'? [*Rom* 3:4]

V3: **concerning his Son, who was born of the seed of David according to the flesh,**

concerning his Son, This gospel of God, which was promised of old, is perfectly summed up in God's Son, who is the brightness of the Father's glory 'and the express image of his person' [*Heb* 1:3]. The One who is co-eternal and co-equal with the Father, is the very Christ whom all Christians worship [cf the confessional 'our' of *v* 4: 'even Jesus Christ *our* Lord'].

who was born of the seed of David according to the flesh, This is the first of the two successive stages of the Messianic vocation. As to the flesh, Christ was born, though not begotten, of David's line in fulfilment of the ancient promise [*Is* 7:14 AV; *Luke* 1:32; *Acts* 2:30; 2 *Tim* 2:8]. The expression 'of the seed of David' implies Christ's willing subjection to mortality for the redemption of his people, a point made explicit in the phrase which follows, 'by the resurrection from the dead.' [cf *Acts* 2:24–32] On the cross the 'Sun of Righteousness' was eclipsed during those awful hours in which he suffered the penal infliction of divine wrath against sin [*Gal* 3:13]. The essential glory of Christ became obscured, when he voluntarily descended into that profound abyss of shame and suffering, which marked the lowest point of his humiliation [*Phil* 2:8].

V4: who was declared to be the Son of God with power, according to the spirit of holiness, by the resurrection from the dead; even Jesus Christ our Lord,

who was declared to be the Son of God with power, This verse describes how the abasement of the Son gave place to the glory of his exaltation. Paul does not say that the resurrection 'made' Christ the Son of God, but that it 'declared' or marked his appointment as 'the Son of God *in power*'. The contrast he draws is between the Son's earthly life of subordination to the Father's will as the 'Servant of the Lord', and the heavenly instatement by which he entered upon 'a new phase of sonship characterized by the possession and exercise of unique supernatural power'. (Geerhardus Vos)

according to the Spirit of holiness (RSV) This enthronement inaugurated the age of the Spirit, whose descent on the day of Pentecost conclusively proved Christ's claim to eternal equality with the Father, for none but the Son of God could send forth the Holy Spirit [*John* 16:7; cf 1 *Cor* 15:45; 2 *Cor* 3:17].

by the resurrection from the dead; The resurrection is that pivotal point in the Incarnate life, which marks the end of Messianic suffering, and the beginning of the transcendent lordship of the Mediator [*Acts* 2:36; *Phil* 2:9–11]. Moreover, the future resurrection of all believers is guaranteed by this triumph of the 'firstborn from the dead' [*Col* 1:18; 1 *Cor* 15:20].

even Jesus Christ our Lord, Since the gospel of God is centred upon his Son, its entire content is expressed in the names that denote the functions he fulfils. The personal name 'Jesus' recalls the historic sacrifice by which he became the Saviour of his people; the official title 'Christ' shows that this gracious design was accomplished in obedience to the Father's will; while 'Lord' denotes the universal sovereignty to which he has been advanced by the resurrection. It is this common confession in the *present* lordship of God's Son over all things, notwithstanding all appearances to the contrary, that unites the apostle with his readers.

*V*5: **through whom we received grace and apostleship, unto obedience of faith among all the nations, for his name's sake;**

through whom we received grace and apostleship, In the experience of Paul, the grace of God in conversion and the call to apostleship coalesced in his encounter with the exalted Mediator through whom he received the double boon [1 *Tim* 1:11–14]. In this second reference to his office [cf *v* 1], he brings out the roving nature of his commission as the apostle to the Gentiles.

unto obedience of faith among all the nations, It is this revelation to Paul of the universal lordship of Christ which explains his unceasing endeavours to bring men of every nation to recognize the reality of that divine rule in their lives [cf *Ps* 2:8 with *Matt* 28:19, 20]. Such obedience to Christ is the fruit of faith in him; whereas the refusal to trust him for salvation is the worst form of disobedience [*John* 16:9].

for his name's sake; It was not primarily to benefit the nations that Paul engaged in this evangelism, but for the sake of 'the name which is above every name' [Phil 2:9]. His paramount concern was not philanthropic but Christocentric. Above all else he sought the honour and glory of his Lord, and in this he faithfully reflected the antecedent design of God.

V6: among whom are ye also, called to be Jesus Christ's:

among whom are ye also, Paul assigns no special place of honour to the Roman church, and his right to address it rests upon its evident inclusion within the terms of his divine mandate to proclaim the faith 'among all the nations' [Rom 16:26].

called to be Jesus Christ's: i.e. they belong to Christ by predestination, redemption, and calling. The apostle never leaves his readers to imagine that they became believers just by voluntary choice, but always traces their salvation back to the effectual calling of God [Rom 8:30, 11:29; 1 Cor 1:9; 2 Tim 1:9f].

V7: to all that are in Rome, beloved of God, called to be saints: Grace to you and peace from God our Father and the Lord Jesus Christ.

to all that are in Rome, beloved of God, called to be saints: Paul recognizes no distinctions in discipleship, for all believers are beloved of God, and all are called to be saints. This is at once a gift and a demand. The distinguishing love of God confers the status of 'sainthood' upon all believers, but it remains their constant vocation to progress in holiness, even though 'sinless perfection' lies beyond this present life [7:21].

Grace to you and peace Paul combines the Greek and Hebrew forms of greeting in this characteristic salutation. Grace is God's undeserved kindness in the gospel. Christ's propitiatory death provides the only basis for a restoration of fellowship between God and man. It is the subjective appropriation of that great objective fact of the gospel, which produces that 'peace of God which passeth all understanding' [cf 5:1; *Eph* 2:13, 14; 1 *John* 4:10].

from God our Father and the Lord Jesus Christ. The juxtaposition of these names is further proof that the absolute deity of Christ was of the very essence of Paul's gospel.

Although the Judaizers persistently opposed Paul's doctrine of grace there is no evidence to suggest that they ever challenged his teaching on this crucial issue. 'The same phenomenon appears everywhere in the Pauline Epistles – the tremendous doctrine of the person of Christ is never defended, but always assumed.' (J. G. Machen)

*V*8: **First, I thank my God through Jesus Christ for you all, that your faith is proclaimed throughout the whole world.**

First, I thank All Paul's epistles, except that to the Galatians, begin with thanksgiving to God for the faith of his readers. He does not congratulate the Romans upon their faith, but fervently thanks God for it. Hence faith must be God's gift to them [*Phil* 1:29; 2 *Pet* 1:1].

my God The knowledge that Paul had of God was neither abstract nor speculative, but living and personal. He could also speak of 'my gospel' because it was first his by experience, and the commission to preach it stemmed from this relationship [2:16, 16:25].

through Jesus Christ Every approach to God must be made through the merits of the Mediator, for in order to know God as Father, it is necessary to recognize Christ as Lord and Saviour [*John* 14:6; 1 *Tim* 2:5]. The solemn truth revealed by Scripture is that, apart from Christ, God is a consuming fire [*Heb* 10:26–29, 12:29].

for you all, The apostle's genuine and undisguised affection for all believers, without respect of persons, was his artless method of securing their reverent attention.

that your faith is proclaimed throughout the whole world. That a witness was maintained in the very capital of the Empire was a great encouragement to Christians everywhere. This reminder of the widespread influence of their example was a stimulus to their continuing fidelity to the gospel.

V9: **For God is my witness, whom I serve in my spirit in the gospel of his Son, how unceasingly I make mention of you, always in my prayers**

For God is my witness, As the believers in Rome could not know of his intense interest in their spiritual welfare, he commends himself to them by drawing their attention to the perfect knowledge which God has of his heart. It is almost an oath. Although God is very far from the thoughts of the wicked, the Christian is constantly conscious of the divine oversight, and he regulates his conduct accordingly [*Ps* 10:4, 139].

whom I serve in my spirit All true service is spiritual, as befits the nature of God [*John* 4:24]. These words show that unlike 'some ungracious pastors', Paul's piety kept pace with his exhortations, for his own service was without reservation of any kind [12:1, 2; *Phil* 4:9]. It follows that no bodily service is acceptable to God, which is not informed and animated by a renewed spirit [8:1–14; *Col* 3:10]. That false mysticism which confines itself to inactive religious veneration is also condemned here, because spiritual worship is ever expressed in rational service [contrast 1:25].

in the gospel of his Son, Despite the general reluctance to believe it, the only 'good news' God has for mankind is to be found 'in the gospel of his Son' [*Luke* 2:10, 11].

how unceasingly I make mention of you, always in my prayers Paul may be 'unknown by face unto' the church at Rome, but the Christians there are no strangers to his prayers.

Their spiritual welfare has a familiar place among the apostle's urgent petitions for the growth and establishment of the whole church of God. If prayer does not 'change things', it is, nevertheless, the appointed means by which God bestows promised blessings upon his people. Ardent prayer is a certain index that such answers of grace are at hand [*Ezek* 36:37]. 'To pray without labouring is to mock God: to labour without prayer is to rob God of his glory.' (Robert Haldane)

*V*10: **making request, if by any means now at length I may be prospered by the will of God to come unto you.**

The specific burden of Paul's prayer was that he might be given the opportunity to visit Rome, yet he consciously subjected this desire to the will of God. Luke's account of the unexpected manner in which his request was fulfilled, and his final arrival in Rome as a 'prisoner of Jesus Christ,' reads like a triumphal progress, which indeed it was [*Acts* 28]. In the pursuit of every lawful project there must be a humble acknowledgement of the divine proviso, 'Thy will be done,' for as Charles Hodge remarks, God's 'providence is to be recognized in reference to the most ordinary affairs of life'. [*James* 4:15]

*V*11: **For I long to see you, that I may impart unto you some spiritual gift, to the end ye may be established;**

Paul now turns to the purpose of his long-awaited visit. As he also expects to be enriched by their meeting together [*v* 12], it seems clear that no particular gift is in mind; what he desires is that the Romans might be strengthened in their faith (James Dunn). Hence he gladly acknowledges the reality of a faith which he only seeks to confirm, and in his modest use of the passive form 'he hides himself by expressing the result'. (A. W. Pink)

God's purpose in the bestowal of individual gifts is achieved in the building up of the whole community. And the glory of the divine prerogative in thus establishing the church is in no way diminished by his use of human instruments to accomplish it.

V12: that is, that I with you may be comforted in you, each of us by the other's faith, both yours and mine.

To avoid giving the impression that the benefits will be all one-sided, Paul assures his readers that he too will be blessed through his fellowship with them. He is not coming to Rome as an aloof benefactor, for he knows that while he is among them ('in you') he will be strengthened and encouraged by their faith. 'There is none so poor in the Church of Christ who may not impart to us something of value.' (Calvin)

However, it is to be carefully noted, that a common faith is the uniting factor in such a fellowship. There can be no mutual edification where there is no mutual faith. John Fawcett gave inimitable expression to this fact of Christian experience in the first verse of his famous hymn. It is only 'the fellowship of kindred minds' which binds hearts together in Christian love. Today many would make 'fellowship' the means of securing a 'common faith', but this is nothing less than a wilful inversion of what is ever the biblical order [2 John].

V13: And I would not have you ignorant, brethren, that oftentimes I purposed to come unto you (and was hindered hitherto), that I might have some fruit in you also, even as in the rest of the Gentiles.

And I would not have you ignorant, brethren, Paul's characteristic way of underlining what he is about to say. See also 11:25; I Cor 10:1, 12:1; 2 Cor 1:8; I Thess 4:13.

that oftentimes I purposed to come unto you (and was hindered hitherto), They must understand that it was not because of indifference that the apostle had not yet made the journey to Rome. But so far he had been hindered from paying them the desired visit, presumably by the need to fulfil his missionary work in the East before turning to the West [cf 15:22–24].

[22]

that I might have some fruit in you also, The quest for spiritual fruit was the mainspring of all the apostle's activity. No doubt it was because Paul saw Rome as an important missionary centre, that he specially wished to strengthen the witness there by a personal visit.

even as in the rest of the Gentiles. Evidently the church at Rome was predominantly Gentile in character.

*V*14: **I am debtor both to Greeks and to Barbarians, both to the wise and to the foolish.**

A study of Paul's sermons in Acts shows that he adapted his presentation of the gospel to suit the particular needs of his listeners [cf *Acts* 14:15ff with 17:22ff]. The apostle was always careful to take account of differences in national character and cultural development (or the lack of it), yet he knew that beneath these superficial classifications, there was the most fundamental division of all, that between the saved and the lost.

Since Paul's unremitting labours were not inspired by those to whom he was sent, but by his abiding sense of the divine obligation which rested upon him, he was not deterred by the unfavourable response his message so often excited. For he knew that all men everywhere needed the gospel, and the solemn fact that they do not by nature desire it had no bearing on his responsibility to make full proof of his ministry [1 *Cor* 9:16].

*V*15: **So, as much as in me is, I am ready to preach the gospel to you also that are in Rome.**

'As far as he was concerned, he was willing to preach in Rome; but whether he should do so or not, rested not with him, but with God.' (Hodge)

*V*16: **For I am not ashamed of the gospel: for it is the power of God unto salvation to every one that believeth; to the Jew first, and also to the Greek.**

For I am not ashamed of the gospel: Although the apostle is proud of the gospel, he is not unaware of the general contempt in which it is held, and so he prefers to say that he is not ashamed of it. The unpopularity of a crucified Christ has prompted many to present a message which is more palatable to the unbeliever, but the removal of the offence of the cross always renders it ineffective [*Gal* 5:11]. An inoffensive gospel is also an inoperative gospel. Thus Christianity is wounded most in the house of its friends.

for it is the power of God unto salvation to every one that believeth; This gives the reason for Paul's pride in the gospel: 'it is the power of God for salvation to every one who has faith.' (RSV) As Anders Nygren makes clear, this does not mean that faith is the *condition* of salvation, as though the gospel really depended upon man's response for its power to save; for in fact the *capacity* to believe is given through the operation of God's power in the gospel (cf comment on 'I thank', *v* 8). This means that whenever the gospel is preached, the power of God is at work for the salvation of men, delivering them from the dominion of darkness, and bringing them into the new age which was ushered in by the appointment of Christ as 'the Son of God *in power*' [*v* 4; cf *Luke* 11:21, 22].

to the Jew first, and also to the Greek. The gospel is for Jews and Gentiles alike ('Greek' here has this wider meaning). It is sent 'first' to the Jew, a priority always recognized by Paul in his missionary practice. But by insisting that it is 'also' for the Gentiles, he 'maintains the radical religious *equality* already proclaimed in the words: "to every one that believeth."' (F. Godet) [*Gal* 3:26–29]

*V*17: **For therein is revealed a righteousness of God from faith unto faith: as it is written, But the righteous shall live by faith.**

For therein is revealed a righteousness of God The gospel is 'the power of God unto salvation' for in it there is the *dynamic* revelation of a *unique* righteousness. Unlike the legal righteousness by which man vainly seeks to attain a right standing before God *through* personal obedience to the law [10:3; *Phil* 3:9], the divine righteousness is that status which God confers upon believers *without* personal obedience because he reckons or imputes to them the obedience of Christ. As the knowledge of such a salvation could never be derived from the natural operation of human reason, this extraordinary righteousness calls for a special revelation in which the unimaginable provision of grace is not only objectively communicated (in the Word of God, whether written or preached) but also subjectively applied (in the experience of believers).

from faith unto faith: 'He saith not, from faith to works, or from works to faith; but "from faith to faith," i.e. only by faith.' (M. Poole) Salvation from first to last is by faith in the justifying righteousness of Christ.

as it is written, But the righteous shall live by faith. As Paul is propounding nothing new, he confirms his doctrine by an appeal to the Old Testament [*Hab* 2:4, also cited in *Gal* 3:11 and *Heb* 10:38]. In this quotation the prophet contrasts the Chaldean invader, whose boastful self-sufficiency shows that he is not upright in heart, with the 'righteous' man who shall live (or be saved) by his faith in the promise of God's deliverance. Thus the faith of the man whom God approves and accounts as righteous [cf *Gen* 15:6 cited in *Gal* 3:6] is the opposite of the spirit of pride which disregards God and invokes his judgment. And it is because salvation always consists in this reliance upon God's righteous intervention in history that it is not an artifice of exegesis for the apostle to find the basis for the ensuing argument in this text.

*V*18: **For the wrath of God is revealed from heaven against all ungodliness and unrighteousness of men, who hinder the truth in unrighteousness;**
This verse begins a terrifying indictment of human sin. The

apostle turns first to the sins of those who are without the light of special revelation [*vv* 18–32]. God will judge the heathen by the light of nature, which is common to all men, and this is sufficient to leave them without excuse [*v* 20]. It may seem strange to some that Paul devotes nearly three chapters to an exhaustive examination of the problem of sin. However, slight views of sin never lead to a fervent appreciation of grace. Man is ever ready to excuse himself. He wears his sins lightly, and tends to dismiss them as mere peccadilloes. In his view they offer no barrier to blessing. After all, forgiveness is God's business![1]

For the wrath of God Paul therefore insists that the gravity of sin must be measured by the strength of the divine reaction it provokes. God is not indifferent to sin. It continually calls forth his holy abhorrence. Sin is an affront to the holiness of God, it is a direct assault upon his majesty, and 'the wrath of God' is an expression which indicates the righteous outflow of divine disfavour upon the sinner. This wrath is not an automatic judgement upon sin by an anonymous cosmic computer, nor can it be entirely explained by the feelings produced in the sinner who is punished. Rather, the phrase 'the wrath *of God*' points to the most intense, personal response to sin within the divine being, though this is without those unworthy human emotions which are normally associated with this word.

is revealed from heaven These words do not demand any supernatural manifestation of God's wrath from heaven. They assert the fact that God's retributive justice is evident in history [*Is* 10:5]. God is no idle spectator of world events; he is dynamically active in human affairs. The commission of sin is constantly punctuated by divine judgment. Truly, 'The history of the world is the judgment of the world.' (Friedrich Schiller)

---

1. 'God will pardon me, it is his trade' were the last words of the poet Heinrich Heine.

against all ungodliness and unrighteousness of men, The stress here lies on the abstract qualities of ungodliness and unrighteousness rather than upon the personal agents through whom they find expression, because God would not punish men if it were not for their sin. The order is also significant. Impiety towards God results in injustice towards men. The derangement in man's primary relationship leads naturally to disturbances in all his transactions with his fellowmen.

who hold down the truth in unrighteousness; (RV) Man unavoidably knows God, for everywhere in the created order he is confronted by 'his everlasting power and divinity' [*v* 20]. But it is because man also knows that he is a sinner that he always seeks to suppress or stifle this true knowledge of God. For though sin has not destroyed man's religious capacities, it has turned them away from the living God, so that he now prefers to worship the finite deities of his own invention [*v* 23].

*V*19: **because that which is known of God is manifest in them; for God manifested it unto them.**

As Calvin says, Although God is in his essence 'incomprehensible, utterly transcending all human thought,' yet he is inescapably revealed within all men through their knowledge of 'the things that are made' [*v* 20], this 'manifestation of the Godhead being too clear to escape the notice of any people, however obtuse.' [Cf *Acts* 14:17, 17:27–29]

*V*20: **For the invisible things of him since the creation of the world are clearly seen, being perceived through the things that are made, even his everlasting power and divinity; that they may be without excuse:**

God's revelation of himself in creation is perspicuous, for there is in it a most glorious display of his divine power. The word translated as 'divinity' (*theiotēs*) occurs only here in the New Testament. On this R. C. Trench wrote, 'It is not to be doubted that St Paul uses this vaguer, more abstract, and less personal word, just because he would affirm that men may know God's power and majesty from his works.' This knowledge of God's creative power renders men responsible, and thus leaves them without excuse. But the knowledge of God's redeeming grace is mediated to mankind solely through his Son in whom 'dwelleth all the fulness of the *Godhead* bodily'. [*Col* 2:9] Paul there uses the word *theotēs* to express the essential deity of the Son, for he 'is declaring that in the Son there dwells all the fulness of absolute Godhead; they were no mere rays of divine glory which gilded him, lighting up his person for a season with a splendour not his own; but he was, and is, absolute and perfect God.'

V21: **because that, knowing God, they glorified him not as God, neither gave thanks; but became vain in their reasonings, and their senseless heart was darkened.**

because that, knowing God, they glorified him not as God, It is because 'the *unseen* things of God are *clearly seen*,' that men cannot plead ignorance for not glorifying him as God (Bengel). The seriousness of this charge lies in the final thrust, 'they glorified him not *as God*'. It shows that all men are destitute of true piety, for all their religious pretensions are based upon a false image they have formed of God. If it is impossible for man to add to the essential glory of God, it yet remains his obligation as God's image-bearer willingly to ascribe unto him that glory which is due to his name.

neither gave thanks; Since man does not like to retain the knowledge of God *as God*, he cannot see him as the benevolent author of all his good. Instead he chooses to live independently in a world of uncertainty, which leaves him free to celebrate his 'good luck', or to praise his superior foresight, as the fancy takes him.

but became vain in their reasonings, The second part of the verse emphasizes the fact that when men reject the truth, they embrace lies in its place. The absence of truth always ensures the presence of error. Men must think something, and when truth is banished, the light that is within them becomes darkness [Matt 6:23].

In thus refusing the true knowledge of God, their understanding 'became vain', an evident allusion to the heathen infatuation with idols, those 'vanities' which are devoid of any correspondence with the truth [Deut 32:21; Acts 14:15].

In the New Testament 'reasonings' bears an unfavourable sense, and denotes the unregulated activity of the mind 'in the service of a corrupt heart'. (Godet) [Luke 5:21, 22] Here it indicates reliance upon the speculative powers of reason to provide a firm basis for religious faith. It is fatal to mistake philosophical enlightenment for spiritual illumination. Every form of heathen gnosis is but a variety of that false fire which ever ends in eternal despair [Is 50:11].

and their senseless heart was darkened. 'The heart' in the Bible stands for the complete self hood of man; it is the moral centre of all his intellectual, emotional, and volitional activity. A heart which is destitute of spiritual understanding is in a condition of darkness which affects the whole man. This gives the *coup de grâce* to the modern myth of man's unaided ascent from primitive animism to the lofty summit of monotheism. It is only in the biblical record of man's fall from his original state of integrity that his present abnormal condition receives an adequate explanation [Eccles 7:29].

V22: Professing themselves to be wise, they became fools,

The effect of sin upon the mind of man is to turn his fancied wisdom into foolishness [1 Cor 1:17-27]. Calvin observed 'that when miserable men do seek after God, instead of ascending higher than themselves, as they ought to do, they measure him by their own carnal stupidity . . . Hence, they do not conceive of him in the character in which he is manifested, but imagine him to be whatever their own rashness has devised.' The folly of idolatry is therefore the logical result of this corrupt imagination (*v* 23). However, when God declares man's wisdom to be foolishness, the whole question of the validity of human knowledge is raised. It is because man 'holds down the truth in unrighteousness' that he becomes a problem to himself. It was by receiving the devil's lie, 'ye shall be as gods,' that man first fell into sin [*Gen* 3:5]. He aspired to an equal ultimacy with God, and thus denied the most basic fact of his own existence, namely, his creature-hood. By refusing to know God *as God*, he lost the only means of identifying *himself*! Every 'problem' in philosophy stems from this primal apostasy. The profound opening sentence of Calvin's *Institutes* expresses this inseparable relationship with unique clarity. 'Our wisdom, in so far as it ought to be deemed true and solid wisdom, consists almost entirely of two parts: the knowledge of God and of ourselves.' It is the loss of the true knowledge of God, which makes the Socratic injunction, 'Know thyself,' an impossible requirement.

No independent knowledge is possible for man. Everything he knows, he knows from God. It is because man refuses to acknowledge this source, and insists upon the originality of his own interpretation of the 'brute facts' of the universe, that his knowledge is poisoned by the fatal error of his fundamental religious presupposition, which is, that there is no self-existent Creator to whom he is indebted for every breath which he draws [*Acts* 17:16–31].

*V*23: and changed the glory of the incorruptible God for the likeness of an image of corruptible man, and of birds, and fourfooted beasts, and creeping things.

In words drawn from *Ps* 106:20 Paul cites man's preference for idolatry as the supreme evidence of his folly. For he thus exchanged the glory of the immortal God for the unreal copy of the figure of mortal man, and even of birds, four-footed beasts, and serpents! But because such an image only represents the deity, idolaters do not regard themselves as idol worshippers. They invoke their god by means of the image; they do not bow down to the image itself.

This sophistry is still favoured by Rome in her vain attempt to justify her wilful departure from the Word of God, yet this is that very thing which the Bible condemns root and branch. Aaron made a golden calf, but he did not have the slightest intention of leading the people to worship this image. He said, 'Tomorrow is a feast *to the Lord*' [*Exod* 32:5]. The calf was simply an aid to devotion, but God's judgment of the matter was very different. 'They made a calf in Horeb, and *worshipped a molten image*. Thus they changed their glory for the likeness of an ox that eateth grass' [*Ps* 106:19, 20].

God has written *ICHABOD* across the elaborate solemnities of all idolaters, whether pagan or 'Christian', for the glory has departed from them [1 *Sam* 4:21, 22; cf *Is* 40:18ff, 44:10ff].

It needs to be further noted that idolatry may not be limited to the mere worship of graven images, it also extends to the unlawful deification of any aspect of created reality, for to break the greatest commandment is still the greatest sin [*Matt* 22:37, 38; 1 *John* 5:21].

V24: Wherefore God gave them up in the lusts of their hearts unto uncleanness, that their bodies should be dishonoured among themselves:

'Wherefore' points to God's justice in giving up those who had dishonoured him to the dishonouring of their own bodies. Three times in five verses the terrible sentence rings out: 'God gave them up' [*vv* 24, 26, 28]. In this handing of them over without restraint to the self-degradation wrought by their own lusts, they receive that 'recompense of their error which was due' [*v* 27; cf *Ps* 81:12]. As R. C. H. Lenski says, 'Men who so love the cesspool of sin are sent into it by justice; what they want, they shall have.'

V25: **for that they exchanged the truth of God for a lie, and worshipped and served the creature rather than the Creator, who is blessed for ever. Amen.**

This verse re-echoes the thought of *v* 23, but it is in no sense a mere repetition of it. Paul's first concern is to vindicate the apparent severity of God's judgment upon idolaters [*v* 24] by emphasizing the heinous nature of their sin. Then again, it might seem from *v* 23 that man had successfully detracted from the essential glory of God by his idolatry, but Paul's fervent ascription of praise here is also a statement of the transcendent blessedness of the Creator. Indeed it is quite impossible for man actually to succeed in his sinful attempt to diminish God's glory. If this were possible, the dividing line between the Creator and the creature would cease to exist, and God would no longer be God. Later in the epistle Paul shows that no creatures can escape paying their tribute to the revenue of the Creator's glory, whether willingly or unwillingly, whether in mercy or in wrath [9:22, 23; *Rev* 4:11].

V26: **For this cause God gave them up unto vile passions: for their women changed the natural use into that which is against nature:**

What was hinted at in *v* 24 is now specified in *vv* 26, 27. The moral degeneracy of the ancient world is exhibited in this awful catalogue of sexual vice, which pagan religion, so far from restraining, actively promoted.

Today the increasing prevalence of those sexual perversions, which are complacently regarded by the avante-garde as 'interesting variants', is a dreadful mark of God's wrath upon a civilization which glories in its 'post-Christian' character.

'Paul first refers to the degradation of females among the heathen, because they are always the last to be affected in the decay of morals, and their corruption is therefore proof that all virtue is lost.' (Hodge)

*V*27: **and likewise also the men, leaving the natural use of the woman, burned in their lust one toward another, men with men working unseemliness, and receiving in themselves that recompense of their error which was due.**

The honourable nature of the married state is grounded in the creative ordinance of God, while the illegitimate desire here described derives its proper name from the city of Sodom, which was destroyed because of it [*Heb* 13:4; *Gen* 19:5]. Poole comments, 'How meet was it that they who had forsaken the Author of nature, should be given up not to keep the order of nature.' So that the frightful physical and moral consequences of indulging these unnatural lusts was the due recompense for their 'error' in 'wandering away' from the true God (*vv* 21-23).

*V*28: **And even as they refused to have God in their knowledge, God gave them up unto a reprobate mind, to do those things which are not fitting;**

Although all men have a knowledge of God, their refusal to acknowledge him shows that they are determined atheists at heart. Paul's word-play is preserved in Charles Williams' translation, 'As they *did not approve* of fully recognizing God any longer, God gave them up to minds that He *did not approve*.' Originally the word translated as 'reprobate' was applied to metals which failed to pass the assayer's test. Here a 'reprobate mind' refers to the mind that God cannot approve and must reject because of its folly in dispensing with its greatest good – the knowledge of himself.

This blinding of the highest faculty in man constitutes the greatest judgment upon man. The religious orientation of man is unmistakably mirrored in his consciousness, and this finds its practical expression in his conduct. Thus man's thoughts can never be regarded as purely theoretical; for it is his mental attitude towards God which determines the quality of his actions towards his fellowmen. What Paul is saying is that man's 'unrighteousness' is the natural consequence of his 'ungodliness', the guilt of which he has just proved.

*V*29: **being filled with all unrighteousness, wickedness, covetousness, maliciousness; full of envy, murder, strife, deceit, malignity; whisperers,**

This is the longest list of sins to be found in Paul's letters (*vv* 29-31). And though it does not furnish an exhaustive catalogue of vice, it certainly conveys a horrifying impression of those sins which enslaved the heathen world in moral chaos. In this verse the inward disposition of apostate mankind is first described in terms of *general motivation* ('being filled with all unrighteousness, wickedness, covetousness, maliciousness') and then of *specific desires* ('full of envy, murder, strife, deceit, malignity'). For 'whisperers' see the next verse. [cf *Mark* 7:21-23]

*V*30: **backbiters, hateful to God, insolent, haughty, boastful, inventors of evil things, disobedient to parents,**

How this evil character manifested itself in daily conduct is next set forth in an apparently random list, which begins with 'whisperers' and extends to the end of *v* 31.

haters of God (ASV margin) 'And so God-murderers. Forasmuch as sinners are God-haters, and could wish there were no God, that they might never come to judgment.' (John Trapp) In those who speak of the 'Death of God', the wish is father to the thought. Secularism seeks to murder God.

inventors of evil things New sins must be discovered by those with jaded palates, and new words must be coined for them. A relevant verdict on the restlessness of present-day society [*Is* 57:20].

*V*31: **without understanding, covenant-breakers, without natural affection, unmerciful:**

without natural affection, Man's inhumanity to man affords striking proof of the biblical doctrine of total depravity. The common practice of infant exposure is a single instance of the senseless brutality which was rife in the ancient world. Nevertheless, modern life is not without its own impressive parallels [cf Paul's prophecy, 2 *Tim* 3:3]. Those who impudently break the first commandment are not likely to be restrained by the second, an unhappy sequence which is fully documented by the history of the present century [*Matt* 22:37–39]. No ultimate moral values can be retained by those who reject belief in God as an anachronistic survival of medieval superstition. Humanistic ethics are doomed to shameful failure because they try to build on sand.

*V*32: **who, knowing the ordinance of God, that they that practise such things are worthy of death, not only do the same, but also consent with them that practise them.**

The fact that the law of God is ineradicably stamped upon man's consciousness means that he can never sin with a clear conscience. But this knowledge of his just exposure to the sentence of death, as only God can inflict it, does not deter him from sinning because he is in love with his lusts. Hence men not only continue to commit sin themselves, but also 'consent' to it in others, i.e. they actually applaud those who do the things which they *know* to be wrong! Paul's examination of the sin of the Gentiles reaches its damning climax in this awful statement. Nothing could exceed the enormity of the concluding indictment. Men enjoy sin simply because it is evil, and they delight to observe others in the same state of condemnation as themselves [*Ps* 10:3; *Prov* 2:14].

CHAPTER TWO

V1: Wherefore thou art without excuse, O man, who-soever thou art that judgest: for wherein thou judgest another, thou condemnest thyself; for thou that judgest dost practise the same things.

As Paul has established the guilt of the Gentiles he now deals with the case of the Jew, who is not actually named until *v* 17. One reason for Paul's use of the generic term 'man' is his concern to prove the strict impartiality of God's judgment [*vv* 1-11]. Another is that he would gain a sympathetic hearing, and his earnestness is evident in the entreaty, 'O man'. The Jew is nonetheless identified in the first verse by the national pastime – censoriousness!

'Wherefore' expresses the apostle's conclusion in advance of his argument. The reasoning appears to be as follows:

> *In judging others,*
> *you also condemn yourself*
> *as you are guilty of the very same sins;*
> THEREFORE *you are without excuse, O man.*

The Jew could heartily endorse the condemnation of the Gentile world, but this verse, which reproduces the Lord's teaching in *Matt* 7:1-3, is nicely calculated to unmask his hypocrisy.

V2: And we know that the judgment of God is according to truth against them that practise such things.

If the Jew commits the same sins as he condemns in the Gentiles, let him not imagine that either privilege or profession can secure him against the just condemnation of God. Paul says 'we know' that God's judgment is strictly in accord with the facts of the case. The word for 'truth' is defined by Cremer as 'the reality lying at the basis of an appearance'.

Man must judge by the outward aspect, and he is often deceived by it; it is otherwise with God who looks upon the heart. [1 Sam 16:7]

Paul is no dissembler, no mute patron of error, and his loyalty to God is the clearest proof of his sincere love for man [Gal 2:11]. It is never a 'kindness' to conceal the truth from men, for as long as they are allowed to indulge a false hope, they must remain strangers to the only hope which 'putteth not to shame' [5:5]. In the kingdom of God, those who would build for eternity, must first dig deep [Luke 6:48].

V3: **And reckonest thou this, O man, who judgest them that practise such things, and doest the same, that thou shalt escape the judgment of God?**

Not content with an abstract statement of an invariable spiritual principle [v 2], Paul presses home its personal application with remorseless logic. If you condemn the Gentiles for these sins, then how can *you* expect your privileged position [Matt 3:8, 9] to secure your immunity from God's judgment when you are practising the same sins yourself? For to be guilty of such works of darkness when enjoying much greater light is far more deserving of blame.

V4: **Or despisest thou the riches of his goodness and forbearance and longsuffering, not knowing that the goodness of God leadeth thee to repentance?**

The Jew imagined that his experience of God's goodness meant that God would not judge him as strictly as the heathen. Not realizing that this kindness was intended to lead him to repentance, he was guilty of holding God in contempt. For he

[37]

mistook the mercy that suspended judgment in the interests of salvation for a moral indifference to sin [*Eccles* 8:11]. And the same fatal mistake is made by anyone who presumes that time given for the turning *from* sin is a divine patronage of the sinner *in* sin. 'There is in every wilful sin an interpretative contempt of the goodness of God.' (Matthew Henry)

V5: **but after thy hardness and impenitent heart treasurest up for thyself wrath in the day of wrath and revelation of the righteous judgment of God;**

The Jew not only fails to benefit from the opportunities for repentance given him by God's longsuffering, but by his continued impenitence he is 'amassing, like hoarded treasure, an ever-accumulating stock of Divine wrath, to burst upon him in the day of the revelation of the righteous judgment of God.' (David Brown) [*James* 5:3].

Although the present age is not without its tokens of God's righteous judgment, the full manifestation of it is reserved until 'the day of wrath' when the complete equity of God's proceedings will be made plain to all his creatures – angels, demons, and men [cf *Ps* 7:11 with *Rev* 6:17].

'There is no judgment of God which is not according to strict justice; there is none that is a judgment of mercy. Mercy and justice are irreconcilable except in Christ, in whom mercy is exercised consistently with justice.' (Haldane)

V6: **who will render to every man according to his works:**

Since the deeds of men afford an infallible index of their character, these acts provide the public evidence by which God judges them [*Prov* 24:12; *Matt* 16:27; 2 *Cor* 5:10; *Rev* 22:12]. It must be remembered that this is not an exposition of Paul's gospel, though it is an essential preliminary to it. The apostle is preaching the full rigour of the law to those who sought to be justified by it [10:1-3]. The application of this principle is unfolded in the following verses [7-10].

'The wicked will be punished on account of their works, and according to their works; the righteous will be rewarded, not on account of, but according to their works.' (Hodge)

The believer's union with Christ is shown by his good works, the reward of which is the reward of God's grace [*Is* 26:12; *John* 15:5].

V7: to them that by patience in well-doing seek for glory and honour and incorruption, eternal life:

The righteous are now described in terms of the principle stated in the preceding verse. In this passage it does not fall within the scope of the apostle's purpose to explain the dynamic from which these good works spring [for that, see 3:21ff].

His present design is to prove to the Jew the complete impartiality of the divine administration. When this section is interpreted as teaching salvation by works, Paul's teaching becomes involved in a hopeless self-contradiction. Against this, it is sufficient to note that the heavenly aspirations which characterize the righteous are not found in a hard and impenitent heart [*v* 5]. They are the fruit of a restored relationship [*Ezek* 36:26, 27]. It is true that many idly dream of glory and honour and immortality, but obedience and perseverance are the invariable marks of those who cherish a living hope [*Col* 1:22, 23]. Such continuance in well-doing is the indispensable condition for the attainment of eternal life [*Matt* 24:13; *Heb* 3:14].

V8: but unto them that are factious, and obey not the truth, but obey unrighteousness, shall be wrath and indignation,

Next the works of the wicked are reviewed. It is better to understand the 'factious' as those who are motivated by that spirit of 'base self-seeking' which thinks only of the immediate gains of sin, and so does not seek after glory, honour and immortality [*v* 7]. Hence they refuse to obey the truth and choose to obey unrighteousness, because they are bent on enjoying the pleasures of sin for a season. As all unrighteousness is *sin* and sin is lawlessness [1 John 5:17; 3:4], such a course of action is a direct attack upon the authority of the Lawgiver and calls forth his righteous reaction of 'wrath and indignation.'

*V*9: **tribulation and anguish, upon every soul of man that worketh evil, of the Jew first, and also of the Greek;**

'Tribulation and anguish' will be the terrible effects of the overflowing of God's 'wrath and indignation' upon all evildoers on judgment day. Paul is not content to say that this unimaginable punishment will be the portion of Jew and Greek alike, but he insists that the Jew has an unenviable priority in the order and degree of his condemnation. For like many professing Christians, the Jew thought that the mere possession of his spiritual privileges was in itself a certain insurance against divine retribution. But when such advantages are scorned, pre-eminence in condemnation is secured and the debt to justice proportionately increased [*Amos* 3:2; *Matt* 11:22; *Luke* 12:47].

*V*10: **but glory and honour and peace to every man that worketh good, to the Jew first, and also to the Greek:**

This completes the application of the principle stated in *v* 6. Paul here repeats two of the terms used in *v* 7 but replaces 'incorruption' with 'peace'. For instead of the 'anguish' felt by the lost, 'peace' is that state of eternal blessedness which is the portion of 'every man that worketh good'. Once more the emphasis falls not on a man's pedigree or pretensions but on his performance. But again the priority of the Jew, whether in condemnation or salvation, neither exempts the Greek from judgment nor excludes him from glory.

*V*11: **for there is no respect of persons with God.**

The inevitable conclusion to be drawn from the foregoing

argument is that God is no respecter of persons [*Deut* 10:17; *Acts* 10:34]. It is impossible to bribe this Judge, whose sentence is strictly in accord with character and is not affected by 'outward state and condition, as country, sex, wealth, wisdom, etc'. (Trapp) Hence the Jew could expect no special treatment on the grounds that he was a member of the chosen race.

*V*12: **For as many as have sinned without the law shall also perish without the law: and as many as have sinned under the law shall be judged by the law;**

Thus God will 'render to every man according to his works'. [*v* 6] The very fact that such a judgment reveals any who are righteous, demands the gospel for their existence. Paul's very precise statement of principle leaves room for this, but an explanation of the gospel is quite alien to his present purpose, and so he does not disclose the basis of their righteousness. In this part of the epistle his object is not only to establish the guilt of the Jew, but also to vindicate the complete equity of the divine procedure in a judgment of condemnation. This restricted design certainly does not require a consideration of justification by faith, but it does demand convincing proof of man's guiltiness before God. Accordingly, the apostle now shows that the judgment of God will be commensurate with the light enjoyed by men. The Gentiles who are without the benefit of special revelation will be judged by the light of nature, their disobedience to which is sufficient to secure their condemnation. On the other hand, the Jew who has been blessed with the written law of God will be judged according to the greater light which he has enjoyed. Great privilege always brings greater responsibility, and if neglected, greater liability to punishment. The heathen are not so blameworthy as the Jew. Nevertheless, both are guilty and both shall perish [*Luke* 12:47, 48].

*V*13: **for not the hearers of the law are just before God, but the doers of the law shall be justified:**

Another uncomfortable fact, conveniently forgotten by the Jew, is rammed home by Paul. It was not enough to be a diligent hearer of the law; it enjoined undeviating obedience to all its precepts. He who seeks justification *by* the law must be perfectly obedient *to* the law. And the implication is that such an exact conformity to its demands is beyond the achievement of sinful man, a fact which receives explicit confirmation in the devastating accusation that begins at *v* 17 [*James* 1:22, 2:10]. The manner in which the word 'justified' here makes its first appearance, affords striking evidence of its forensic character.

*V*14: **(for when Gentiles that have not the law do by nature the things of the law, these, not having the law, are the law unto themselves;**

The heathen are not in possession of the written law [*v* 12], yet their own judgments and actions are an acknowledgment that the moral law has been stamped upon their constitution by the Creator. For whenever they attempt to follow the dictates of conscience, they are confronted with the obligation to bring their conduct into conformity with this law that is revealed within them.

This partial and external obedience to 'the things of the law' is not said to be a fulfilment of the law, and should not be confused with the spiritual and perfect obedience that Paul attributes to the 'doers' of the law in the previous verse. As W. G. T. Shedd observes, the phrase denotes a fractional obedience to particular parts of the law, and not the law as a whole. The pagan does not obey the law in its entirety. It is obvious that such a piecemeal 'obedience' cannot please God, when it even fails to silence the witness of an 'accusing' conscience (*v* 15).

*V*15: **in that they show the work of the law written in their hearts, their conscience bearing witness therewith,**

and their thoughts one with another accusing or else excusing them;)

There is a close resemblance between the English and the Greek words for 'conscience'. The literal sense of the latter is given by W. E. Vine as 'a knowing with', and hence 'co-knowledge with oneself'. Conscience is that innate faculty to distinguish between right and wrong, which passes its independent judgment on a man's conduct. It is regarded by John Murray as 'an evidence of our indestructible moral nature, and is proof of the fact that God bears witness to himself in our hearts'.

The conscience of the natural man is blurred, though not extinguished, by sin, but in the Christian it is enlightened by the word of God, and quickened by the Holy Spirit. That this verse refers to the activity of conscience in the unregenerate is finely brought out by Murray's perceptive remark, 'Paul does not say that the law is written upon their hearts'. It is true that the law of God is indelibly written in their hearts, but it has not been engraved by grace upon their hearts [cf *Jer* 31:33]. If then the imperfect witness of the conscience of the natural man convicts him of his sinfulness, how much more will the Author of conscience condemn it?

*V*16: in the day when God shall judge the secrets of men, according to my gospel, by Jesus Christ.

Paul now sums up the whole paragraph by showing that the principle laid down in *v* 6, that God 'will render to every man according to his works', will be exhibited on the day of judgment to the eternal confusion of those who only 'glory in appearance'. For it was through trusting in the perfunctory performance of an external code that Jewish hypocrisy was fostered. And it is to warn against such a delusive confidence in appearance that the apostle reminds his kinsmen of the Day when the 'secrets of men' will be infallibly judged [*vv* 28, 29; 1 *Cor* 4:5]. Moreover, the Judge of all men is Jesus Christ, whose ability to discern the hidden depths of every heart supplies further proof of his deity [*Acts* 17:31; 2 *Cor* 5:10]. 'According to my gospel' registers Paul's conviction that he was not only commissioned to preach the gospel of grace, but also to warn of 'the judgment to come' [*Acts* 24:25].

*V*17: **But if thou bearest the name of a Jew, and restest upon the law, and gloriest in God,**

What follows proves that it is not the hearers, but the doers of the law who shall be justified [*v* 13]. Having reached this point in the argument, Paul is ready to identify the man he is addressing [*v* 1], and here begins an ironical rehearsal of the privileges in which the Jew gloried [*vv* 17–20].

The Jew bore his name proudly for it was the theocratic title of honour which marked him out as a member of the chosen race. He rested upon the law, confident that his salvation was assured by the mere possession of it. Worst of all, in boasting that his nation was the sole recipient of the divine favour he transferred to himself the glory that belonged to God alone [cf *Jer* 9:24].

*V*18: **and knowest his will, and approvest the things that are excellent, being instructed out of the law,**

The superior discernment of the Jew and his mental approval of the divine will were the results of his possession of the written Word of God in which he was instructed from childhood. But unlike the Psalmist, he failed to see that this light was given to guide his steps into the path of obedience [*Ps* 119:105].

*V*19: **and art confident that thou thyself art a guide of the blind, a light of them that are in darkness,**

The Jew was proud of his knowledge and looked with contempt upon the Gentiles who were given over to idolatry. Although those who were sickened by the excesses of heathen worship were generally welcome as proselytes, there was always the danger that these converts from paganism would be corrupted by the inconsistencies they constantly observed in their guides [*Matt* 15:14; 23:15, 16].

*V*20: **a corrector of the foolish, a teacher of babes, having in the law the form of knowledge and of the truth;**

The Jew took great pride in his ability to correct and teach these Gentile converts, because he knew that in the law he possessed the 'form', the correct embodiment, of absolute knowledge and truth. Paul does not contest the claim, but next shows that the Jew's failure to do what he *knew* to be right was far more inexcusable than the heathen ignorance he despised [*vv* 21–24].

*V*21: **thou therefore that teachest another, teachest thou not thyself? thou that preachest a man should not steal, dost thou steal?**

This series of rhetorical questions reaches a crescendo of searing indignation as Paul compares the profession of the Jew with his practice. For in teaching others, he had failed to teach himself [*Matt* 23:3], and in these verses he is accused of theft, adultery, and sacrilege. Thus the Jew is himself found guilty of the very sins he professed to abhor in others. On his proneness to theft and adultery, see *Ps* 50:18 and *Jer* 5:8.

*V*22: **thou that sayest a man should not commit adultery, dost thou commit adultery? thou that abhorrest idols, dost thou rob temples?**

Plainly this is a list of such glaring inconsistencies as would excite the contempt of the heathen [*v* 24]. And this was especially the case when the well-known Jewish hatred of idolatry was overcome by a rapacity which did not scruple to steal idolatrous objects or offerings, notwithstanding the ban imposed by *Deut* 7:25f. So that by the violation of his professed abhorrence of all idols, the Jew destroyed his own distinctiveness and in fact became a practising pagan!

V23: thou who gloriest in the law, through thy transgression of the law dishonourest thou God?

The final antithesis announces the astonishing verdict. The Jew who glories in the law is the very person who is dishonouring God by his transgression of the law.

'God is dishonoured by the transgressions of his people, in a manner in which he is not dishonoured by the same transgressions in the wicked, who make no profession of being his.' (Haldane)

V24: For the name of God is blasphemed among the Gentiles because of you, even as it is written.

The conclusion Paul draws from this damning indictment is that the religious perversity of the Jew caused the Gentiles to blaspheme the name of God, for they judged the character of the Deity by the conduct of those who claimed to be his people. Unbelievers who have ample opportunity to observe the sins which are committed by professors are not thereby encouraged to assume the mantle of true religion themselves.

So far from the Gentiles having a monopoly in sin, Paul has proved from Scripture that the guilt of the Jew is aggravated by the fact that he always sins against the light [Is 52:5].

V25: For circumcision indeed profiteth, if thou be a doer of the law: but if thou be a transgressor of the law, thy circumcision is become uncircumcision.

The Jew had one last hope left, and that was his unbounded confidence in circumcision as a sufficient security against condemnation. Paul proceeds to demolish this false hope by arguing against the Jew on his own terms. In such a context it was not germane to the apostle's purpose to speak of circumcision as a sign of the covenant of grace. As such it would be spiritually profitable to all those who share in Abraham's justifying faith.

However, the Jew placed his reliance upon his physical descent from Abraham, and he trusted in the law of Moses [*Matt* 3:9; *John* 8:39]. 'Very well,' says Paul, 'even on that basis circumcision is profitable, but only if you keep the law. Should you fail to do this, the sign is nullified by your disobedience.' In effect Paul only mentions the possibility of keeping the law in order to dismiss it. The Jew looked for his deliverance in the law, but in reality it sealed his doom [5:20; 10:5; *Gal* 3:19-22].

Hodge's practical remark on this verse is worthy of note: 'Whenever true religion declines, the disposition to lay undue stress on external rites is increased . . . The Christian Church, when it lost its spirituality, taught that water in baptism washed away sin. How large a part of nominal Christians rest all their hopes on the idea of the inherent efficacy of external rites!'

V26: If therefore the uncircumcision keep the ordinances of the law, shall not his uncircumcision be reckoned for circumcision?

Since the privilege of circumcision was cancelled by Jewish disobedience, it logically followed that the disadvantage of uncircumcision was removed by Gentile obedience. The obedience that Paul has in view is not the pagan's sporadic observance of 'the things of the law' [*v* 14], but the believer's fulfilment of the law's righteous requirements through the power of the indwelling Spirit [cf *Rom* 8:4]. Hence the apostle is referring 'to those many Gentiles converted to the gospel who, all uncircumcised as they are, nevertheless fulfil the law in virtue of the spirit of Christ, and thus become the *true* Israel, *the Israel of God, Gal* 6:16.' (Godet)

V27: and shall not the uncircumcision which is by nature, if it fulfil the law, judge thee, who with the letter and circumcision art a transgressor of the law?

Therefore if those who remain in their naturally uncircumcised state are found to fulfil the law, it is evidence that their obedience will condemn the Jew who, despite the advantage of the written law and circumcision, is still a transgressor of the law [*Matt* 12:41, 42]. As Paul here relentlessly insists, the Jew's failure to profit from these privileges only served to increase his guilt. For the law engraved on tables of stone finds no accomplishment in a stony heart of unbelief, and its unfulfilled commands thus become a swift witness against the transgressor [cf 2 *Cor* 3:6, 7]. And though circumcision, like the New Testament ordinances of Baptism and the Lord's Supper, was of divine appointment, yet there was no value in the 'outward and visible sign' unless it was accompanied by 'inward and spiritual grace'.

*V*28: **For he is not a Jew who is one outwardly; neither is that circumcision, which is outward in the flesh:**

*V*29: **but he is a Jew who is one inwardly; and circumcision is that of the heart, in the spirit, not in the letter; whose praise is not of men, but of God.**

In passing this crushing verdict upon the spiritual bankruptcy of Judaism, the apostle completely reverses the Jew's own ideas of his Jewishness. For he boasted of his birth, trusted in external rites, and like all who are content with an outward show, he expected the praise of men [*Matt* 6:5; *John* 5:44]. In denying the validity of this confidence, Paul makes a play on the word 'Jew', which means 'praise'; 'whose praise is not of men, but of God'. Moreover, the spiritual significance of circumcision was clearly taught by the prophets [*Deut* 10:16, 30:6; *Jer* 4:4, 9:26]. Therefore the true circumcision is that of the heart which is renewed by the Holy Spirit. It is true that the doctrine of the Spirit finds no formal place in this part of the letter, but Paul's veiled reference to the results of believing the gospel demands such an acknowledgment of the Spirit's regenerating activity. Matthew Henry effectively transposes the verse into Christian terms.

> He is not a Christian, that is one outwardly, nor is that baptism, which is outward in the flesh; but he is a Christian, that is one inwardly, and baptism is that of the heart, in the spirit, and not in the letter; whose praise is not of men, but of God.

CHAPTER THREE

*V*1: **What advantage then hath the Jew? or what is the profit of circumcision?**

If the 'privileges' of the Jew served only to increase his condemnation, then it would appear that they were a serious liability which he could well do without. Paul anticipates and answers the objections which his teaching in the previous chapter would raise in the Jewish mind.

In the same way, a nominal Christian when faced with God's rejection of his empty profession, will always ask what is the advantage of his creed and baptism if they cannot save him from condemnation? (Godet)

*V*2: **Much every way: first of all, that they were intrusted with the oracles of God.**

This verse sheds a remarkable light on Paul's view of Scripture. He does not here complete his enumeration of the spiritual blessings of the Jews [for that see, *Rom* 9:4, 5], but sums them all up in this one supreme privilege. 'First of all,' before everything else, God conferred upon them the dignity of being the depositaries of the divine oracles [*Acts* 7:38]. Indeed the Jews would not have so carefully preserved the written record of God's dealings with their race in judgment as well as grace, apart from the sustained conviction that such a special revelation had been entrusted to them by God. And as a true son of Israel, the apostle shared that conviction in full measure. 'For

[50]

Paul the *written* Word is God's speech, and God's speech is conceived of as existing in the form of a "trust" to Israel; divine oracles have fixed and abiding form . . . And Paul was not afraid of being accused of bibliolatry when he thus assessed the inscripturated Word.' (John Murray) But when the Jews were thus assured that the message of salvation was in their hands, it was all the more tragic that they failed to see the fulfilment of the Messianic promises in the One whom they had despised and rejected [cf *Is* 53].

*V*3: **For what if some were without faith? shall their want of faith make of none effect the faithfulness of God?**

It may seem surprising that Paul refers to the Jews' widespread rejection of the gospel as the unbelief of 'some'. But though the 'some' are many, they are not the whole. This 'some' therefore points to the other 'some' in whom God's purpose according to the election of grace is fulfilled [cf 11:1-7]. As we also live in a world which appears largely indifferent if not actively hostile to the Word of God, it is important to remember that this Word always accomplishes the purpose for which he sends it forth [*Is* 55:11], for he will never permit the want of faith in 'some' to nullify his own faithfulness.

*V*4: **God forbid: yea, let God be found true, but every man a liar; as it is written,**
That thou mightest be justified in thy words,
And mightest prevail when thou comest into judgment.

Not content with the negative answers implied in the preceding questions, Paul dismisses any suggestion of God's unfaithfulness with total abhorrence. For God must be found true, even though every man should turn out to be a liar [cf *Ps* 116:11]. The falsehoods of men are so often said to invalidate the veracity of God that the apostle's vehement protest is exactly to the point. And this is our warrant to defend the unchanging truthfulness of God's Word against all the objections of unbelief, whether voiced in the form of apostate science, philosophy, or theology! 'Whenever, then, the Divine testimony is contradicted by human testimony, let man be accounted a liar.' (Haldane)

This affirmation is confirmed by an appeal to *Ps* 51:4: 'that Thou mayest be justified when Thou speakest, and win the case when Thou enterest into judgement'. (F. F. Bruce) The image is that of a court in which God condescends to plead his case against men so that his Word may be publicly vindicated. It is clear that God must always emerge the victor from such a contest. For when men argue with God they only succeed in covering themselves with shame.

V5: **But if our unrighteousness commendeth the righteousness of God, what shall we say? Is God unrighteous who visiteth with wrath? (I speak after the manner of men.)**

However, it may be objected that if man's unrighteousness thus serves to show forth the righteousness of God, is it not therefore unjust of God to reward this contribution to his glory with the infliction of his wrath? Paul's indignant disclaimer, 'I speak after the manner of men,' indicates that his reluctant statement of this sinful mode of reasoning was only in order to refute it with all the energy at his command.

V6: **God forbid: for then how shall God judge the world?**

Paul's repugnance to this impiety is again expressed in the exclamation, 'God forbid'. It is a folly that does not deserve a reply, though he provides one in the form of a question. This announces a truth which would command the assent of his imaginary Jewish objector, for clearly a God divested of rectitude would be quite unable to judge the world [cf *Gen* 18:25]. It is because God *is* righteous that he is bound to punish evildoers who have no intention of serving him, even though the actions which evoke his wrath may also unwittingly redound to his glory [v 5]. It should be noted that Paul does not try to prove the fact of universal judgment, he simply asserts it as a fundamental element of the revelation which has been entrusted to him. According to John Murray, the significance of the apostle's answer is that it shows what must always be true in regard to the ultimate facts of revelation: 'These facts are ultimate, and argument must be content with categorical affirmation. The answer to objections is proclamation.'

V7: **But if the truth of God through my lie abounded unto his glory, why am I also still judged as a sinner?**

In this more vivid re-statement of the cavil raised in *v 5*, Paul now plays the part of the ungodly objector. In the boldness of its questioning of God's rectitude, it reveals an attitude of mind that constitutes the very essence of ungodliness.

V8: **and why not (as we are slanderously reported, and as some affirm that we say), Let us do evil, that good may come? whose condemnation is just.**

The most outrageous application of this principle is found in the lawless perversion of the gospel which was slanderously attributed to the apostle by his enemies [cf 6:1]. 'By reducing the reasoning of the Jews to a conclusion shocking to the moral sense he thereby refutes it . . . Any doctrine, therefore, which is immoral in its tendency or which conflicts with the first principles of morals, must be false, no matter how plausible may be the arguments in its favour.' (Hodge)

By contrast Ignatius Loyola taught his followers to suppress their own moral feelings. 'If anything shall appear white to our eyes which the Church has defined as black, we likewise must declare it to be black.' (cited by L. Boettner) The enthusiastic adoption of such a system of moral casuistry made the name of 'Jesuit' infamous throughout Europe.

Paul's concurrence with God's judgment of condemnation is based on the recognition that this verdict is just, and is therefore not to be deprecated. It must be acknowledged that the apostles of Christ were unacquainted with the all-pervasive moral anaemia which nowadays is euphemistically described as Christian tolerance. R. L. Dabney points out 'that the inspired men of both Testaments felt and expressed moral indignation against wrong-doers, and a desire for their proper retribution at the hand of God . . . Sympathy with the right implies reprobation of the wrong.'

*V*9: **What then? are we better than they? No, in no wise: for we before laid to the charge both of Jews and Greeks, that they are all under sin;**

This verse begins the apostle's summing up of what he has separately demonstrated, namely, that the Gentiles and the Jews are alike guilty before God. Although Paul has insisted upon the value of the privileges enjoyed by the Jew [*v* 2], he vigorously denies that these advantages enhance their standing before God. Those gripped by sin are also under its condemning power. The guilty have no 'rights'; they must sue for grace [*v* 19ff].

*V*10: **as it is written,**
There is none righteous, no, not one;

This community in condemnation is confirmed by an impressive chain of Old Testament quotations, appropriately headed by a free rendering of *Ps* 14:3, which denies the possibility of finding even one righteous man. What unites all men is their solidarity in guilt, for every man lacks the righteousness which God demands. 'Righteousness is the criterion by which sin is judged and the absence of righteousness means the presence of sin.' (John Murray)

*V*11: **There is none that understandeth,**
There is none that seeketh after God;

Once again the thought, rather than the precise words of the Psalmist, is reproduced by Paul [*Ps* 14:2, 53:3]. It is because man's mind has been blinded by sin, that there is no movement of his will towards God. God is man's greatest good; it is man's inability to recognize and act upon this truth which reveals the extent of his depravity [*Eph* 4:18].

*V*12: **They have all turned aside, they are together become unprofitable;**
   There is none that doeth good, no, not so much as one:

This is an exact quotation of *Ps* 14:3, 53:4 from the Greek version of the Old Testament. It diagnoses the condition of mankind as one of universal apostasy [cf 1:21]. All have turned aside from God the source of life, with the result that humanity has become soured, corrupted, and completely unprofitable to God. Not a single soul does anything that is good, because 'all are rotten to the core' [*Ps* 14:3 NEB].

*V*13: **Their throat is an open sepulchre;**
   With their tongues they have used deceit:
   The poison of asps is under their lips:
*V*14: **Whose mouth is full of cursing and bitterness:**

The vices of the tongue are next described in words which are again taken from the Psalms [cf 5:9, 139:4, 10:7]. Perhaps nothing more vividly demonstrates the wickedness of man than his vile debasement of the noble faculty of speech, 'for out of the abundance of the heart the mouth speaketh' [*Matt* 12:34]. First, the *throat* is likened to an open grave, which may either suggest the desire to devour its intended victim, or the pollution that is spread by the foul odours of corruption. By contrast the deceitful *tongue* accomplishes its evil designs with sugared words of flattery. The third figure compares the calumny and falsehood which emerges from malignant *lips* with the serpent's infusion of its deadly poison. Finally, the *mouth* is said to be full of the cursing and bitterness that manifests the hatred of a heart bent on murder (Godet).

V15: **Their feet are swift to shed blood;**
V16: **Destruction and misery are in their ways;**
V17: **And the way of peace have they not known:**

These verses are from *Is* 59:7, 8. This hatred is also expressed in deeds; only the *feet* are mentioned because they carry the body and its members on their campaigns of violence. The horrifying picture is drawn in three graphic strokes: ruthless, devastating feet crushing and shattering; leaving trails of destruction and wails of misery in their wake; and all because they have not known the *one* way of peace, which is only followed by those who obey the Prince of peace [*Matt* 5:9]. (Lenski)

V18: **There is no fear of God before their eyes.**

The final quotation is taken from *Ps* 36:1. Practical atheism is the root cause of man's unrighteousness. In the natural man there may be a theoretical belief in God's existence, but his behaviour constantly belies his profession. In his conduct he is neither constrained by reverential awe, nor restrained by the fear of future punishment. All the evils described in the preceding verses are but the logical outcome of the truth set forth here. 'The absence of this fear means that God is excluded not only from the centre of thought and calculation but from the whole horizon of our reckoning; God is not in all our thoughts. Figuratively, he is not before our eyes. And this is unqualified godlessness.' (John Murray)

V19: **Now we know that what things soever the law saith, it speaketh to them that are under the law; that every mouth may be stopped, and all the world may be brought under the judgment of God:**

It is an indisputable axiom that those who are 'under the law' are obliged to render a perfect obedience to it. The charge has a particular relevance to the Jew who did not realize that his sinfulness made the law the instrument of his own condemnation. It is plain that Paul's use of the word 'law' here includes the whole of the Old Testament, for his quotations were drawn from the Psalms and Isaiah. However, the fact that the Gentiles have not received the written Word does not place them beyond the scope of its condemnation, for their failure to live up to the light of nature leaves them without excuse [2:14, 15].

Man's conduct is in mournful conformity with the character given to him in the Word of God, and he is therefore justly exposed to the wrath of God.

The condemnation of all men is the inevitable consequence of a broken law, which passes impartial judgment upon all transgressors. The purpose of the law is to bring the whole world *under judgment* (*hupodikos*). The word appears only here in the New Testament. It describes the plight of an accused person who has no hope of averting the sentence of condemnation because he cannot refute the charge brought against him. Every mouth is silenced by the law; it leaves man without a word to utter in his own defence [*Job* 40:4; *Ps* 130:3].

*V*20: **because by the works of the law shall no flesh be justified in his sight: for through the law cometh the knowledge of sin.**

In language borrowed from *Ps* 143:2 this gives the reason for the preceding assertion. The guilt of all men must be established *because* no man can be declared just on the basis of his deeds when 'the law calls nothing obedience, but perfect obedience.' (Shedd) Certainly if any man could perfectly obey the law, he would be justified by that obedience [2:13]. But in fact this theoretical possibility is never realized, for 'there is none righteous, no, not one' [*v* 10]. The cause of this universal failure resides in the inability of the 'flesh' to fulfil a 'spiritual' law. For however much the 'flesh' may impress its own kind, it shall not 'be accounted righteous in his sight' (ASV margin). The verse states the inescapable conclusion to be drawn from the foregoing arguments. The sin which disqualifies man from all hope of being justified by his personal obedience to the law of God, also condemns him for his total inability to meet its righteous demands.

But this negative conclusion is not without positive value, 'for through the law cometh the knowledge of sin'. A correct understanding of the true function of the law is an essential element in the effective proclamation of the gospel. The heart of man must be deeply furrowed by the sharp plough of God's law before there can be a profitable reception of the seed of life. Paul's doctrine of grace is firmly based upon an adequate doctrine of sin, because he knew that it is only the convicted sinner who desires an interest in the Saviour from sin. Thus the proper use of the law is to convince man of his guilt before God, for no unawakened heart is able to appreciate gospel grace [*Gal* 3:22].

V21: **But now apart from the law a righteousness of God hath been manifested, being witnessed by the law and the prophets;**

The whole of Paul's gospel is embraced in the antithesis between the 'then' of man's misery and the 'now' of God's grace [cf *Eph* 2:12f]. Here his emphatic 'but now' rivets the attention upon the dramatic change effected by the action of God. For now 'apart from the law' – i.e. taking no account whatever of man's abortive attempts to comply with its demands – God's righteousness has been revealed (for this see comment on 1:17).

Moreover, what is now so clearly manifested was also attested by the law and the prophets. The entire Old Testament gave witness to this 'righteousness without works'; it was foreshadowed in the rites of the law, and foretold in the promises of the prophets [cf *Luke* 24:27, 44].

V22a: **even the righteousness of God through faith in Jesus Christ unto all them that believe;**

Man is put into possession of a divine righteousness through (*dia*) the instrumentality of faith. The preposition used shows that faith is not a meritorious work; it is simply the hand that lays hold of the merits of Another. Here for the first time in the epistle, Paul directly relates the righteousness of God with the redemptive achievement of Christ. As this statement *limits* the gift of righteousness to the faith which is specifically directed to Jesus Christ, so it also *includes* all those who exercise such faith in him – it is 'unto all and upon all them that believe' (ASV margin). This fullness of expression emphasizes the fact that the same blessing is extended to every believer. It is the glory of the gospel that 'there is no discrimination among believers – the righteousness of God comes upon them *all* without distinction'. (John Murray)

*V*22b: **for there is no distinction;**

*V*23: **for all have sinned, and fall short of the glory of God;**

There is also no distinction between Jew and Gentile in regard to their common need of an interest in Christ, because they are both equally guilty before God. 'For all sinned and (do) come short of the glory of God.' (David Brown) 'The sinning of each man is presented as an historical fact of the past' (H. A. W. Meyer cited by Hodge). Dr Hodge's own comment here is, 'The sinning is represented as past; the present and abiding consequence of sin is the want of *the glory of God*' [cf 5:12]. The natural result of the disfiguration of God's image in man through sin, is found in man's complete ethical disablement. All men do constantly fall short of the glory of God, because all have sinned in Adam, and all are sinners by practice.

*V*24: **being justified freely by his grace through the redemption that is in Christ Jesus:**

After the digression of *vv* 22b, 23, the present participle, 'being justified', shows how God's righteousness is even now conferred upon all believers [*v* 22a]. God at once declares them righteous by putting the righteousness of Christ to their account. The double description used by Paul safeguards the character of justification as an absolute grant to the undeserving. Those who are 'freely' justified 'by his grace' clearly must receive it as God's gift. The total incapacity of man to make any contribution to this divine donation could not be more strongly emphasized. The riches of God's grace and the imaginary 'merits' of man cannot be allowed to co-exist together for one moment. Church history has proved that the maintenance of this truth is the crucial element in the preservation of Paul's gospel from corruption. It was the re-discovery by Martin Luther of the doctrine of God's free justification of the ungodly which heralded the greatest revival of true religion since the days of the apostles. It is the verdict of history that Christianity languishes whenever this doctrine is obscured.

The cost of this 'free' justification is met by the One who gave his life 'a ransom for many' [*Matt* 20:28]. Paul used the original word in its strengthened form, which, as Trench points out, does not signify a mere recall from captivity, 'but recall of captives from captivity through the payment of a ransom for them'. Thus redemption in the New Testament may not be reduced to the idea of simple deliverance, for the emancipation of which it speaks is the purchase of Christ's blood [*Eph* 1:7; *Col* 1:14; 1 *Pet* 1:18, 19]. And there can be no experience of redemption apart from a personal knowledge of the Redeemer in whom 'this redemption resides in its unabbreviated virtue and efficacy'. (John Murray)

*V*25: **whom God set forth to be a propitiation, through faith, in his blood, to show his righteousness because of the passing over of the sins done aforetime, in the forbearance of God;**
*V*26: **for the showing, I say, of his righteousness at this present season: that he might himself be just, and the justifier of him that hath faith in Jesus.**

These verses provide the clearest statement of God's method of salvation to be found in the whole of Scripture. Such a revelation of what the Cross means to God is obviously of supreme importance to man, since it unalterably determines the content of saving faith. The cross is not an unexplained symbol, a mysterious event which saves irrespective of the kind of response it evokes in man: for salvation literally depends upon receiving God's interpretation of its significance.

whom God set forth to be a propitiation, The heart of the gospel is that on the cross God publicly set forth Christ as a 'propitiatory offering', i.e. as the appointed means by which God's wrath against sinners is averted.[1] Having proved at length that the wrath of God rests upon 'all ungodliness and unrighteousness of men' [1:18], Paul now points every convicted sinner to the one sacrifice which satisfied all the claims of divine justice. The dreadful reality of God's wrath against sin required appeasement, but the magnitude of God's love was manifested in the very provision of that propitiation which sin demanded [1 John 4:10]. This means that faith must find its pardon in Christ's sufferings for the guilty. For there can be no pacification of man's conscience apart from a believing interest in the blood which pacified God's wrath.

> *If Thou hast my discharge procured,*
> *And freely in my room endured*
> *The whole of wrath divine;*
> *Payment God cannot twice demand –*
> *First at my bleeding Surety's hand,*
> *And then again at mine.*

> Augustus M. Toplady.

1. Recent energetic attempts to make 'propitiation' mean 'expiation' – a sinister feature of many modern translations – have been ably refuted by Leon Morris in his important linguistic study, *The Apostolic Preaching of the Cross*, Tyndale 1965. On this passage he says that more than expiation is required, for to speak of expiation is to deal in sub-personal categories (cf. Bushnell: 'we propitiate only a person, and expiate only a fact, or act, or thing'), 'whereas the relationship between God and man must be thought of as personal in the fullest sense.' p. 201.

through faith, in his blood, These two clauses further define the concept of propitiation: 'Propitiation does not take place except through faith on the part of the saved, and through blood on the part of the Saviour.' (Godet) The first limits the propitiatory power of Christ's sacrifice to those who exercise faith in him; the second locates that power in the blood that was poured out in a violent death, vicariously borne to save sinners from receiving the wages they had earned by their disobedience [6:23].

to show his righteousness because of the passing over of the sins done aforetime, in the forbearance of God; God's purpose in setting forth Christ as a propitiation was to demonstrate his judicial righteousness by punishing sin with the severity it deserved. Such a vindication of God's character was necessary, because his forbearance in passing over sins in former times was widely misinterpreted by sinful men as an indifference to the claims of justice [Acts 14:16, 17:30]. However, this was only the suspension and not the revocation of the punishment which was due; payment of the debt was postponed, but the charges were not cancelled. And though that delay in the day of reckoning then ministered to a false sense of security in sin, no such illusion can now be entertained when the cross exhibits God's determination to avenge every breach of his law.

for the showing, I say, of his righteousness at this present season: God's past forbearance in passing over sins without exacting their proper penalty was only possible because he had in view the demonstration of his righteousness 'at this present season', i.e. the epoch of Christ's manifestation as the propitiation for the sins of the world [1 John 2:2]. 'And the implication is, that apart from this sacrifice, the justice of God would have no more allowed "forbearance" and delay of penalty, in the instance of mankind, than it did in that of the fallen angels.' (Shedd) And with respect to the future, this manifestation of God's righteousness at Golgotha was for the purpose of providing a righteous pardon for his people.

that he might himself be just, and the justifier of him that hath faith in Jesus. God's provision of Christ as a 'propitiatory offering' was the public vindication of his justice, and at the same time the means of justifying (declaring just) the ungodly [4:5]. If God had executed judgment upon the guilty he would have shown himself to be just, but he could not justify the ungodly by inflicting upon them what his justice demanded. Thus for God both to vindicate his own righteousness, and put righteousness within the reach of the sinful, it was necessary that instead of executing this judgment upon sinners he should provide a propitiation for their sins (Denney). Hence the cross exhibits the unfathomable wisdom of God, for it is only in the penal sufferings of his Son that his inflexible determination to punish sin, and his sovereign will to exercise mercy are seen to harmonize [*Ps* 85:10; *Gal* 3:13; *2 Cor* 5:21].

Paul's final words again stress the indispensable rôle of faith in justification, and specifically, of faith 'in Jesus'. Here the human name 'Jesus' becomes a poignant reminder of the cost of the Christian's 'free' justification [Heb. 2:9f].

V27: Where then is the glorying? It is excluded. By what manner of law? of works? Nay: but by a law of faith.
V28: We reckon therefore that a man is justified by faith apart from the works of the law.

Now that Paul has explained God's way of putting sinners right with himself [*vv* 21–26], he asks, 'What room is left for boasting in this gospel?' The question is applicable to all men, though it has particular point for the Jew who gloried in his privileges and boasted of his works [cf 2:17–25; *Luke* 18:9–12; *Phil* 3:4–6]. His answer is, 'It is entirely shut out'. The law (or principle) which for ever excludes such boasting is not that of works but of faith. And this is because: 'Faith is *self-*

renouncing; works are *self*-congratulatory. Faith looks to what God does; works have respect to what we are.' (John Murray) The apostle therefore concludes that a man is justified by the faith which receives the gift of God's righteousness, quite apart from 'the works of the law'. Since these principles are mutually exclusive, it is impossible for a man to be justified by faith, while he seeks righteousness by his own obedience to the law. Hence Luther was true to the spirit of the passage when he insisted that justification is by faith *alone*. 'Here St Paul shows himself a pure Lutheran.' (Trapp)

*V*29: **Or is God the God of Jews only? is he not the God of Gentiles also? Yea, of Gentiles also:**

*V*30: **if so be that God is one, and he shall justify the circumcision by faith, and the uncircumcision through faith.**

Paul further shows that the old racial distinctions have been abolished in the gospel of God's free grace [cf *Eph* 2:11-18]. As all Jews know there is but one God [*Deut* 6:4], it follows that he is God of both Jews and Gentiles [*Is* 45:21, 22]. Then since this *one* God is the same for all, he cannot have *two* ways of declaring men righteous, one for Jews and another for Gentiles (Lenski). In the matter of their acceptance with God, Jews therefore enjoy no superiority over Gentiles. Salvation is neither guaranteed by circumcision, nor precluded by uncircumcision, because anyone whom God justifies is justified 'by' or 'through' faith (a difference in expression which warrants no distinction in meaning). Such a recognition of faith as the decisive factor in salvation depends upon the realization that all men have been reduced to the same common level of need by sin [3:23].

*V*31: **Do we then make the law of none effect through faith? God forbid: nay, we establish the law.**

Finally, Paul asks whether this insistence upon faith does away with the law. Is not God's commandment made void by the claim that *no* contribution is made to justification by *any* works of legal obedience? Recoiling from the suggestion in disgust, he shows that the righteousness of faith does not abrogate but actually establishes the law. For by faith 'we attain a perfect righteousness, we are interested in the most complete obedience of Christ to the moral law; and that hereby every type, promise, and prophecy is fulfilled; see *Matt* 5:17; *Luke* 16:17.' (Poole)

CHAPTER FOUR

*V*1: **What then shall we say that Abraham, our fore-father, hath found according to the flesh?**

Paul has claimed that his gospel is but the manifestation of what was foretold in the law and the prophets [1:2, 3:21]. Now he shows that the fundamental continuity which exists between the promises and their fulfilment also extends to the justification of believers in Old Testament times. The apostle's appeal to the experience of Abraham and David provides confirmation of the fact that believers in both dispensations are justified in exactly the same way, by faith in God's promise. The precise interpretation of the verse depends on whether the phrase 'according to the flesh' goes with 'forefather' or 'hath found'. Those who favour the latter alternative take the question to mean: What did Abraham obtain according to the flesh? Did the patriarch gain righteousness by any works of his own? [cf *Phil* 3:3, 4] If the former construction is adopted the question would be: What then shall we say of the case of Abraham, our forefather according to the flesh? It seems better to understand the phrase in this physical sense, 'because the contrast with another kind of fatherhood belonging to Abraham is already in the apostle's thoughts: see *v* 11'. (Denney)

*V*2: **For if Abraham was justified by works, he hath whereof to glory; but not toward God.**

*V*3: **For what saith the scripture? And Abraham believed God, and it was reckoned unto him for righteousness.**

A Jewish objector to the teaching that men are justified by faith alone would naturally appeal to the case of his illustrious ancestor. And certainly *if* Abraham had been justified on the basis of his works he would have had a ground for boasting. But he was not justified by works as is seen from the fact that he had no such ground of boasting before God; an assertion which the apostle proves by citing the testimony of Scripture, *Gen* 15:6.

This states that Abraham simply believed God, he rested on the bare promise of God [*vv* 18-22], 'and it was reckoned unto him *for* (*eis*) righteousness'. As the whole weight of Paul's argument is directed against justification by works [*vv* 4, 5], it is obvious that 'faith' is not to be understood as a work which is reckoned *as* righteousness by God. The preposition (*eis*) must rather mean that faith is *unto* righteousness; it is the instrument through which the believer becomes personally interested in the justifying righteousness of Christ.

Righteousness was reckoned to Abraham as a matter of grace and not of debt [*v* 4]. It was not acquired by his own merit, but conferred upon him by sovereign grace. There is, however, nothing fictional or unreal about this gracious act of imputation by which the sinner is justified. For God declares none righteous save those whom he constitutes righteous in Christ. Hence the unrighteous can be judged righteous only because Christ's perfect righteousness is actually put to their account.

*V*4: **Now to him that worketh, the reward is not reckoned as of grace, but as of debt.**
*V*5: **But to him that worketh not, but believeth on him that justifieth the ungodly, his faith is reckoned for righteousness.**

Despite legalistic assumptions to the contrary, the case of

Abraham cannot be compared with that of a worker, whose pay is never allotted by grace but is 'reckoned according to debt' – a phrase which aptly applies to the Jewish recording of merits (cf *TDNT*, Vol. IV, p. 291). For whenever merit-mongers seek to accumulate a credit balance with God, they only succeed in putting themselves hopelessly in the red!

Having indicated the impossibility of attaining righteousness by works, Paul sets forth God's method of grace in an antithesis which absolutely excludes boasting [*v* 5]. It is a general statement of the principle that holds good in the case of every sinner who is justified. The significance of the singular is well brought out by Hodge's remark, 'God does not justify communities'. When a man has been brought to realize his own ungodliness, he no longer tries to work for his acceptance by God. He abandons the ground of merit as a lost cause, and instead believes on him who justifies 'the ungodly'. The strength of Paul's paradox serves to magnify the miracle of God's grace in freely justifying the ungodly. 'The man is taken as ungodly, "just as he is", and is forgiven. He is not first made perfectly holy, and then pronounced just. Neither is he first made imperfectly holy or partially sanctified, and then pardoned. Pardon and justification is the very first act (after election, 8:30) which God performs in reference to the "ungodly".' (Shedd) And he is justified in spite of his ungodliness, 'because his *faith* is reckoned for righteousness' (cf comment on *v* 3).

In the Old Testament judges are instructed to 'justify the righteous, and condemn the wicked,' but in the gospel it is God's unique prerogative to justify the 'ungodly' and that without injustice, as *Rom* 3:26 makes clear [*Deut* 25:1]. But once the sinner *is* justified he neither remains ungodly [1 *Cor* 6:11], nor is barren of the 'works' by which he is later 'justified' [*James* 2:20ff]. As such deeds are the *consequence* of God's transforming verdict it is obvious they can add nothing to it, but they do afford the visible proof of the reality of the saving change that has taken place.

*V*6: **Even as David also pronounceth blessing upon the man, unto whom God reckoneth righteousness apart from works,**

*V*7: **saying,**

> **Blessed are they whose iniquities are forgiven,**
> **And whose sins are covered.**

*V*8: **Blessed is the man to whom the Lord will not reckon sin.**

The fundamental importance of *Gen* 15:6 in showing that faith is 'reckoned' for righteousness is confirmed by the use which is made of the same word in *Ps* 32:1, 2. As John Murray observes, it is particularly pertinent to Paul's purpose that the man whom David pronounced blessed is not the man who has good works put to his account 'but whose *sins* are *not* laid to his account'. And the apostle rightly interprets this non-reckoning of sin as the positive imputation of righteousness. For though justification embraces much more than the remission of sin [cf 5:17–21], he is able to take the part for the whole, because God's forgiveness necessarily implies the complete reinstatement of the sinner.

*V*9: **Is this blessing then pronounced upon the circumcision, or upon the uncircumcision also? for we say, To Abraham his faith was reckoned for righteousness.**

*V*10: **How then was it reckoned? when he was in circumcision, or in uncircumcision? Not in circumcision, but in uncircumcision:**

Paul now asks, Is this blessedness of which David spoke confined to those who are circumcised? He has already denied that circumcision is necessary to justification [3:29–31], but here reverts to the example of Abraham to explain why this rite must not be imposed upon Gentile believers [*vv* 9–12].

Circumcision was a question of critical importance in the Early Church. In the Jewish mind it was not a sign of God's grace, but the first meritorious act of obedience to the law, which became a symbol of an adherence to a scheme of salvation by works. It had taken pride of place in Paul's repentant recital of his former self-righteousness [*Phil* 3:5]. Judaizers, who claimed to be Christians, constantly dogged the apostle's footsteps and endeavoured to force his Gentile converts to submit to circumcision. Paul sternly warned the Galatians that to consent to this demand was to fall from grace, for it became a token of their debt to fulfil the whole law [*Acts* 15:9, 10, 24; *Gal* 5:1-4; *Phil* 3:2, 3].

According to the indisputable testimony of Scripture Abraham's faith 'was reckoned for righteousness', but it must be further asked, How – i.e. under what circumstances – was his faith thus reckoned to him? Was it when he was in the state of circumcision or uncircumcision? That it was when he was still uncircumcised is the answer that lies on the very surface of the Old Testament record. 'Abraham's justification is narrated in *Gen* 15, his circumcision not till *Gen* 17, some fourteen years later: hence it was not his circumcision on which he depended for acceptance with God.' (Denney)

*V*11: **and he received the sign of circumcision, a seal of the righteousness of the faith which he had while he was in uncircumcision: that he might be the father of all them that believe, though they be in uncircumcision, that righteousness might be reckoned unto them;**
*V*12: **and the father of circumcision to them who not only are of the circumcision, but who also walk in the steps of that faith of our father Abraham which he had in uncircumcision.**

In correcting the Jews' misplaced confidence in circumcision, Paul is careful not to discredit its real value as an ordinance of divine appointment. It was given to Abraham by God as a sign and seal of his *faith*. It was the external mark (sign) which was the authentication (seal) of the righteousness that was his by faith while he was still virtually a Gentile. As the visible token of his justification, it assured Abraham of the genuineness of his faith. But it added nothing to that faith, nor did it dispense with its necessity. Consequently it was no more of an automatic passport to salvation for unbelieving Jews, than are the sacraments today for unbelieving Gentiles.

Moreover, it was in the purpose of God that Abraham was justified by faith before he was circumcised since he thus became 'the father of all them that believe'. This shows that spiritual kinship and not physical descent is the determining factor. It is only those who share Abraham's faith, who are accounted his spiritual heirs. All uncircumcised believers are appropriately included among the children of Abraham, because the righteousness which was reckoned to him in that state, is also imputed to them upon exactly the same terms.

On the other hand, it must not be supposed for a moment that circumcision is a hindrance to faith. The circumcised who also share Abraham's 'uncircumcision-faith' may equally claim him as their father. 'Circumcision is not an excluding factor and neither is it a contributing factor to that by which we become the children of Abraham. All who are of faith "these are the sons of Abraham" [*Gal* 3:7].' (John Murray)

*V*13: **For not through the law was the promise to Abraham or to his seed, that he should be heir of the world, but through the righteousness of faith.**

Having shown that Abraham was justified by faith alone [*vv* 1-8], and that this 'uncircumcision-faith' made him the father of all believers [*vv* 9-12], Paul now confirms his argument by another consideration, namely, 'that law and promise are mutually exclusive ideas'. (Denney) For it was 'not through law' (ASV margin) *of any kind* that the promise was given to Abraham. John Murray points out that the absence of the article here serves to emphasize that the Mosaic economy is not in view, but simply law as law demanding obedience. God had acted unilaterally in giving Abraham a great promise, which was not suspended upon his obedience to any law, for that would have ruled out its fulfilment as the unconditional bestowment of grace. The promise is antithetical to law.

The gracious provisions of the promise apply not only to Abraham but also to his seed, who are his *spiritual* offspring, i.e. all believers [cf *vv* 16, 17; whereas in *Gal* 3:16 the 'seed' is Christ]. The words 'that he should be heir of the world' are not an exact quotation but a summary of the promises God made to Abraham [cf *Gen* 12:3, 18:18, 22:18]. Abraham was saved by his faith in the promise, but it is evident that neither he nor his seed have yet inherited the world. Hence this ultimate fulfilment of the promise still awaits Christ's return in glory [cf *Matt* 5:5; 2 *Pet* 3:13].

V14: For if they which are of the law be heirs, faith is made void, and the promise is made of none effect:

Faith is made void and the promise is nullified if the inheritance is to be earned by an obedience to law, whether written upon the conscience or inscribed upon tables of stone. Paul here exposes the futility of Jewish unbelief in seeking righteousness by means of law, because law rules out both faith and the promise on which it rests (Lenski). Thus the man who seeks justification by works has substituted trust in his own ability for faith in the promise. But the true heirs rest upon the promise, for they know that they could never *merit* God's great salvation [cf 10:1-10].

V15: For the law worketh wrath; but where there is no law, neither is there transgression.

Paul now reveals the real result of this false faith to dash all hope of inheriting by law. For instead of producing the expected blessing, law works nothing for sinful men but wrath! This is the wrath of God which is called forth by man's constant contradiction of his law [1:18]. Without law there would be no sin, for sin is any lack of conformity to the demands of law [1 *John* 3:4]. As these demands are always spurned by man's transgressions, law unavoidably works wrath. 'The sin is as wide as the law; and the law has been shown to be as wide as the race [2:12-16].' (Shedd) Therefore justification by law is an impossibility [*Gal* 3:10-12].

*V*16: **For this cause it is of faith, that it may be according to grace; to the end that the promise may be sure to all the seed; not to that only which is of the law, but to that also which is of the faith of Abraham, who is the father of us all**

This states the conclusion that must be drawn from the preceding argument. Since an adherence to law only brings conviction of sin and ministers wrath, the one way in which sinners may receive the inheritance is through the faith which embraces the provisions of grace. 'Faith and grace cohere; law and the promised inheritance are contradictory.' (John Murray)

God's purpose in determining that the inheritance should be 'of faith' was to make the promise sure to *all* the seed; not only to believers who are 'of *the* law' (i.e. those born under the Mosaic economy, Jews), but also to believing Gentiles having Abraham's faith if not his blood (Shedd). In describing Abraham as 'the father of us all', the apostle makes a unit of the two groups because their common faith has made them members of the same family [cf *Gal* 3:9].

*V*17: **(as it is written, A father of many nations have I made thee) before him whom he believed, even God, who giveth life to the dead, and calleth the things that are not, as though they were.**

The parenthetical appeal to *Gen* 17:5 proves that Abraham's spiritual fatherhood extends to Gentiles as well as Jews, for this quotation from the Greek version of the Old Testament renders 'nations' by the same word that Paul uses for 'Gentiles' = *ethnē* (so C. K. Barrett).

who is the father of us all . . . before him whom he

believed, The connection is with the preceding verse: Abraham is our father because he is so before God. In the eternal purpose of God Abraham was destined to be the spiritual prototype of all who believe. For Abraham this purpose of God was as certain when it was expressed in the form of promise as if it had already passed into the sphere of accomplishment, and herein lies the distinctive character of his faith. As the promise given to Abraham appeared to face insuperable difficulties, it demanded an omnipotent God for its fulfilment. It was to just such a God that Abraham's faith was directed [*v* 20].

First, he is the God 'who giveth life to the dead'. The promise of an heir to this aged couple called for nothing less than the supernatural impartation of life [*v* 19]. Similarly, all spiritual vivification belongs to God alone [*Eph* 1:19, 20].

Secondly, he 'calleth the things that are not, as though they were'. 'The word "call" is used of God's effectual word and determination.' (John Murray) God's decree gives a certain future to those things which are without present existence. Because Abraham believed that the declared purpose of God must come to pass, he received the promise as though it were the fulfilment [cf *Heb* 11:1].

*V*18: **Who in hope believed against hope, to the end that he might become a father of many nations, according to that which had been spoken, So shall thy seed be.**

'Who in hope believed against hope' is a striking description of Abraham's faith. 'It was both contrary to hope (as far as nature could give hope), and rested on hope (that God could do what nature could not).' (Denney) And Abraham so believed against every evidence to the contrary, in order that God's declared purpose might be fulfilled through him. He faced the obstacles that stood in the way of his becoming a father at all without any weakening of faith [*v* 19], because every time he looked at the stars in the heavens he was reminded of the Promiser's creative power (though Paul quotes only part of *Gen* 15:5, Lightfoot says 'his readers would mentally continue it'). 'It is the nature of faith to believe God upon his bare word . . . It will not be, saith sense; it cannot be, saith reason; it both can and will be, saith faith, for I have a promise for it.' (Trapp)

*V*19: **And without being weakened in faith he considered his own body now as good as dead (he being about a hundred years old), and the deadness of Sarah's womb;**

In order to show that the fulfilment of God's promise was strictly supernatural in character, Abraham and Sarah were denied an heir until all natural hope was extinguished. 'This explains why, in the life of Abraham, so many things proceed contrary to nature . . . Abraham was kept childless until an age when he was "as good as dead", that the divine omnipotence might be evident as the source of Isaac's birth [*Gen* 21:1-7; *Rom* 4:19-21; *Heb* 11:11; *Is* 51:2].' (Geerhardus Vos, *Biblical Theology*, p. 81).

The omission of 'not' in the best texts is important (cf AV: 'he considered *not* his own body now dead'). For it shows that though Abraham was not blind to the empirical facts of the situation, he did not allow them to have an adverse effect upon his faith in the promise. He faced up to his own and his wife's 'deadness' without doubting God's word.

*V*20: **yet, looking unto the promise of God, he wavered not through unbelief, but waxed strong through faith, giving glory to God,**
*V*21: **and being fully assured that what he had promised, he was able also to perform.**

It was because Abraham's attention was fixed upon the promise, that he was not inwardly torn by distrust; but was rather strengthened in faith, giving glory to God. Believing God's word always gives glory to God. It honours *his promises* by taking him at his word, and it honours *his power* by acknowledging his ability to do the impossible [*Mark* 10:27]. Unlike the unbelieving [1:21], Abraham glorified God as God, by recognizing him as the all-powerful Creator who could not fail to keep his covenanted word (so Barrett).

V22: **Wherefore also it was reckoned unto him for righteousness.**

'Wherefore also' indicates the consequence of the faith described in verses 20, 21. Abraham's specific and unqualified reliance on God's promise was the necessary condition, but not the ground of his justification. Since this unwavering faith glorified God by reckoning upon his faithfulness, God also reckoned it to Abraham for righteousness [*Gen* 15:6, see also comment on *v* 3].

V23: **Now it was not written for his sake alone, that it was reckoned unto him;**
V24: **but for our sake also, unto whom it shall be reckoned, who believe on him that raised Jesus our Lord from the dead,**
V25: **who was delivered up for our trespasses, and was raised for our justification.**

In conclusion Paul drives home the lesson to be learned from the history of Abraham [cf 1 *Cor* 10:11]. For the same divine reckoning by which Abraham was justified will be reckoned to all who believe after the pattern of his faith. This identical method of reckoning shows that Abraham was not justified by a faith which was radically different from that of the Christian. In fact there is an identity of belief which makes his example of abiding significance for the Christian. 'He believed in God as quickening the dead, that is, as able to raise up from one as good as dead, the promised Redeemer.' (Hodge) Therefore Christ declared, 'Abraham rejoiced to see my day; and he saw it, and was glad.' [*John* 8:56] However, the Christian enjoys the fulfilment of that which Abraham only received in the form of promise, for Paul succinctly describes this as believing 'on him that raised Jesus our Lord from the dead'. In the New Testament, belief in the gospel is frequently expressed as a belief in the resurrection, because this climactic event is at once the ultimate vindication of Christ's claim to be the Son of God, and the decisive proof of God's acceptance of his redeeming work [10:9; *Acts* 1:22, 4:33, 17:31; 1 *Cor* 15].

It should be noticed that Paul knows nothing of a 'Jesus' worship, which would force God the Father into the background of men's minds. He explicitly states that saving belief is focussed on him who 'waked' Jesus. As Geerhardus Vos says, The Father's power was exercised in the resurrection of Jesus, so that through him it may work upon others.

who was delivered up for our trespasses, and was raised for our justification. In this brief sentence of profound import and eloquent simplicity, there is distilled the very sum of saving knowledge. It is best to take both expressions as having prospective reference: 'He was delivered up on account of our offences – to make atonement for them; and he was raised on account of our justification – that it might become an accomplished fact.' (Denney) Christ's death and resurrection are inseparable because they form one redemptive act; neither makes sense without the other, so that whenever one is mentioned the other is always implied. Here again our attention is directed to the action of God the Father in delivering up his Son to make atonement for our sins [8:32; *Acts* 2:23], and in raising him for our justification [6:4; *Acts* 3:15; *Gal* 1:1]. And we are thereby taught to ascribe all the glory of our salvation to God who designed, provided, and executed this great work of redemption.

Paul here says that Christ was raised for our justification, for though the work of atonement was finished on the cross, the righteousness by which we are justified is forever embodied in the living Lord through whom this grace is mediated to us [John Murray; cf 5:2, 1 *Cor* 1:30]. But it would have been equally legitimate to say that he died for our justification, since his redeeming death is the basis of our reinstatement before God [cf 5:9; *Eph* 1:7]. However, the verse as it stands, serves to show that Paul never thought of the cross by itself, for 'he knew Christ only as the Risen One who had died, and who had the virtue of his atoning death ever in him'. (Denney)

CHAPTER FIVE

In what follows Paul expounds the blessed consequences that flow from Christ's having been raised for our justification. As Nygren puts it, All who have this new life in Christ are free from wrath [*ch* 5], free from sin [*ch* 6], free from law [*ch* 7], and free from death [*ch* 8].

*V*1: **Being therefore justified by faith, we have peace with God through our Lord Jesus Christ;**

Although 'let us have peace with God' (RV) is the better attested reading, it is rejected by most scholars because it is inconsistent with the context. Exhortation is entirely out of place in a passage where Paul is speaking of the objective benefits of justification [*vv* 10, 11], and there can be no doubt that his meaning is 'we *have* peace with God' (as in AV, ASV, RSV).

'Therefore' introduces the conclusion to be drawn from the preceding argument [cf 12:1]. '*Therefore,*' says the apostle, 'having been justified by faith, we have peace with God.' This means that God's wrath no longer threatens us, because we are accepted in Christ [*v* 9]. What is indicated is not a change in our feelings, but a change in God's relation to us. And this objective peace with God is not only the purchase of Christ's blood but also the fruit of his continued mediation. 'All spiritual blessings are *in* Christ. But they are also enjoyed *through* Christ's continued mediatory activity.' (John Murray)

[79]

V2: **through whom also we have had our access by faith into this grace wherein we stand; and we rejoice in hope of the glory of God.**

It is also through the mediation of Christ that we have had our 'introduction' by faith into this grace of justification in which we have come to stand. The idea suggested by the word is that of introduction to the presence-chamber of the king. As Sanday and Headlam observe, 'The rendering "access" is inadequate, as it leaves out of sight the fact that we do not come in our own strength but need an "introducer" – Christ.' Having once been ushered into this state of grace and favour, it is our immutable privilege to enjoy unhindered communion with the Father.

It would be strange if these blessings did not promote within the believing heart a lively sense of assurance and confident hope. Indeed the word translated as 'rejoice' really means an exultant boasting, which is inspired by the certainty that 'we have peace with God' [*v* 1]. This glorying is faith's present anticipation of the glory to be revealed at the consummation of God's eternal purpose in Christ, when our chief end shall be realized as we 'glorify God and enjoy him for ever' [cf 8:17–25; 2 *Cor* 3:18; *Col* 3:4; 1 *John* 3:2].

V3: **And not only so, but we also rejoice in our tribulations: knowing that tribulation worketh stedfastness;**
V4: **and stedfastness, approvedness; and approvedness, hope:**

But our boasting is not confined to the hope of future glory; we also see our present trials as a cause for exultation! This glorying in tribulation is a fruit of faith, for as Calvin says, 'this is not the natural effect of tribulation, which, as we see, provokes a great part of mankind to murmur against God, and even to curse him.' It is only the knowledge that these tribulations are the appointment of his heavenly Father, which enables the Christian to rejoice in them, for in themselves

they are evil, grievous and not joyous [*Heb* 12:6; *Rev* 3:19].
Paul's own experience was in line with his teaching, 'that we
must through much tribulation enter into the kingdom of
God' [*Acts* 14:22]. There is no short cut to glory. The believer
must follow the path marked out for him by his Saviour, for
the cross always precedes the crown [*Phil* 1:29, 30].

We can glory in tribulation because we have come to
know that it works in us a spirit of brave endurance. It is by
the exercise of this grace that the Christian approves himself
and shows that he is no fair-weather professor [*Matt* 13:21].
Hence the endurance of these trials provides the Christian
with subjective evidence of his own sincerity. His Christian
character is proved by his patience in tribulation, which in
turn assures him of the genuineness of his hope [1 *Pet* 1:7].
John Murray draws attention to the fact that the apostle has
described a circle which begins and ends in hope. He insists
that 'glorying in tribulations is subordinate – they subserve the
interests of hope'. Accordingly, the believer's present trials
must always be viewed in the light of their eternal sequel
[1 *Pet* 4:12, 13].

V5: **and hope putteth not to shame; because the love of
God hath been shed abroad in our hearts through the
Holy Spirit which was given unto us.**

This is the one hope that is well founded, and so, unlike those
who have embraced a delusory hope, we are not put to shame
[cf *Ps* 25:20]. On the contrary, it is the hope in which we
glory even in the midst of our afflictions. Haldane here points
out the connection between the Christian's hope and his
power to witness; 'Just in proportion as his hope is strong,
will he make an open and bold profession of the truth . . .
This shows the great importance of keeping our hope un-
clouded. If we suffer it to flag or grow faint, we shall be
ashamed of it before men.'

We are able to sustain this hope in such straits, 'because the
love of God has been poured out in our hearts through the

Holy Spirit who was given to us.' It is evident from the context that Paul refers to God's love for us [v 8], and not our love for him as Romish expositors maintain on dogmatic grounds following Augustine (cf Nygren's vigorous protest). It is not without significance that in this verse both the love of God and the Holy Spirit are mentioned for the first time in the epistle, for only he can communicate to us the *sense* of God's love. This is in fact a concise statement of the theme which is fully developed by Paul in Chapter 8. 'Poured out' indicates the lavish diffusion of this love which carries with it the irrefragable assurance of salvation [cf *Acts* 2:17, 18, 33, 10:45; 'poured out upon us richly,' *Titus* 3:6]. The sphere of the Spirit's operation is the heart to which he has immediate access; it being his special work to apply the benefits of redemption to those for whom the Saviour suffered. 'Who was given to us' harks back to the time of conversion, for it is only in the Spirit that a man can savingly confess 'Jesus is Lord' (1 *Cor* 12:3; cf 8:9].

'Though sinners should hear ten thousand times of the love of God in the gift of his Son, they are never properly affected by it, till the Holy Spirit enters into their hearts, and till love to him is produced by the truth through the Spirit.' (Haldane)

*V*6: **For while we were yet weak, in due season Christ died for the ungodly.**

The supreme demonstration of the love of God is seen in Christ's death for the ungodly. This love is at once original and unmerited, for it is extended to those who are completely powerless to help themselves. 'Sinful' seems to be the meaning of 'weak' here, for 'while we were yet weak' is almost synonymous with 'while we were yet sinners' (v 8). It was therefore while we were under the condemning power of sin, while we were wholly disabled by sin, that Christ died for our benefit. God could find nothing in the 'ungodly' to constrain his love [cf 4:5]. The amazing character of God's love thus lies in the fact that it was exercised towards those whose natural condition was absolutely repugnant to his holiness. And it is only as we are taught by grace to acknowledge this unpalatable truth that the boundless nature of God's love begins to dawn upon us. 'In due season' means that Christ died at the time appointed by God, and in accordance with his eternal purpose [*John* 8:20, 12:27, 17:1; *Gal* 4:4; *Heb* 9:26].

*V*7: **For scarcely for a righteous man will one die: for peradventure for the good man some one would even dare to die.**
*V*8: **But God commendeth his own love towards us, in that, while we were yet sinners, Christ died for us.**

It is not likely that Paul is drawing a contrast between a righteous and a good man, and it is better to understand both epithets as describing the same individual. As John Murray explains it, 'In the human sphere scarcely for a *righteous* and *good* man will one die but God exhibits and commends *his* love in that it was for *sinners* Christ died.' It is obvious that 'righteous' and 'good' are used *relatively* of man's judgment, for the universal dominion of sin has already been proved at length. A man may indeed be prepared to make the ultimate sacrifice to save someone whom he *deems* to be worthy of it, but God gave up his Son to the death of the cross for those whom he *knew* to be utterly vile and worthless! The comparison thus brings out the unique character of God's love, which reached its zenith in Christ's death for sinners [*John* 3:16; 1 *John* 4:10]. From this it follows that conviction of sin is the essential prerequisite to an interest in Christ [*Mark* 2:17]. Hence those who imagine that they are without sin necessarily exclude themselves from all the blessings which Christ purchased for sinners by his death [1 *John* 1:8–10]. 'While we were yet sinners' implies that the readers are no longer in that state of condemnation [cf 1:7], 'for he died to save us, not *in* our sins, but *from* our sins; but we were yet sinners when he died for us.' (Matthew Henry) [*Matt* 1:21]

*V*9: **Much more then, being now justified by his blood, shall we be saved from the wrath of God through him.**

The Christian faith is not groundless optimism, but a confident hope based upon cogent reasoning. The argument is that if Christians were justified by the death of Christ when they were lost in sin, how much more shall they be saved from wrath now that they are restored to God's favour. In this section the one-sided nature of God's action in salvation is strongly brought out by Paul's graphic description of man's plight. In verse 6, 'powerless' (NEB) indicates a total inability to obey God's commands, while 'ungodly' points to the inevitable connection which exists between godlessness and the lack of godliness. In verse 8 the word 'sinners' describes those who are by nature and by inclination addicted to disobedience, and in verse 10 'enemies' means those who hate God, and who are by reason of their sin, hateful to God. Thus, it was for man, helpless and hopeless, that Christ died. Paul 'assumes that Christ's death put sinners on a new footing, a new standing before God; in a word, that it rectified their relation. And then he argues: "If justified as sinners by his blood, much more shall we as friends be saved from wrath through him." ' (Smeaton)

The hope of glory necessarily includes the assurance that through Christ we shall be saved from the wrath to come [*John* 3:36]. 'It was a virile conception of God that the apostle entertained and, because so, it was one that took account of the terror of God's wrath. Salvation from the future exhibition of that terror was an ingredient of the hope of glory.' (John Murray) [2:5, 8; 1 *Thess* 1:10, 5:9]

*V*10: **For if, while we were enemies, we were reconciled to God through the death of his Son, much more, being reconciled, shall we be saved by his life;**

The argument of this verse is based on the two states of Christ, for if reconciliation was made by means of his humiliating death, then how much more shall his glorious resurrection life ensure the final salvation of those for whom he suffered.

As Denney rightly insists, 'enemies' must be given the passive meaning it undoubtedly has in 11:28. We were *God's* enemies, not merely ourselves hostile to God, but in a real sense the objects of his hostility by reason of our sin. This meant that our restoration to divine favour depended entirely upon God, the Offended One, taking the initiative in reconciling the offenders to himself. And this he did by removing the sin, which was the ground of that enmity, through the death of his Son. Therefore to suggest that what is in view is the laying aside of our hostility is to miss the point of the whole passage. 'Paul is demonstrating *the love of God*, and he can only do it by pointing to what *God* has done, not to what *we* have done . . . The subjective side of the truth is here completely, *and intentionally*, left out of sight; the laying aside of *our* hostility adds nothing to God's love, throws no light on it; hence in an exposition of the love of God it can be ignored.' (Denney)

'Much more' indicates an indissoluble connection between Christ's death and resurrection, because it assures all who are reconciled to God by Christ's death of their perseverance to glory by virtue of his endless life.

*V*11: **and not only so, but we also rejoice in God through our Lord Jesus Christ, through whom we have now received the reconciliation.**

Having spoken in the previous verse of reconciliation in terms of its objective accomplishment, the apostle now describes the glorying in God which attends its subjective application. The knowledge that God is a reconciled Father in Jesus Christ suffuses the believing heart with exultant joy. Salvation is a present reality for the Christian. And as God was reconciled by the death of the Mediator, even so believers receive this reconciliation *through* the mediation of their exalted Redeemer. As the concluding words of the verse unmistakably show, reconciliation 'is not a change in our disposition toward God, but a change in his attitude toward us. We do not *give* it (by laying aside enmity, distrust, or fear); we *receive* it, by believing in Christ Jesus, whom God has set forth as a propitiation through faith in his blood. We take it as God's unspeakable gift.' (Denney)

*V*12: **Therefore, as through one man sin entered into the world, and death through sin; and so death passed unto all men, for that all sinned:**

It was the Puritan Thomas Goodwin who said, 'In God's sight there are two men – Adam and Jesus Christ – and these two men have all other men hanging at their girdle strings' (cited by F. F. Bruce). This passage makes it clear that Paul regarded Adam as the first man, whose disobedience to God's commandment had far-reaching consequences for the human race. But for those modern scholars who regard the Fall as a mythical statement of what is nevertheless a valid religious truth, Adam becomes a sort of religious Everyman. It would be frivolous to reproduce such a view as an exposition of the apostle's teaching in this place. The right to be regarded as a serious interpreter of Paul's gospel rests upon a willingness to remain within the boundaries of his thought. It does not consist in expounding what the apostle would have taught if only he had been better informed! According to Paul, Adam is a type of Christ, but only by way of complete contrast. Adam's transgression involved the whole race in sin, condemnation and death, whereas Christ's obedience purchased righteousness, justification, and life for his people. His design is to show that God's justification of the ungodly proceeds on the same principle by which Adam's sin was imputed to his posterity. Therefore a rejection of solidarity in sin is also a denial of solidarity in grace.

Unhappily the big guns of modern 'science' have persuaded most scholars today to make a strategic withdrawal from the front line of biblical supernaturalism to take up a position which they imagine can be more easily defended against the attacks of unbelief. However, J. G. Vos has pointed out the consequences of this capitulation to the prevailing climate of scepticism: 'This argument of Paul in *Romans 5* depends absolutely for its validity on the fact that as Jesus was a historical person so Adam was a historical person. There cannot be a proper parallel between a mythical Adam and an historical Christ. Adam is as essential to the Christian system of theology as Jesus Christ is. Christ is, indeed, called in Scripture "the second Adam" or "the last Adam". Any theory which tends, as the common form of evolution does, to eliminate Adam as a real historical person, is destructive of Christianity. Yet this very thing is done by the common form of evolutionary theory. It has no more room for a real Adam than it has for a real fall of mankind into sin. And if Christ as the second Adam came to undo the harm done by the first Adam, then we must needs continue to believe in the reality of the first Adam.' (*Surrender to Evolution: Inevitable or Inexcusable?* p. 20)

Therefore, as through one man sin entered into the world, and death through sin; How much of the preceding context is summed up in this 'therefore' is a matter of dispute. Nygren does not take it to refer to any particular verse or statement, but to the presupposition which underlies all that Paul has said. It introduces an explicit statement of what has so far only been implied, namely, that Adam and Christ are the respective heads of the two ages; Adam is the head of the old age of *death*, and Christ is the head of the new age of *life*. 'As' begins a comparison which has no corresponding 'so' to complete it. This is because the extraordinary content of the verse called for an explanatory parenthesis [*vv* 13–17]. John Murray notes that each part of the verse has a distinct emphasis. 'In the first half the accent falls upon the *entrance* of sin and death through *one man*. In the second part the accent falls upon the universal *penetration* of death and the sin of *all*.'

Adam was not the originator of sin, 'for the devil sinneth

from the beginning,' but humanity was introduced to sin by Adam's failure to obey God [1 *John* 3:8]. As the image-bearer of God, Adam's life consisted in communion with his Maker, so separation from God resulted in Adam's death [*Gen* 2:17, 3:19]. Sin meant that Adam could no longer live in fellowship with God in the garden. 'The root of death is in having been sent forth from God.' (Vos) Death is not natural to the constitution of man, but is the penal consequence of sin [6:23]. If Adam had not sinned, he need not have died. In that case it is probable that eternal life would have been imparted to him by means of the tree of life [*Gen* 3:22]. 'After man should have been made sure of the attainment of the highest life, the tree would appropriately have been the sacramental means for communicating the highest life.' (Vos, *Biblical Theology*, p. 28) But by disobeying God he partook instead of the sacrament of death (James Philip).

and so death passed unto all men, for that all sinned: Although it is possible to understand this statement as referring to the voluntary sins of all men, the context clearly forbids this interpretation, because Paul, no less than five times, explicitly states that the universal sway of death is due to the single sin of one man [*vv* 15, 16, 17, 18, 19]. The only satisfactory solution to the problem is to be found in the representative relation which Adam sustained to the race. 'In Adam all die' [1 *Cor* 15:22] can only be explained by the fact 'that in Adam all sin'. Sin is traced back to Adam, 'because we are in Adam in a peculiar manner, not only as our seminal root but also as our representative head.' (John Murray, *The Imputation of Adam's Sin*, p. 82)

V13: for until the law sin was in the world; but sin is not imputed when there is no law.
V14: Nevertheless death reigned from Adam until Moses, even over them that had not sinned after the likeness of Adam's transgression, who is a figure of him that was to come.

The purpose of Paul's parenthesis is to prove his statement that 'death passed unto all men' through the single sin of Adam. This is made evident by the fact that sin was in the world up to the time that the law was given by Moses. But in accordance with the principle already stated in 4:15, the presence of sin always implies the existence of some kind of law, for the simple reason that 'sin is not imputed when there is no law'. Yet from Adam to Moses death reigned 'even over them that had not sinned after the likeness of Adam's transgression,' i.e. over those who unlike Adam stood outside the pale of special revelation and did not therefore openly and willingly violate the positive command of God. Paul's assumption is that *this universal reign of death cannot be explained except by the transgression of an expressly revealed commandment*, and since that cannot be laid to the charge of each and every member of the race, the only sin that can account for it is the sin of Adam and the participation of all in that sin (so John Murray).

In the concluding clause of *v* 14 Adam is said to be 'a figure of him that was to come'. It is because Adam's one act of disobedience is imputed to others, whose activity was not personally and voluntarily engaged in its performance, that he is here described as a type of Christ. For as the sin of Adam was the ground of our condemnation, so the righteousness of Christ is the ground of our justification. Adam's one sin sufficed to ruin the race, but Christ's obedience conferred righteousness upon his people. Just as 'death reigned over those who did not sin after the similitude of Adam's transgression' so the apostle is 'chiefly interested in demonstrating that men are justified who do not act righteously after the similitude of Christ's obedience'. (John Murray)

*V*15: **But not as the trespass, so also is the free gift. For if by the trespass of the one the many died, much more did the grace of God, and the gift by the grace of the one man, Jesus Christ, abound unto the many.**

Verses 15–17 qualify the final clause of the previous verse,

[89]

'who is a figure of him that was to come,' so that Paul does not complete the comparison begun in *v* 12 until *v* 18. This verse begins with an emphatic negation, calculated to dispel any illusion that there is an exact correspondence between the sin of Adam and the work of Christ. Certainly the free gift is not like the transgression, for we gain far more in Christ than ever we lost through Adam [cf *Eph* 2:4-7]. As the 'much more' indicates, we have here another *a fortiori* argument which extols the munificence of God's grace in our salvation [cf *vv* 9, 10, 17]. It was through the trespass of the *one* that *the many* died ('many' is used for the sake of emphasis, though of course all mankind is meant). But grace not only annuls the sentence of condemnation, it also abounds unto justification and life! John Murray draws attention to the piling up of expressions which throws into relief the free grace of God. God's gratuitous favour is manifested in the free gift of righteousness [*v* 17], which is the gift by the grace of the one man Jesus Christ. In speaking of the smaller company who are thus blessed, Paul probably alludes to *Is* 53:11, 'where the Servant of the Lord justifies "the many".' (F. F. Bruce)

*V*16: **And not as through one that sinned, so is the gift: for the judgment came of one unto condemnation, but the free gift came of many trespasses unto justification.**

Another compressed statement serves to introduce a fresh point of contrast. The gift far exceeds one man's sinning. For through the single sin of one man the judgment of condemnation came upon all men, but the free gift took account of many transgressions which were all embraced in the one verdict of justification. This is the amazing grace that not only reverses our just condemnation in Adam, but also declares us righteous because Christ has completely satisfied the claims of divine justice on our behalf [2 *Cor* 5:21]. 'Christ has done far more than remove the curse pronounced on us for the *one* sin of Adam; he procures our justification from our own innumerable offences.' (Hodge)

*V*17: **For if, by the trespass of the one, death reigned through the one; much more shall they that receive the abundance of grace and of the gift of righteousness reign in life through the one, even Jesus Christ.**

The final contrast shows that the terrible consequences of the fall are more than overcome through the justifying righteousness of Christ which is freely put to our account ('imputed not infused' – Sanday and Headlam; cf 3:21, 22, 10:3; *Phil* 3:9). If Adam's one trespass brought the whole race *under the reign* of death, then how much more shall they who receive the abundance of grace and the gift of righteousness *reign in life*, both now and in the glory to come, through the continuous mediation of the one, Jesus Christ. 'If the union with Adam in his sin was certain to bring destruction, the union with Christ in his righteousness is yet more certain to bring salvation.' (Shedd)

*V*18: **So then as through one trespass the judgment came unto all men to condemnation; even so through one act of righteousness the free gift came unto all men to justification of life.**

This verbless summary brings the parallel which was begun in *v* 12 to a striking conclusion: 'So then as through one trespass – unto all men condemnation; even so through one act of righteousness – unto all men to justification of life.' If the second 'all' is co-extensive with the first, then the passage teaches a universalism that is contrary to the total testimony of Scripture. What Paul has in view is not the numerical extent of those saved; he is showing what the respective acts of Adam and Christ mean for those they represent. All who are condemned are condemned through the *one trespass* of Adam, and all who are justified are justified because of the *one righteous act* of Christ. Christ's whole earthly course, culminating in the death of the cross, is here referred to as a single act, because his complete obedience purchased for his people a righteousness as indivisible as that seamless robe which once he wore [cf *Matt* 3:15; *John* 8:29; *Gal* 4:4; *Phil* 2:8]. The phrase 'justification of life' means 'justification entitling to, and issuing in, the rightful possession and enjoyment of life'. (David Brown)

*V*19: **For as through the one man's disobedience the many were made sinners, even so through the obedience of the one shall the many be made righteous.**

As it is by the imputation of Adam's disobedience that many are 'constituted sinners', so it is through the imputation of Christ's obedience that many are 'constituted righteous'. 'Viewed from the standpoint of personal, voluntary action the disobedience in the one case is that of Adam and the obedience is that of Christ. But the effect of the "constituting" act is that others, not personally and voluntarily engaged, come to have property, indeed propriety, in the personal, voluntary performance of another.' (John Murray, *The Imputation of Adam's Sin*, p. 88) As the representative head of his people, Christ came to render a perfect obedience to all the *precepts* of the law in order to fulfil all righteousness on their behalf [cf *v* 18]. But because a broken law also called for the willing endurance of the *penalty* it pronounced against its transgressors, it was necessary for the Surety of a sinful people to exhaust that penalty in his own body on the tree [1 *Pet* 2:24]. Only Christ could render such a perfect obedience to God, and this he did for those he represented [*John* 17:2].

Our being placed in the category of the righteous is the blessed consequence of Christ's 'one act of righteousness'. This is not a bare declaration; it is also a constitutive act. Justification means that our participation in the benefits of Christ's righteousness is as real as was our involvement in the misery of Adam's sin. And this is because the same principle is at work in each of the 'constituting' acts. The future tense does not mean that justification is an act which is reserved for the consummation, but that it continues as an operative principle to

[92]

the end of the age in order to include all who shall be justified by Christ's obedience. This doctrine was given beautiful expression by the writer of the Epistle to Diognetus, 'O the sweet exchange, O the inscrutable creation, O the unlooked-for benefits, that the sin of many should be put out of sight in one Righteous Man, and the righteousness of one should justify many sinners!' (quoted by F. F. Bruce)

*V*20: **And the law came in besides, that the trespass might abound; but where sin abounded, grace did abound more exceedingly:**
*V*21: **that, as sin reigned in death, even so might grace reign through righteousness unto eternal life through Jesus Christ our Lord.**

In making his comparison between Adam and Christ, Paul has already referred to the Mosaic law [*vv* 13, 14], and now he explains its particular bearing upon the situation that was brought into being through Adam's trespass. In the purpose of God it 'came in alongside' in order that the trespass might abound. 'Adam's trespass was disobedience to expressly revealed commandment. When the law came in through Moses, there was henceforth a multiplication of the kind of transgression exemplified in Adam's trespass, that is to say, transgression of clearly revealed commandment.' (John Murray) So though the Jews imagine the law to be the very citadel of sanctity, it is in fact the divine searchlight that not only shows up sin for what it is, but also arouses the enmity of the heart so that it actually provokes further transgressions [cf 7:8, 11, 13]. Such a 'law-work' is a necessary preparation for the profitable reception of the gospel, for it is only through the work of the law that a man becomes convinced of his need of an interest in the Saviour from sin.

but where sin abounded, grace did abound more exceedingly: This superabounding provision of grace does not apply to *all* who have abounded in sin; it is 'particular, and peculiar to the elect; to them only the grace of God is super-abundant after that they have abounded in sin, and by how much the greater is their guilt, by so much the greater is the grace of God in the free forgiveness thereof.' (Poole)

that, as sin reigned in death, even so might grace reign through righteousness unto eternal life This wholly unexpected boon was the result of the divine design. For it was God's purpose that the benefits of redemption should vastly exceed the evils of man's rebellion. 'The issues of a *divine* act working salvation are much more sure, than the issues of a *human* act working ruin.' (Philippi) Adam's sin had introduced the seemingly interminable reign of death, but God savingly intervened to strip sin of its sovereignty [6:23]. He made provision for the reign of grace, even the grace that reigns *through righteousness* unto eternal life. The righteousness contemplated is that which was wrought out by the Second Adam, whose complete obedience purchased a title to eternal life for all he represented. 'Grace did not, could not, deliver the lawful captives without paying the ransom. It did not trample on justice, or evade its demands. It reigns by providing a Saviour to suffer in the room of the guilty. By the death of Jesus Christ, full compensation was made to the law and justice of God.' (Haldane)

through Jesus Christ our Lord. Paul's reverence for his exalted Lord is very evident here, and is consistent with apostolic usage. The human name 'Jesus' may suffice to describe or emphasize the humiliation of the Incarnate life, but the undimmed glory of his Resurrection life demands the full title, 'Jesus Christ our Lord'. As the Christian's life is 'hid with Christ in God', his gaze must ever be directed to the beatific vision of the glorified Lord [*Col* 3:1-4]. Eternal life, together with every other spiritual blessing, is conveyed to believers *through* the continual mediation in heaven of their enthroned Priest-King.

CHAPTER SIX

V1: **What shall we say then? Shall we continue in sin, that grace may abound? God forbid.**

A grace which superabounds over sin may prompt a carnal heart to reason, 'The more I sin, the more God's grace is glorified in my justification.' Paul puts the objection in the form of a question, 'partly to show his dislike that his doctrine should be so perverted, and partly to show the peace of his own conscience, that he was far from such a thought'. (Poole) This licentious inference is at once energetically rejected by the apostle as an abuse of grace.

V2b: **We who died to sin, how shall we any longer live therein?**

The absurdity of supposing that Christians can live in sin is exposed by giving the reason for its rejection in the form of a question. They are not only 'dead to sin' (as the AV inadequately translates) but they 'died' to it in the past – the tense pointing to a definitive, once-for-all act. Thus the question is, 'We, being as we are persons who died to sin, how shall we any longer live therein?' The impossibility of the believer living in sin is this way asserted in the strongest possible manner. The force of Paul's thought and the foundation of the ensuing argument is the fact that *believers have died to sin*, and it is this decisive breach with sin which constitutes their identity.

Therefore, 'the person who has died to sin no longer lives and acts in the sphere or realm of sin ... There is a kingdom of sin, or darkness, and of death. The forces of iniquity rule there. It is the kingdom of this world and it lies in the wicked one [cf 2 *Cor* 4:3, 4; *Eph* 2:1-3; 1 *John* 5:19]. The person who has died to sin no longer lives there; it is no more the world of his thought, affection, will, life, and action. His well-springs are now in the kingdom which is totally antithetical, the kingdom of God and of his righteousness.' (John Murray, *Principles of Conduct*, pp. 204-205) [*Gal* 1:4; *Col* 1:12, 13; 1 *Pet* 4:1-4]

V3: Or are ye ignorant that all we who were baptized into Christ Jesus were baptized into his death?

Another question at once serves to substantiate the apostle's thesis and to reprove his readers for failing to grasp the implications of their baptism (the same method is used extensively in 1 Corinthians, see for example 1 *Cor* 3:16, 6:15). As Denney says, 'There is no argument in the passage at all, unless all Christians were baptized.' In accordance with the command of Christ and the practice of the apostles, all who were converted by the preaching of the gospel in the Early Church confessed their faith in Christ in baptism [*Matt* 28:19; *Acts* 2:38]. The force of the question therefore lies in its appeal to what all believers know from experience, *viz.* baptism 'into Christ' signifies union with Christ in his death. But they must further recognize that this not only means that they died with him, but that in doing so *they also died to sin*!

V4: We were buried therefore with him through baptism into death: that like as Christ was raised from the dead through the glory of the Father, so we also might walk in newness of life.

This verse shows that baptism not only sets forth the union of believers with Christ in his death, but that it also has the positive purpose of identifying them with him in his resurrection life. 'They were, in fact, "buried" with Christ when they were plunged in the baptismal water, in token that they had died so far as their old life of sin was concerned; they were raised again with Christ when they emerged from the water, in token that they had received a new life, which was nothing less than participation in Christ's own resurrection life.' (F. F. Bruce) And the terms in which this truth is expressed impressively illustrate the glory and dignity of the new life which is theirs in Christ. For just as Christ was raised by the Father's glorious power, so they have been raised to walk 'in a new state, which is life.' (Lightfoot) [cf *Eph* 1:19, 20; 2:1]

Although the New Testament commonly refers to believers as those for whom Christ died, a number of passages also state that they died in Christ [6:3–11; 2 *Cor* 5:14, 15; *Eph* 2:4–7; *Col* 3:3]. 'All for whom Christ died also died in Christ. All who died in Christ rose again with Christ. This rising again with Christ is a rising to newness of life after the likeness of Christ's resurrection. To die with Christ is, therefore, to die to sin and to rise with him to the life of new obedience, to live not to ourselves but to him who died for us and rose again. The inference is inevitable that those for whom Christ died are those and those only who die to sin and live to righteousness.' (John Murray, *Redemption Accomplished and Applied*, p. 70)

V5: For if we have become united with him in the likeness of his death, we shall be also in the likeness of his resurrection;

The preceding reference to our new life in Christ is proved by the fact that identity with him in the likeness of his death must be followed by identity with him in the likeness of his resurrection. On the word 'likeness', John Murray says that it shows Paul is not speaking of '*our* physical death and resurrection; he is dealing with our death to sin and our resurrection to spiritual life.' To denote the certainty of this the apostle uses the future tense ('we shall be'). The verse is therefore 'another reminder that the death and resurrection of Christ are inseparable. Those for whom Christ died are those for whom he rose again and his heavenly saving activity is of equal extent with his once-for-all redemptive accomplishments.' (*Op. cit.*, p. 71)

V6: knowing this, that our old man was crucified with him, that the body of sin might be done away, that so we should no longer be in bondage to sin;

An appreciation of this argument should lead us to acknowledge that 'our old man was crucified with him'. This means that the old man *no longer lives*, our unregenerate self was crucified with Christ. Paul speaks of a completed act and not of a continuing process. It is because the old man is dead and buried that the believer's struggle with indwelling sin cannot be explained in terms of an antithesis between the old man and the new man. 'The believer is a new man, a new creation, but he is a new man not yet made perfect. Sin dwells in him still, and he still commits sin. He is necessarily the subject of progressive renewal . . . But this *progressive* renewal is not represented as the putting off of the old man and the putting on of the new.' (1 John Murray, *Principles of Conduct*, p. 219. For a detailed consideration of *Col* 3:9, 10 and *Eph* 4:20–24, see pages 214–218 of his book.) The apostle's teaching is that in virtue of his vital union with Christ the believer enjoys *the inalienable status of a man who has been sanctified by a definitive act*. It is this act which provides the basis for his increasing conformity to Christ, as it also affords the guarantee of his complete glorification [2 *Cor* 3:18; *Phil* 1:6]. This lays the solemn responsibility upon him to live like the new man he is, for the old man is dead and so can no more be blamed for his sins [cf the awful warning of 1 *Cor* 6:15, 16].

Paul further states that this took place in order that 'the body of sin' ('that body of which sin has taken possession' – Sanday and Headlam) might be done away. He does not use the word 'body' to suggest a materialistic conception of sin, as though the body were the source and seat of sinfulness, but because sin finds its concrete expression through 'the body as conditioned and controlled by sin'. (John Murray) Thus sin is not the controlling factor in the Christian, because the old man has been crucified.

The final clause sets forth the purpose for which this was effected. It was in order to terminate our bondage to sin. This introduces the theme of freedom from the bondservice of sin that is developed in the following verses. For having been marvellously delivered from our compulsory serfdom to sin, we must not voluntarily continue to render service to it.

*V*7: **for he that hath died is justified from sin.**

'Justified' does not here refer to our acquittal from sin's guilt, but to our being 'quit' of sin's power. The thought is that sin has no power over a dead man. For as death clears men of all claims, so 'it clears us, who have died with Christ, of the claim of sin, our old master, to rule over us still.' (Denney) Hence Christians are to realize and reckon on the fact that they have been delivered from their former servitude to sin in order to become the servants of righteousness [6:11ff].

*V*8: **But if we died with Christ, we believe that we shall also live with him;**

Paul here prepares the way for the personal application of the truth that believers have died to sin [cf *vv* 3, 5]. The 'if' of reality denotes the certainty of our identity with Christ in his death. If that is true (as it is), then it must follow that we shall also live with him. Although this living with Christ doubtless includes the future resurrection state of glory, the primary reference is to our present participation in the resurrection life of Christ. As Christians cannot live at all without Christ, 'we believe' expresses the assurance of faith that we shall so live in union with him.

*V*9: **knowing that Christ being raised from the dead dieth no more; death no more hath dominion over him.**

This assurance is grounded upon the finality of the resurrection, which is the guarantee that believers must continuously share in Christ's resurrection life. In that state of glory, 'death hath no more dominion over him,' but this implies that he was once under its power. For in assuming the burden of sin he became subject to the penalty of sin. Yet in the death he died the price was paid which for ever broke death's lordship over his people. So his resurrection is the pledge that this victory over sin will be repeated in the experience of every believer.

V10: **For the death that he died, he died unto sin once: but the life that he liveth, he liveth unto God.**

The once-for-all character of Christ's death is stressed in this verse, and this is an emphasis which is frequent in the New Testament [*Heb* 7:21, 9:12, 28, 10:10; 1 *Pet* 3:18]. By taking the form of a servant for our salvation Christ entered into the state of humiliation that was conditioned by the sin with which he was vicariously identified (John Murray). But this connection with sin was terminated by his atoning death, and in his resurrection he entered upon a state of life that was not conditioned by sin. His death thus completely severed his relationship *to sin*, so that the life which he now lives in glory he lives *to God*. This is of course no reflection on the fact that the whole of Christ's earthly course was marked by his total devotion to God. The contrast drawn is between his vicarious relation to sin on earth, and his lack of any connection with sin in heaven. 'As Christ, then, once entered upon this life and glorious activity, does not depart from it to return back again, so the believer, once dead to sin and alive to God in Christ, cannot return to his old life of sin. *v* 11 explicitly draws this conclusion, held in suspense since *v* 8, and prepared for in verses 9 and 10.' (Godet)

V11: **Even so reckon ye also yourselves to be dead unto sin, but alive unto God in Christ Jesus.**

It should be noted that it is only after Paul has unfolded the full implications of union with Christ that doctrine at last gives place to exhortation. The content of the command presupposes what has already been proved. For if believers are not dead to sin, they could not reckon to be true what was in fact not the case. Two acts of reckoning are called for, the first being preparatory to the second. It is because we can reckon on having died to sin that we can also reckon on being alive to God. And this we are 'in Christ Jesus'. This is the first time in the epistle that Paul uses this pregnant phrase, which here points to the divine initiative in our salvation. For we are 'in Christ' only through the gracious act of God that put Christ's righteousness to our account (C. E. B. Cranfield). 'We may forget what we should be; we may also (and this is how Paul puts it) forget what we *are*. We are dead to sin in Christ's death; we are alive to God in Christ's resurrection; let us regard ourselves as such *in Christ Jesus*.' (Denney)

*V*12: **Let not sin therefore reign in your mortal body, that ye should obey the lusts thereof:**

This command must be understood in the light of the assurance that 'sin shall not have dominion over you' [*v* 14]. Sin does not lord it over believers, and it is only because this is true that the command, 'Let not sin therefore reign,' becomes meaningful. 'To say to the slave who has not been emancipated, "Do not behave as a slave" is to mock his enslavement. But to say the same to the slave who has been set free is the necessary appeal to put into effect the privileges and rights of his liberation. So in this case the sequence is: sin does not have the dominion; therefore do not allow it to reign.' (John Murray)

On the other hand, the exhortation would be pointless if sin did not exist in the believer. For though he died to sin and his life is hid with Christ in God [*Col* 3:3], his mortal body is still very much alive to the pull of those unlawful physical and mental desires, by which sin seeks to regain the mastery over

[101]

his life. But he is to realize that through Christ he now has the power to resist the prohibited cravings he once helplessly indulged. It is probable that Paul refers to the body as 'your *mortal* body' to illustrate the incongruity of any yielding to its sinful demands on the part of those who are 'alive from the dead' [*v* 13].

*V*13: **neither present your members unto sin as instruments of unrighteousness; but present yourselves unto God, as alive from the dead, and your members as instruments of righteousness unto God.**

Since believers have died to sin, they must not *go on presenting* their bodily members to sin as the 'weapons of unrighteousness' (ASV margin) to wage warfare in its service. 'Sin is regarded as a sovereign (who reigns, *v* 12), who demands the military service of subjects (exacting obedience, *v* 12), levies their quota of arms (weapons of unrighteousness, *v* 13), and gives them their soldier's-pay of death (wages, *v* 23).' (Lightfoot) But they are to present themselves and their members *once for all* to God as befits those who are 'alive from the dead'. For as the radical renewal of the whole man involves his total dedication to God, this necessarily includes the surrender of his faculties and members to God's service. These are now to be used as the 'weapons of righteousness' in the fight against their former master. That the apostle took no quiescent view of the Christian life is shown by his frequent use of military metaphors, which reflect the seriousness of the struggle that no good soldier of Jesus Christ can avoid [cf *Eph* 6:10ff].

*V*14: **For sin shall not have dominion over you: for ye are not under law, but under grace.**

The encouragement to fulfil these imperatives is provided by the promise given in the first part of the verse. This future should not therefore be taken as a disguised exhortation; it rather expresses the certainty of the fact asserted. We can indeed so present ourselves and all our members to God for his service, because sin *shall not* have lordship over us. For to come under the government of redeeming grace in Christ is to be freed from the dominion of sin. This is neither freedom from sinning nor freedom from conscious sin. 'Sin as indwelling and committed is a reality; it does not lose its character as sin. It is the contradiction of God and of that which a believer most characteristically is. It creates the gravest liabilities. But by the grace of God there is this radical change that it does not exercise the dominion. The self-condemnations which it evokes are the index to this fact. It is this destruction of the power of sin that makes possible a realized biblical ethic.' (John Murray, *Principles of Conduct*, pp. 220–221)

We owe this deliverance to the fact that we are no longer under law but under grace. 'Under law' (no article) does not mean 'under the Mosaic economy', for many who lived under the dispensation of law were the recipients of grace. To be under law is to be under its commands, and under its condemnation for every failure to meet its righteous demands. This means that law can do nothing to justify law-breakers; it simply confirms them in their helpless bondage to sin. But by Christ's mighty rescue we are placed under the sovereignty of grace instead. As 'under grace' indicates, independence is not an option that is open to man. For it is through the justifying provisions of grace that we are filled with the spiritual power which enables us 'to trample unrighteousness under foot and to work righteousness'. (Lenski) [cf 13:8–10; *Gal* 5:6]

V15: **What then? shall we sin, because we are not under law, but under grace? God forbid.**

As Paul is aware of the way in which such spiritual teaching can be perverted by blind logic, he now returns to consider the question raised in verse 1 from a different point of view. There his reference to superabounding grace had prompted the false inference of continuing in sin that it might abound all the more. Here the removal of the restraint of law could be misconstrued as a free licence to sin, and again the suggestion

is summarily rejected by his 'God forbid'. For though in 'one
sense the believer is not "under law", in another sense he is
[cf 1 Cor 9:21]'. (John Murray) The monstrous nature of this
reasoning is exposed in the following verses.

*V*16: **Know ye not, that to whom ye present yourselves
as servants unto obedience, his servants ye are whom ye
obey; whether of sin unto death, or of obedience unto
righteousness?**

Paul's readers know or certainly *ought* to know that they have
been released from the bondage of sin for the service of
righteousness [*v* 3]. No absolute freedom is conferred upon the
Christian, *for his position is simply that of a slave who has changed
masters* (Nygren). Formerly he was the slave of sin, rendering
willing obedience to the lusts that bring death in their train.
But now that he has become the slave of righteousness [*v* 18],
he must see to it that his obedience in its service is equally
whole-hearted [cf *Luke* 16:13].

*V*17: **But thanks be to God, that, whereas ye were servants of sin, ye became obedient from the heart to that
form of teaching whereunto ye were delivered;**

The Christians in Rome clearly do not owe their deliverance
to the power of their own choice. For as Nygren well says,
'Paul does not *praise* them for having made a better and
happier choice; he *thanks* God for taking them out of the old
bondage.' It was through the exercise of divine power that
they who *were* the slaves of sin, *became* obedient to the pattern
of teaching to which they were delivered [cf 2 *Tim* 1:13]. The
apostolic gospel is here likened to a pattern or mould into
which molten metal is poured to set. This mould is the
authoritative norm that shapes the thought and conduct of
all who are delivered up to its teaching. One would expect
doctrine to be handed over to the hearers, rather than the
hearers to the doctrine. But Christians are not the masters of
a tradition like the Rabbis, for they are created by the word of

God and they remain in subjection to it (so Barrett). As an ex-Pharisee Paul knew better than anyone else the frustration and futility of an external obedience. But Christianity is not legalism because it renders to God that heart obedience which is the mark of the new creation.

*V*18: **and being made free from sin, ye became servants of righteousness.**

These passives again point to the action of God in releasing us for his service: 'and having been liberated from sin, you were enslaved to righteousness'. This paradoxical way of expressing the truth shows that the effectual call of God makes our commitment to righteousness as absolute as was our former slavery to sin. 'The striking thought is the fact that our emancipation is a new enslavement. In *v* 20 we are shown what a sad liberty we enjoyed when we were slaves of sin; here we are shown what a glorious liberty we obtained when we were made slaves to righteousness.' (Lenski)

*V*19: **I speak after the manner of men because of the infirmity of your flesh: for as ye presented your members as servants to uncleanness and to iniquity unto iniquity, even so now present your members as servants to righteousness unto sanctification.**

In thus speaking of believers being 'enslaved to righteousness' Paul has illustrated the truth in a figure drawn from human relations. This is in order to meet the weakness of their spiritual understanding [cf 1 *Cor* 3:1]. But this illustration requires further explanation, for 'enslavement to righteousness' could look as if holiness were a matter of sheer compulsion. 'It is not so; "*for* as you once willingly and entirely surrendered yourselves to sin, and were in *this* way slaves of sin, so now willingly and entirely surrender yourselves to righteousness, and be in *this same* voluntary manner slaves of righteousness." ' (Shedd) Paul's point is that though their service is now of a different kind and is directed to a different end, yet it calls for *the same dedication* they once showed in the service of sin. 'Unto holiness' (AV) is better fitted to convey 'the once-for-all breach with sin and commitment to righteousness' than 'sanctification' which is often used to denote a process (John Murray).

*V*20: **For when ye were servants of sin, ye were free in regard of righteousness.**

As an incentive to obedience Paul now bids his readers consider the unprofitable nature of their former course [*vv* 20, 21]. At that time they were 'free in regard of righteousness'. As responsible subjects they were not exempt from the claims of righteousness upon them, but they were devoid of righteousness and they gloried in their supposed freedom from its restraints. But this was a spurious liberty since it involved them in the guilt which was the inevitable consequence of their iniquity. 'Sinful inclination (which is as really *inclination* as holy inclination) is *false* freedom, because it conflicts with the moral law, and is forbidden by it.' (Shedd)

*V*21: **What fruit then had ye at that time in the things whereof ye are now ashamed? for the end of those things is death.**

The question Paul asks implies the negative reply, 'No fruit whatever!' As sinners they had then imagined that there was some gain in their sin, but as believers they know that there was no fruit in the things of which they are now ashamed. In that state of sin they could bear no fruit unto God, because they were infatuated with 'the unfruitful works of darkness' whose only end is death [cf *Gal* 5:22; *Eph* 5:9]. 'As soon as the godly begin to be enlightened by the Spirit of Christ and the preaching of the Gospel, they freely acknowledge that the whole of their past life, which they lived without Christ, is worthy of condemnation. So far from trying to excuse themselves, they are in fact ashamed of themselves. Indeed, they go farther, and continually bear their disgrace in mind, so that the shame of it may make them more truly and willingly humble before God.' (Calvin)

V22: But now being made free from sin and become servants to God, ye have your fruit unto sanctification, and the end eternal life.

From the fruitlessness, shame, and condemnation of that bondage of death, Paul gratefully turns to contemplate the glorious transformation wrought in them by the grace of God. 'But now, you have been liberated from sin and en-slaved to God, you have your fruit unto holiness, and the end eternal life.' Paul's conclusion thus proves that grace can never minister to licence, for it always produces fruit which leads to holiness and issues in eternal life [cf *Heb* 12:14].

V23: For the wages of sin is death; but the free gift of God is eternal life in Christ Jesus our Lord.

Having explained these two contrasting forms of bondservice, Paul now sums up their respective results in a final statement that leaves nothing more to be said. On 'wages' H. W. Heidland makes three significant comments. 1. As 'wages' were paid to meet the costs of living, sin is here shown to be the deceiver that promises life but pays out death. 2. Because these 'wages' are not confined to a single payment, the shadow of the final penalty already overhangs this present life. For just as eternal life is the present possession of the believer, so sin already offers its slaves deadly poison from the cup of death. 3. Since 'wages' is a legal term, this shows that man has rights only in regard to sin, and these rights become his judgment (*TDNT*, Vol. 5, p. 592). This death has the same duration as the life that belongs to the future age. Both are endless because the future age is endless. The term 'death' does not therefore point to the annihilation of the sinner. 'To pay any one is not to put him out of existence; it is rather to make him feel the painful consequences of his sin, to make him reap in the form of corruption what he has sowed in the form of sin [*Gal* 6:7, 8; *2 Cor* 5:10].' (Godet)

Although Paul has referred to the fruit borne by believers, he does not regard this as meriting eternal life. This is the free gift of God in Christ Jesus our Lord; it is given to us *in Him* who has merited it *for us* [cf *1 Cor* 1:30]. For unlike sin, righteousness is not self-originated, consequently its reward must be gracious. Eternal life is a gift 'because the imputed righteousness of a believer is a gratuity, and his inherent righteousness is the product of the Holy Spirit moving and inclining his will'. (Shedd) Pen and ink cannot conceal the apostle's exultant joy as he thus celebrates the triumph of God's grace in our salvation.

CHAPTER SEVEN

V1: Or are ye ignorant, brethren (for I speak to men who know the law), that the law hath dominion over a man for so long time as he liveth?

Having proved that believers have died to sin [ch 6], Paul next explains the way in which they have become dead to the law [ch 7]. He had touched on this topic in his reference to the fact that believers are not under law [6:14], but the immediate need to refute the false inference that might be drawn from this proposition had then prevented his positive exposition of how this came about. But now the Christians in Rome have their attention turned to this subject, whose importance is impressed upon them by the pastoral concern which is reflected in the repeated address of 'brethren' [vv 1, 4]. The apostle begins his discussion by reminding them that the law only has authority over a man for as long as he lives, and he is confident that this general principle will be self-evident to everyone who knows anything about law.

V2: For the woman that hath a husband is bound by law to the husband while he liveth; but if the husband die, she is discharged from the law of the husband.
V3: So then if, while the husband liveth, she be joined to another man, she shall be called an adulteress: but if the husband die, she is free from the law, so that she is no adulteress, though she be joined to another man.

To illustrate this general principle Paul refers to the law of marriage. If during the lifetime of her husband the woman marries another man, she is guilty of adultery. However, if her husband dies, the marriage tie is dissolved and she is legally free to marry again [1 *Cor* 7:39]. As a wife she was under the law regarding husbands, but as a widow she is altogether free of that law. The comparison suits Paul's purpose very well, because it shows that a person can be set free from a law without the overthrow of the law itself. For it is clear that the law regarding husbands continues in full force, though she is herself freed from it. The point is that this death not only ends one relationship, but it legally opens the way for her to enter into another union. 'So we Christians, no longer under law, are now in a most blessed new relation: under grace [6:14, 15]. Paul's illustration is perfectly chosen.' (Lenski)

*V*4: **Wherefore, my brethren, ye also were made dead to the law through the body of Christ; that ye should be joined to another, even to him who was raised from the dead, that we might bring forth fruit unto God.**

Those who try to turn this simple illustration into a complex allegory or parable accuse the apostle of confusion of thought because the parallel is not exactly carried through in this verse. But this is to mistake his purpose, for in fact he here confines himself to a single point of comparison. *And this is the principle that legal obligation is severed by death.* As the husband's death released his wife from the marriage bond, so there is a death by which we are freed from the law. *For through Christ's death we have received our discharge from all the claims of the law upon us.* 'We were made dead to the law through the body of Christ,' i.e. through his vicarious endurance of the law's curse on our behalf [*Gal* 3:13].

The positive purpose of our severance from the law was that we should be joined to another, 'even to him who was raised from the dead'. Christ having been thus raised from the dead dies no more [6:9], and it is by our participation in his endless life that the permanence of this new union is secured [John 14:19]. The great end served by this union with Christ is 'that we might bring forth fruit unto God' [cf 6:22; Gal 5:22, 23]. Had Paul wished to continue the marriage metaphor 'bear offspring' would have been a more suitable word than 'bear fruit', in addition to which this fruit is borne 'for God' and not 'for Christ', as a woman bears children for her husband. This fruit-bearing is the unexpected sequel to our severance from the law that confounds all legalists, who think that the relinquishing of law is fatal to the production of good works; we next see what it does produce (so Lenski).

V_5: For when we were in the flesh, the sinful passions, which were through the law, wrought in our members to bring forth fruit unto death.

This verse shows why such fruitfulness was impossible under the law. Here for the first time in the epistle Paul uses the expression 'in the flesh' to describe the old unregenerate life of sin in contrast to the new life 'in the Spirit' [v 6]. The basis for this usage is doubtless to be found in the distinction made by our Lord: 'that which is born of the flesh is flesh; and that which is born of the Spirit is spirit' [John 3:6]. 'The *reason* why we are naturally generated in sin is that, whenever we begin to be, we begin to be as sinful because of our solidarity with Adam in his sin . . . Natural generation we may speak of, if we will, as the means of conveying depravity, but, strictly, natural generation is the means whereby we come to be and depravity is the correlate of our having come to be.' (John Murray, *The Imputation of Adam's Sin*, pp. 92–93) To be 'in the flesh' is therefore to be in that condition in which it is impossible to please God [8:8].[1]

1. Since 'the Word became flesh, and dwelt among us' it is impossible to suppose that sinfulness belongs to the flesh as flesh. However, it must be remembered that Christ's entry into the world was as unique as his departure from it. 'The knowledge of the virgin birth is impor-

While we were in that sinful state the law aroused in us those sinful passions, which were powerfully at work in our members to bring forth 'fruit' – well yes, if you wish to call it that, but it was *fruit for death*! According to the apostle to be 'in the flesh' and 'under the law' is a sure prescription for death, because the law kindles in a corrupt nature the very desire it is supposed to suppress. For as he presently explains, its holy prohibitions are then the incitement to transgression [vv 7–13]. Thus lawlessness is the paradoxical result of being under the law! This in no way conflicts with what Paul says elsewhere on the function of the law in exercising a restraint upon evil-doers [13:3, 4; 1 Tim 1:9, 10], for though the fear of punishment restrains the criminal passions, it does not eradicate them and only restrains to a degree, and even then not always. As Denney says, 'Death is personified here as in *v* 17: this tyrant of the human race is the only one who profits by the fruits of the sinful life.'

V6: But now we have been discharged from the law, having died to that wherein we were held; so that we serve in newness of the spirit, and not in oldness of the letter.

But now we have been discharged from the law – a bondage which was terminated through our having died to the law! *With the result* that we are now serving in newness of the Spirit, and not in oldness of the letter (cf 6:4 which states the

---

tant because of its bearing upon our view of the solidarity of the race in the guilt and power of sin. If we hold a Pelagian view of sin, we shall be little interested in the virgin birth of our Lord; we shall have little difficulty in understanding how a sinless One could be born as other men are born. But if we believe, as the Bible teaches, that all mankind are under an awful curse, then we shall rejoice in knowing that there entered into the sinful race from the outside One upon whom the curse did not rest save as he bore it for those whom he redeemed by his blood.' (Gresham Machen, *The Virgin Birth*, p. 395) The validity of the title 'the last Adam' as applied to Christ really rests upon the supernatural fact of the virgin birth.

purpose of our being raised with Christ). The 'newness' of this service consists in the life, power, and effectiveness which it derives from its Author, the Holy Spirit. Before his conversion Paul had vainly tried to serve God 'in oldness of the letter', but it was a service which he later described as a 'confidence in the flesh' [*Phil* 3:3, 4]. What is set out below gives more simply the substance of a note by Shedd:

The Two Kinds of Service

The 'oldness of the letter'	The 'newness of the Spirit'
is a service of bondage,	is a service of liberty,
a mechanical and false	a spontaneous and real
obedience enforced by a	obedience inspired by a
fearful spirit of servitude,	joyful spirit of adoption,
which seeks to perform	which actually fulfils
by an effort of will	by an inward inclination
the letter of the law.	the intent of the law.
Here the law is written	Here the law is written
in the heart [*Rom* 2:15],	*upon* the heart [*Jer* 31:33],
and is therefore	and is therefore
external to the will.	internal to the will.
'*For the letter killeth,*	*but the Spirit giveth life.*'
	[*2 Cor* 3:6]

*V*7: **What shall we say then? Is the law sin? God forbid. Howbeit, I had not known sin, except through the law: for I had not known coveting, except the law had said, Thou shalt not covet:**

As Paul has insisted that the law cannot deliver the sinner but merely makes his bondage more bitter, some might be ready to infer that the law itself was sinful; a suggestion that meets with his customary expression of intense aversion. On the contrary, he emphatically rejects this false idea by an appeal to his own experience of the law's real effect. For it was through the law that he came to realize that he was himself a sinner. If then the law shows up sin for what it really is, it cannot itself be sinful!

In the second part of the verse Paul describes how the law brought this knowledge of sin home to his heart. He had imagined himself to be 'blameless' for as long as he was able to entertain the notion that external obedience could satisfy the demands of the law [Phil 3:6]. Conviction of sin came to him with the realization that the law condemned not only outward breaches of the commandments but also the first secret stirrings of sinful desire within the heart [Matt 5:21-30].

V8: **but sin, finding occasion, wrought in me through the commandment all manner of coveting: for apart from the law sin is dead.**

The word here rendered 'occasion' (*aphormē*) 'was used to denote a base of operations in war', so Paul is saying that the law provided sin with the base it needed for mounting its attack against him (Vine). So that instead of being crushed by the commandment which forbade coveting, he found that it stimulated in him all kinds of covetousness. 'The more the light of the law shines upon and in our depraved hearts, the more the enmity of our minds is roused to opposition, and the more it is made manifest that the mind of the flesh is not subject to the law of God, neither can be.' (John Murray, *Principles of Conduct*, p. 185) Hence it was Paul's experience that apart from the law sin was dead. This means that he had no consciousness of sin until the law aroused within his heart every sort of sinful desire. 'By means of this poker in the hands of sin the slumbering fire in Paul was stirred to shoot out all its flames.' (Lenski)

V9: **And I was alive apart from the law once: but when the commandment came, sin revived, and I died;**

Paul was 'alive' in his own self-esteem until his conscience was awakened by the commandment. His intimate acquaintance with the letter of the law could not puncture his proud self-righteousness, but when the law was powerfully applied to his heart by the Holy Spirit he lost that good opinion of himself. The hopeless nature of Paul's plight was revealed by the law, which not only condemned his sin, but what was still more alarming, stimulated the once dormant depravity of his heart to vigorous activity; thus when sin 'revived' Paul 'died'.

*V*10: **and the commandment, which was unto life, this I found to be unto death:**

When Paul discovered within himself this violent contradiction of the law's demands, he found that the commandment which promised life upon obedience had become for him nothing more than a sentence of death [*Lev* 18:5]. 'How vain therefore is it to expect salvation from the law, since all the law does, in its operation on the unrenewed heart, is to condemn and to awaken opposition! It cannot change the nature of man.' (Hodge)

*V*11: **for sin, finding occasion, through the commandment beguiled me, and through it slew me.**

However, this tragic result was not the fault of the law. For it was really sin that took advantage of the law to 'beguile' Paul, and through it slew him [cf 2 *Cor* 11:3]. This word recalls Eve's deception by Satan, who made the commandment seem an unreasonable obstacle to the gratification of a harmless desire, from which no evil but only good could come [*Gen* 3:1-13]. Such forbidden fruit always seems sweet in prospect, but bitter experience proves that death is always the aftermath of disobedience. In Eve's case it brought death upon the race [5:12]; in Paul's case it brought the fact of his already existing deadness home to his consciousness.

*V*12: **So that the law is holy, and the commandment holy, and righteous, and good.**

Paul now states the conclusion to be drawn from the preceding verses [*vv* 7-11]. As the law is holy, so each of its stipulations including that mentioned in *v* 7 'is holy, and righteous, and good'. Thus in spite of the bad use that sin makes of the law, the apostle insists that the resultant misery is no fault of the law itself [*v* 13]. For the adjectives used point to the fact that the law perfectly reflects the character of its divine author. Hence John Murray observes, 'As "holy" the commandment reflects the transcendence and purity of God and demands of us the correspondent consecration and purity; as "righteous" it reflects the equity of God and exacts of us in its demand and sanction nothing but that which is equitable; as "good" it promotes man's highest well-being and thus expresses the goodness of God.'

*V*13: **Did then that which is good become death unto me? God forbid. But sin, that it might be shewn to be sin, by working death to me through that which is good; – that through the commandment sin might become exceeding sinful.**

Since Paul 'died' when the commandment came [*vv* 9, 10], was this mournful result to be attributed to the good law? The very wording of the question shows what the answer must be, for no good thing can bring about the death of anybody (Lenski). But not content to leave the inference to be drawn, he again utters his strong exclamation of denial. No, the real culprit for this tragic reversal of his expectations is sin, which is shown up in its true character by working evil through that which is good! However, the final purpose clause makes it plain that the perversity of sin in abusing the law was not outside the scope of God's redemptive design. For he has ordered the operation of the law to be the means of impressing upon the sinner the excessive sinfulness of sin. Accordingly, when sin wields the law as a weapon of death, the sinner's false sense of security is shattered and the hopelessness of his situation is agonizingly revealed.

These verses are therefore an instructive account of Paul's experience before conversion as they explain how the law of

God was used to bring conviction of sin to his heart [*vv* 7–13]. Nowadays when such birth pangs are distinctly unfashionable it is worth recalling the practical remark of Charles Hodge on this passage: 'If our religious experience does not correspond with that of the people of God, as detailed in the Scriptures, we cannot be true Christians.'

*V*14: **For we know that the law is spiritual: but I am carnal, sold under sin.**

The clue to the interpretation of this controversial passage is to remember the purpose for which it was written [*vv* 14–25]. In this chapter the apostle's theme is freedom from the law, but this truth is conditioned by the fact that the believer is not only 'in Christ' but he is also still 'in the flesh'. And this inevitably means that there is a dualism in his present experience between the 'now' and the 'not yet'. The paradoxical consequences of living in this state of tension are well drawn out by Nygren:

> Chapter 6: We are *free from sin* – yet we must battle against it.
> Chapter 7: We are *free from the law* – yet we are not righteous according to its criterion.
> Chapter 8: We are *free from death* – yet we long for the redemption of our bodies.

When this distinction is understood there is no difficulty in referring Paul's persistent use of the present tense in these verses to a present conflict within himself. There is here no indulgence in self-analysis for its own sake, but a practical concern to prove that the law can neither justify nor sanctify. For as the law was powerful to convict but powerless to save the sinner [*vv* 7–13], so it is quick to detect but impotent to remove the sin that remains in the believer [*vv* 14–25]. From this it follows that the law can never be the means of salvation, neither in its attainment nor in its retention. The believer's righteousness is not of the law, but is nothing less than the righteousness of God in Christ [*Phil* 3:9].

For we know that the law is spiritual: The reason Paul here uses the plural 'we' is to associate all believers with this judgment, which is an evaluation of the law that is peculiar to the regenerate. They know that the law is spiritual because they can discern that it is inspired and indited by the Holy Spirit. This statement therefore refers to the divine origin and character of the law.

but I am carnal, sold under sin. This contrasts the spirituality of the law with the inner contradiction of its holy perfection which marks the life that is lived in the flesh. When Paul thus confesses that he is 'carnal', or 'fleshly', this must not be confused with the condition of the unregenerate, who are as to their *state*, 'in the flesh' [7:5, 8:8], whose *conduct* is 'after the flesh' [8:4, 5], and whose *thought* is governed by a 'carnal mind' [8:6, 7]. But 'fleshly' certainly does point to a condition of life that falls far short of the absolute holiness of the law. It frankly indicates a participation in the weakness that inescapably belongs to the flesh. For though the apostles claimed infallibility for their teaching, and could exhort believers to follow their example, even they never claimed to be sinlessly perfect [cf *Gal* 2:11; 1 *Cor* 9:26, 27; *Phil* 3:12–14; 1 *John* 1:8]. As set against the standard of God's holiness, Paul in common with all other believers is not completely holy [cf *Job* 40:4; *Ps* 38:1–10, 40:12, 51:1–12, 69:5, 90:7, 8, 119:96, 120, 176; *Is* 6:5; *Matt* 26:41; *Rom* 8:23; *Eph* 6:12; *Heb* 12:1].

'He is still to some extent, and he feels it to be no small extent [*v* 24], ruled by *flesh*. But he is not wholly and completely ruled by it. He is inwardly inclined to good [*vv* 15, 19, 21]; is disinclined to, and hates evil [*vv* 15, 16, 19]; "delights in the law of God" [*v* 22]; and "serves the law of God" [*v* 25]. The natural man is not thus described in Scripture. That a regenerate man may be called "carnal" is proved by 1 *Cor* 3:1, 3.' (Shedd)

As the strong expression 'sold under sin' recalls Elijah's word to Ahab, some have contended that it could not describe a regenerate person. But there is an important difference between what is passively experienced and what is actively determined. Paul complains that he *has been sold* under sin, whereas it is said of Ahab that he *sold himself* to do that which is evil in the sight of the Lord [1 *Kings* 21:20]. Paul thus finds himself taken captive by a power that forces his members to serve sin against his will, but he knows that this is only because no good thing dwells 'in his flesh' [*v* 18]. And though constantly betrayed by the flesh, he also knows that he is no longer the slave of sin but the willing servant of righteousness [6:17, 18]. Hence we should not fail to appreciate the fact that the force of the apostle's language is due to the intensity of his feeling against this *partial bondage of the flesh* (which is not the same thing as his former absolute bondage to sin).

*V*15: **For that which I do I know not: for not what I would, that do I practise; but what I hate, that I do.**

This substantiates the indictment of the previous verse. 'For that which I do *I know not*,' i.e. Paul does that which *he does not love and delight in* [cf 'know' in *Ps* 1:6, 36:10; *Amos* 3:2; *Matt* 7:23; *John* 10:14; 1 *Cor* 8:3; 2 *Tim* 2:19]. The second 'for' explains that his actions are a strange contradiction of his affections. For what commands the consent of *his inmost will*, he fails to practise; but what he hates with a holy detestation, that he does. As Paul represents himself as doing that which he does not will, the passage presents something of a psychological problem, since no act can be performed without the motivation of the will. Moreover, it is equally evident that he does not claim coercion as an excuse to evade the moral responsibility for his actions [cf *v* 24]. But as already hinted above, Paul is here using 'will' in the 'highly restricted sense of that determinate will to the good, in accordance with the will of God, which is characteristic of his deepest and inmost self, the will of "the inward man" [*v* 22]. It is that will that is frustrated by the flesh and indwelling sin. And when he does the evil he does what is not the will of his deepest and truest self, the inward man. This explains both types of expression, namely, that what *he wills* he does not do and what *he does not will* he does.' (John Murray) Furthermore, as the same author says, it is not to be supposed that in thus delineating the conflict between these carnal and spiritual principles Paul is giving a '*statistical* history of the outcome' or that 'his determinate will to the good came to no effective fruition in practice.'

V16: But if what I would not, that I do, I consent unto the law that it is good.

What Paul does that is contrary to his inward inclination evokes the self-condemnation which really amounts to an endorsement of the spirituality of the law [*v* 14]. As Calvin indicates in his commentary, it is quite illegitimate to draw a parallel between Ovid's confession, 'I see what is better and approve of it; I follow what is worse,' and what is taught here, for such similarities are purely verbal. The heathen could never 'consent unto the law that it is good'. That is the testimony of the regenerate heart! 'There is no conflict between the law and the believer; it is between the law and what the believer himself condemns.' (Hodge)

V17: So now it is no more I that do it, but sin which dwelleth in me.

This is yet another declaration which could only be made by a regenerate man. Paul now regards the sin that he commits as so foreign to his renewed *egō* that he can say that it is *no longer* 'I that do it, but sin which dwelleth in me' [*v* 20]. This is not a convenient method of escaping the blame for the sin; it is an affirmation that in the struggle against sin, the self stands on God's side. For there are not two egos in Paul contending for the mastery. There is but one acting subject, the new man in whom sin has been deposed from its regency, though not yet expelled from its residency. So that sin is now a 'squatter', and not the true inhabitant, the figure being taken from a house into which an intruder has crowded (Shedd). 'There is a total difference between surviving sin and reigning sin, the regenerate in conflict with sin and the unregenerate complacent to sin. It is one thing for sin to live in us: it is another for us to live in sin.' (John Murray, *Redemption Accomplished and Applied*, p. 145)

*V*18: **For I know that in me, that is, in my flesh, dwelleth no good thing: for to will is present with me, but to do that which is good is not.**

The preceding statement is now confirmed by a further explanation of this strange duality. Paul knows from personal experience that in him, *that is*, in his flesh, there dwells nothing good. His care in distinguishing 'in me' from 'in my flesh' is significant. It provides an additional proof that he is speaking of *his present experience as a believer*, for a man who is unregenerate is nothing but flesh! So Paul cannot let the statement stand without qualification. For he is also a man in whom the Holy Spirit dwells. Hence it would be untrue to say that there was no holiness in him. But that aspect of the truth is alien to his present purpose, which is to show that his remaining sin ('dwells' looks back to *v* 17) prevents him from fulfilling what he desires to do.

Thus what Paul wills he fails to accomplish in practice. 'He does not mean that he has nothing but an ineffectual desire, but he denies that the efficacy of his work corresponds to his will, because the flesh hinders him from the exact performance of what he is doing.' (Calvin) The new man cannot completely carry out the desires of his heart, for he is frustrated by the flesh in two ways. 1. Even when he obeys, which is his general habit, he never comes perfectly up to the ideal of the law which is *spiritual* [*v* 14]. 2. He sometimes yields to inward corruption, and actually transgresses the law (so Shedd).

*V*19: **For the good which I would I do not: but the evil which I would not, that I practise.**

In this repetition of the thought of *v* 15, the thing willed is defined as the 'good' and that which is not willed but practised as the 'evil'. It must not be forgotten that it is in the light of God's law that Paul makes this evaluation of himself [*v* 14]. It is precisely because the Christian is painfully aware of the 'spiritual' nature of the law of God that he realizes the impossibility of ever bringing 'the flesh' into conformity with its demands. Thus the practical importance of the passage for us lies in its disclosure of the apostle's experience of this inner conflict that is characteristic of and restricted to the regenerate.

*V*20: **But if what I would not, that I do, it is no more I that do it, but sin which dwelleth in me.**

How much Paul deplores this inability is shown by his repeated disavowal of the sin that still lodges in his flesh [*v* 17]. Regenerate Paul is forced to live with it, but he will neither recognize it nor come to terms with it. This is not a denial of responsibility for the obedience that sin coerces from his members, but it is a refusal to acknowledge its right to do this [*v* 23]. For after the city of Mansoul has been liberated by King Emmanuel, the forces of Diabolus continue their resistance to his rule, though they no longer have any real claim to the city (see John Bunyan's instructive allegory, *The Holy War*).

*V*21: **I find then the law, that, to me who would do good, evil is present.**
*V*22: **For I delight in the law of God after the inward man:**
*V*23: **but I see a different law in my members, warring against the law of my mind, and bringing me into captivity under the law of sin which is in my members.**

As 'then' indicates, Paul is now ready to sum up the condition described in the preceding verses [vv 14-20]. 'I find, then, this law in operation, that when I desire to do what is good, evil lies ready to hand.' (F. F. Bruce) 'The law' has nothing to do with the Mosaic law as this translation clearly shows; it is 'the law of sin' [v 23] which habitually opposes Paul's will to do good.

Hence John Owen observes: '*Believers have experience of the power and efficacy of indwelling sin.* They *find* it in themselves; they find it as a *law*. It hath a self evidencing efficacy to them that are alive to discern it. They that find not its power are under its dominion. Whoever contend against it shall know and find that it is present with them, that it is powerful in them. He shall find the stream to be strong who swims against it, though he who rolls along with it be insensible of it.' (*Treatise on the Remainders of Indwelling Sin in Believers*, Works, vol. 6, p. 159)

What Paul predicates of himself in verse 22 is unquestionably the utterance of a regenerate man. For no one who is a stranger to the grace of God can say, 'I *joyfully* agree with the law of God' (Arndt-Gingrich). So far he has used only 'I' in his struggle to explain what he essentially is, but now he adds the term 'the inward man'. This points to the transformation which has brought about his delighted concurrence with the divine will. 'The inward man' is therefore 'the "new man" in Christ that is daily being renewed in the Creator's image [cf 2 *Cor* 4:16; *Col* 3:10].' (F. F. Bruce)

But though Paul thus delights in God's law, he sees 'a different law' – 'the law of sin' – that is constantly at war with his whole-hearted assent to 'the law of God', which he calls 'the law of my mind'. This spiritual discernment is the fruit of regeneration, for the natural man cannot even *see* the things of God, let alone describe them as the law of his mind [cf *John* 3:3; I *Cor* 2:14]. The reference is to the governing principle of his life, since 'the mind' here includes both the understanding and the will. 'The understanding is enlightened, and the will is enlivened by the Holy Spirit, who dwells in the *mind*,

thus regenerated, as the source and support of its divine life.'
(Shedd)

However, the apostle's complaint is that he finds the law of
his mind opposed by the law of sin in his members. He finds
this rebellious principle warring against his allegiance to God
and bringing him into captivity. These participles point to an
unceasing warfare, but because they are present and not
aorist participles they tell us nothing of the ultimate success
of the campaign [cf 1 *Pet* 2:11; *James* 4:1]. Hence this captivity cannot be regarded as a permanent condition which has
been secured by a decisive victory. Moreover, the fact that
Paul *twice* refers to the law of sin *in* his members shows that
this is no longer the law *of* his members. He speaks of a foreign
power that forces his members to revolt against the rule of his
mind which they would otherwise obey [cf 6:19]. But just as
no sovereign in his capital can view an insurrection in his
provinces with complacency, so Paul deeply deplores this
violent contradiction of his regenerate will in his members –
as the next verse eloquently demonstrates.

V24: **Wretched man that I am! who shall deliver me out of the body of this death?**

In thus giving expression to the real distress he feels as he
watches the course of this conflict, Paul is not giving way to
blank despair. For though he condemns himself in such
unsparing terms, he remains confident that his cry for deliverance will be heard [*v* 25]. This is neither the wail of a lost soul,
nor the bewildered appeal of a man under conviction but
without hope. 'He does not inquire who is to deliver him, as if
he were in doubt, like the unbelievers, who do not understand that there is only one deliverer. His language is that of a
man who is panting and almost fainting, because he sees that
his help is not close enough.' (Calvin) What he longs for is the
redemption of his body [8:23], which will end the struggle
that he knows will go on for as long as he inhabits 'the body of

this death', i.e. the physical body in whose members the law of sin is still operative. It is precisely because the believer's present emancipation from the thraldom of sin is not a deliverance to a state of absolute sinlessness that his final salvation remains a matter of hope [8:24].

V25: **I thank God through Jesus Christ our Lord. So then I of myself with the mind, indeed, serve the law of God; but with the flesh the law of sin.**

I thank God through Jesus Christ our Lord. The groan for deliverance from 'the body of this death' is answered by this triumphant thanksgiving which looks forward to the resurrection hope of all believers [1 *Cor* 15:56, 57]. 'Paul does not say that he already has this deliverance. It has been confused with our deliverance. It has been confused with our deliverance from the guilt of sin in justification. This has led to the mistaken idea that Paul is here dramatizing his past unregenerate state. This converts Paul into a show actor.' (Lenski)

So then I of myself with the mind, indeed, serve the law of God; but with the flesh the law of sin. Such is the situation that continues until the glorious day of consummation [8:11]; until then this strange duality remains. Paul however is careful to emphasize his personal responsibility for all the acts he has described; he does not shift the blame for his forced surrender to the law of sin upon an old ego! But it should also be noted that in placing 'I myself' next to the law of God, he shows 'that he regards this as the prominent fact of his present experience and moral state . . . Paul does not serve sin so much as he serves holiness.' (Shedd)

Haldane therefore justly concludes: 'Beyond this no child of God can go while in this world; it will ever remain the character of the regenerate man . . . In every believer, and in no one else, there are these two principles, – sin and grace, flesh and spirit, the law of the members and the law of the mind. This may be perverted by the opposer of divine truth into a handle against the gospel, and by the hypocrite to excuse his sin. But it gives ground to neither. It is the truth of God, and the experience of every Christian.'

CHAPTER EIGHT

*V*1: **There is therefore now no condemnation to them that are in Christ Jesus.**

From the contradiction of 'the flesh' which believers still find within themselves, Paul now turns to the determinative aspect of their experience by explaining the full implications [*vv* 1–11] of what was summarily stated in 7:6 (cf comment there). They have been discharged from the law, having died to its *condemning* power, because the sentence of condemnation which they deserved was fully borne by Christ on their behalf. So that there is now no condemnation of any kind for those who are 'in Christ Jesus' [6:3–11]. This means that they have not only been liberated from all liability to punishment, but also that in Christ they have been delivered from the enslaving power of sin in order that they might serve God 'in newness of the spirit'.

*V*2: **For the law of the Spirit of life in Christ Jesus made me free from the law of sin and of death.**

'For' advances the reason for the assurance just given. This is the last time that Paul sets forth his own experience ('me') to illustrate the experience of all believers. He was freed once for all from the lordship of 'the law of sin and death' when the power of God brought him under the governance of another principle, 'the law of the Spirit of life in Christ Jesus'. Although the tense of the verb shows that this liberation was effected in his justification, the apostle's purpose is not to revert to justification but to advance to the blessed life-giving consequences that flow from it.

Sin was able to turn God's holy law into the law of death [7:10, 11], but thanks to the grace which delivered him from all condemnation that same law is now the rule of his life [7:23: 'the law of my mind']. The Spirit's law of life is *qualitatively* different, but it is not *quantitatively* different in the sense that the Holy Spirit impels to any action not already prescribed by the law of God (see note on 7:6 and compare 13:8-10). It must be acknowledged that life in the Spirit is not an external obedience to a killing code, but neither is it a formless mysticism which has no relation to the revealed will of God. 'After his liberation Paul freely adopts and obeys God's law, and sin's law is deposed and is able to disturb him only from the outside through his members.' (Lenski) When the Holy Spirit thus puts a man 'in Christ' the reign of sin is broken, but even this 'victorious' chapter does not relieve him of the necessity of putting to death the deeds of the body [8:13]! Is this then so very different from the struggle described [7:23-25] in the previous chapter of 'defeat'?

V3: **For what the law could not do, in that it was weak through the flesh, God, sending his own Son in the likeness of sinful flesh and for sin, condemned sin in the flesh:**

This second 'for' traces the Spirit's work in the believer back to its objective basis, i.e. to the act by which God condemned sin in the flesh. What God did establishes what the law could not do; it was unable to condemn 'sin in the flesh' because 'it was weak through the flesh'. The law could condemn the sinner but it could not break the dominion of sin. For though sin had no place in the original constitution of man, once he fell a prey to this alien power, the law could only confirm its usurped lordship, since all breakers of the law lie helplessly under the curse [*Gal* 3:10]. Sin consigns man to the debtor's prison, and then makes the law his gaoler. 'Verily I say unto thee, Thou shalt by no means come out thence, till thou hast paid the last farthing' [*Matt* 5:26].

God, sending his own Son This points to the pre-existence of the Son. He was God's own Son before he was sent into the world. Here, as always in Scripture, God the Father is represented as taking the initiative in the salvation of mankind. 'His own Son' (see also *v* 32) is the Pauline equivalent to the Johannine title, 'only begotten Son' and both point to an eternal and essential relationship [*John* 1:14, 18, 3:16, 18; 1 *John* 4:9].

in the likeness of sinful flesh Paul sails between the Scylla of denying the reality of Christ's humanity ('in the likeness of flesh') and the Charybdis of compromising his sinlessness ('sinful flesh'). He uses this unique and exact expression to show us that the Incarnation brought the Son into the closest connection with our sinful condition, short of actually becoming sinful himself. And his meaning is that when the Son entered into our lot he overcame sin in the flesh, i.e. in the same realm which sin had made its own.

and for sin, To introduce the idea of a 'sin-offering' (RV) here is an unwarranted restriction of the apostle's thought. The whole purpose of God's sending his own Son in the likeness of sinful flesh was to judge and destroy *sin*! For apart from sin there would have been no need for his coming at all.

condemned sin in the flesh: Although the law is powerful to condemn sin in the flesh in a purely declarative sense, it is impotent to destroy sin's power over the flesh. But it was in the flesh of Christ that God both pronounced and executed his sentence upon sin [8:1]. 'In that same nature which in all others was sinful, in that very nature which in all others was dominated and directed by sin, in that nature assumed by the Son of God but free from sin, God condemned sin and overthrew its power. Jesus not only blotted out sin's guilt and brought us nigh to God. He also vanquished sin as power and set us free from its enslaving dominion. And this could not have been done except in the "flesh". The battle was joined and the triumph secured in that same flesh which in us is the seat and agent of sin.' (John Murray)

V4: that the ordinance of the law might be fulfilled in us, who walk not after the flesh, but after the Spirit.

in order that the just requirement of the law might be fulfilled in us, (RSV) This statement does not refer to the justifying righteousness of Christ, but to the work of the Holy Spirit within the believer. According to Jeremiah, God's promise to write his law upon the hearts of his people was to be a distinguishing feature of the New Covenant of which he prophesied [*Jer* 31:31–34, see also *Ezek* 36:26–28]. This 'New Covenant is not indifferent to law. It is not contrasted with the old because the old had law and the new has not. The superiority of the new does not consist in the abrogation of that law but in its being brought into more intimate relation to us and more effective fulfilment in us.' (John Murray, *The Covenant of Grace*, p. 29) Paul speaks of such a fulfilment in this verse. The righteous requirement of the law is fulfilled in believers through 'the law of the Spirit of life in Christ Jesus' [*v* 2]. 'That their obedience is not *perfect* is no more a truth than that it is a *real* and *acceptable* obedience through Christ.' (David Brown)

who walk not after the flesh, but after the Spirit. The apostle has *all* believers in view [cf *v* 9]! Negatively, they are described as those whose life-style is no longer determined by the dictates of the flesh. Positively, they are shown to be those who are willingly walking (a walk is a voluntary progress!) under the gracious direction of the Holy Spirit. 'For Paul, the human spirit is dormant or dead until it is aroused to life by the Spirit of God; hence to "walk . . . after the *pneuma*" implies the action of the human spirit in response to the guidance of the divine Spirit.' (F. F. Bruce) This contrast between the flesh and the Spirit is the theme of the next section [vv 5-13].

V5: **For they that are after the flesh mind the things of the flesh; but they that are after the Spirit the things of the Spirit.**

Paul now proceeds to explain the difference between these two mutually exclusive ways of living. To walk after the flesh [v 4] is the course of conduct that naturally results from a life which is determined by the flesh ('after the flesh'), and a mind which is therefore set upon the things of the flesh. The man who is thus dominated by the flesh has no capacity to discern the things of the Spirit, which are foolishness to him because he is dead towards God [1 Cor 2:14]. On the other hand, the believer is no longer of the flesh for he has been divinely quickened; his life is under the direction of the Spirit so that he fixes his mind upon spiritual things. It must be realized that an absolute distinction is in view here. The apostle is not contrasting the lower nature of the flesh with the higher nature of the spirit in one individual; he is insisting that men are *either* 'in the flesh' *or* 'in Christ'.

V6: **For the mind of the flesh is death; but the mind of the Spirit is life and peace:**

The natural man has the mind of the flesh; the believer the mind of the Spirit. To have the mind of the flesh is to exist in that state of spiritual death which reaches its culmination in the second death, the eternal death which is the wages of sin [6:23; Eph 2:1]. But to have the mind of the Spirit is to enjoy the first-fruits of life now, and to reap the full harvest hereafter [v 11]. This life is therefore spiritual life and the peace that accompanies it is the feeling of inward tranquillity that results from a restored relationship with God [5:1].

V7: because the mind of the flesh is enmity against God; for it is not subject to the law of God, neither indeed can it be:

This verse gives the reason why 'the mind of the flesh is death'. It is 'enmity against God', the author of life! 'Alienation from him is necessarily fatal.' (Denney) This hostility is actively expressed in its total opposition to the declared will of God. As if this were not enough, Paul adds that it is *incapable* of submission to the law of God. Because *self-will* is enthroned in the 'mind of the flesh' it cannot obey the will of its Creator, Sustainer, and Judge! This is a constitutional impossibility which neither the promise of reward nor the threat of punishment can remove. 'The expulsion of the sinful inclination, and the origination of the holy inclination, in the human will, is a revolution in the faculty which is accomplished only in its regeneration by the Holy Spirit. Self-recovery is not possible to the human will, though self-ruin is [*Hosea* 13:9].' (Shedd)

V8: and they that are in the flesh cannot please God.

This re-states the thought of verse 7 in more personal terms, and so paves the way for Paul's direct address to the readers in verse 9. 'The mind of the flesh' is not an abstraction; it belongs to those who cannot please God. They *ought* to please God, but they *cannot* please him. This total inability of the natural man is due to his total depravity – his 'natural' aversion to God [*v* 7]. Those who object to this doctrine, which has its basis in this passage, often do so because they think that total depravity means absolute depravity. It is however a term 'of *extensity* rather than *intensity*. It is opposed to *partial* depravity; to the idea that man is sinful in one moment and innocent or sinless in another; or sinful in some acts and pure in others. It affirms that he is all wrong, in all things, and all the time. It does not mean that man is as bad as the devil, or that every man is as bad as every other, or that any man is as bad as he may possibly be, or may become. But there is no limit to the universality or *extent* of evil in his soul. So say the Scriptures, and so says every awakened conscience.' (Tayler Lewis, quoted by Alexander Whyte in his *Commentary on the Shorter Catechism*, p. 40)

*V*9: **But ye are not in the flesh, but in the Spirit, if so be that the Spirit of God dwelleth in you. But if any man hath not the Spirit of Christ, he is none of his.**

Paul here thankfully turned to the believers in Rome who are 'not in the flesh, but in the Spirit'. By the grace of God they now belong to an entirely different realm. But though they have been delivered from the dominion of the flesh, they are still living in a body which is subject to death because of sin [*v* 10]. And this means that they are called to resist the unceasing attempts of the flesh to re-assert its authority over them [*vv* 12, 13]. It is the Holy Spirit who initiates this conflict and sustains the believer in it, because a man is nothing but flesh until he is in the Spirit and the Spirit is in him. There is a quietism that tends to equate peace with the absence of all strife, and there is an enthusiasm that can neglect the duty of putting to death the deeds of the body. But this constant struggle with the flesh is a surer evidence of the presence of the indwelling of the Spirit!

The apostle does not doubt that this is the experience of his readers, but the 'if so be' which qualifies his assurance shows that this is to be confirmed by self-examination [2 *Cor* 13:5]. Because if any man has not the 'Spirit of Christ' [*John* 16:7], he is none of his [*Jude* 19]. As any man who lacks the Spirit is no Christian, so every man who belongs to Christ is indwelt by his Spirit. Consequently *all* believers are 'Spiritual' and no distinction can be made between those who are 'in the Spirit' and those who are not 'in the Spirit' (John Murray).

*V*10: **And if Christ is in you, the body is dead because of sin; but the spirit is life because of righteousness.**

but the Spirit is life because of righteousness. (AV) This is a reference to the Holy Spirit and not to the human spirit, for we contribute nothing to this life which is given to us through the justifying righteousness of Christ. 'If then Christ dwells in your heart through the Spirit, though your body is doomed to die because of sin, you have life in the Spirit because of righteousness.' Eternal life is our present possession on account of the righteousness of God, accomplished for us by Christ and applied to us by the Holy Spirit, who will also quicken even our mortal bodies on that great day when our salvation shall be consummated [v 11]. 'Now, if all men die on account of sin, as the apostle here teaches, then no man can have life by his own righteousness.' (Haldane)

*V*11: **But if the Spirit of him that raised up Jesus from the dead dwelleth in you, he that raised up Christ Jesus from the dead shall give life also to your mortal bodies through his Spirit that dwelleth in you.**

The spiritual resurrection of believers is the guarantee of their participation in the resurrection of the body, for the Spirit through whom God raised Jesus from the dead already dwells in their hearts. 'It should be noticed how significantly Paul varies in this connection the name of Christ. First he speaks of the raising of *Jesus* from the dead. Here the Saviour comes under consideration as to himself, his own human nature. Then he speaks of the raising of *Christ Jesus* from the dead. Here the Saviour comes under consideration as the Messiah in his representative capacity, which furnishes a guarantee that his resurrection must repeat itself in that of the others.' (Geer-hardus Vos, *The Pauline Eschatology*, p. 163) What an incentive such a glorious prospect affords believers for mortifying the deeds of the body!

*V*12: **So then, brethren, we are debtors, not to the flesh, to live after the flesh:**

All Christians are perpetual debtors to grace, but they owe no debt to the flesh. Hence those who are the temples of the Holy

Spirit must no longer obey the insistent demands of the flesh [1 *Cor* 3:16.] The conclusion is drawn in negative terms in order to underline the utter inconsistency of such a course. The positive implication is that all who are so graciously indwelt by the Spirit will yield themselves without reserve to his government of their lives.

*V*13: **for if ye live after the flesh, ye must die; but if by the Spirit ye put to death the deeds of the body, ye shall live.**

The paradoxical nature of this utterance strikingly sets forth the reason why believers are under no obligation to the flesh: To *live* after the flesh brings on *death*; to put to *death* the deeds of the body preserves *life*!

for if ye live after the flesh, ye must die; Eternal death is the inevitable consequence of living after the flesh. It is because this cause can never be separated from its death-dealing effect that believers must never think that it is safe to yield to the lusts of the flesh. Anyone who thinks otherwise has clearly mistaken a false sense of security *in* sin for a true experience of salvation *from* sin. 'Let not that man think he makes any progress in holiness who walks not over the bellies of his lusts. He who doth not kill sin in his way takes no steps towards his journey's end.' (John Owen)

but if the Spirit This essential qualification rules out all asceticism, all fleshly ideas of mortifying the flesh [cf *Col* 2:18-23]. 'Mortification from a self-strength, carried on by ways of self-invention, unto the end of a self-righteousness, is the soul and substance of all false religion in the world.' (John Owen)

ye put to death the deeds of the body, ye shall live. As the only true life is spiritual life, believers must put to death the deeds of the body, i.e. the *physical* body that sin still uses as its ally in its war against the soul [cf 7:23: 'the law of sin which is in my members']. It is not spiritual to overlook the fact that sin comes to its concrete expression through the body. Having been freed from the law of sin and death [*v* 2], believers are now under an abiding obligation to deny sin this use of the body for its development to the detriment of their life [*Col* 3:5]. As John Owen says, 'Be killing sin or it will be killing you'. And this is a work which is peculiar to believers, for those who are still under the dominion of sin cannot be called upon to mortify particular sins but are first to be summoned to a saving interest in Christ (cf Owen, *Of the Mortification of Sin in Believers*, *Ch* 7).

*V*14: For as many as are led by the Spirit of God, these are sons of God.

Those who faithfully engage in this daily work of mortifying the flesh enjoy the assurance that they are indeed sons of God. '*For* as many as are being led by the Spirit of God, *these* are sons of God.' The believer's submission to the leading of the Spirit in the fight against indwelling sin is thus a sure mark of true sonship. Paul 'had pointed to the very fact of this conflict as a banner of hope. For he identifies the fact of the conflict with the presence of the Holy Spirit working in the soul; and in the presence of the Holy Spirit is the earnest of victory. The Spirit would not be found in a soul which was not purchased for God and in the process of fitting for the heavenly Kingdom. Let no one talk of living on the low plane of the seventh chapter of Romans. Low plane, indeed! It is a low plane where there is no conflict. Where there is conflict – with the Spirit of God as one party in the battle – there is progressive advance towards the perfection of Christian life. So Paul treats it.' (B. B. Warfield, 'The Spirit's Testimony to Our Sonship' in *Faith and Life*, pp. 189–190)

This leading of the Spirit can *never* contradict the testimony of God's word but is *always* in conformity with it. It 'excludes all fanaticism, all auto-suggestion, all hearing fictitious, imaginary inward voices. We have the *written* Word with

which to test every inward Word that we have absorbed.'
(Lenski) It is of the greatest importance to note that the Spirit
who led Jesus into the wilderness to be tempted also helped
him to gain the victory over the devil by bringing God's
written Word to his remembrance [cf *Luke* 4:1, 4, 8, 12, 14;
Eph 6:17].

V15: **For ye received not the spirit of bondage again
unto fear; but ye received the spirit of adoption, whereby we cry, Abba, Father.**

'Ye received' is in the aorist tense and it looks back to the time
when Paul's readers became Christians. You did not then
receive the Holy Spirit as a spirit of bondage 'again unto fear'
[cf *Gal* 4:1-9]. Their former state was characterized by a
slavish dread of punishment. 'They were then not under
grace, but under law [6:14]; and "the law worketh wrath"
[4:15]. The legal spirit has nothing genial or spontaneous in
it: no enjoyment. This wretched spirit, or frame of mind, was
not introduced a second time, by the reception of the Holy
Ghost.' (Shedd) For it is the function of the Spirit to bring men
into a state of liberty and not bondage [2 *Cor* 3:17].

In the second part of the verse the verb is repeated for the
sake of emphasis. On the contrary, you received in conversion
the Holy Spirit as the Spirit of adoption through whom you
were assured of your acceptance into the family of God! This
is the adoption of grace whereby those who were God's
enemies are not merely made his friends but are advanced by
him to the status of sons [1 *John* 3:1]. 'Adoption confers the
name of sons, and a *title* to the inheritance; regeneration confers the *nature* of sons, and a *meetness* for the inheritance.'
(Haldane) [*John* 1:12, 13]

And it is because they have not only the *status* but also the
heart of sons that they are impelled to cry, 'Abba, Father!'
(Denney). This crying recalls the urgent invocation of God
which is frequently found in the Psalms (Cranfield notes that
the same word is used more than forty times in the Greek

translation of this book, e.g. *Ps* 3:4, 18:6, 34:6 etc.). But here it is the Spirit of adoption who moves us to call upon God as our Father. As *Mark* 14:36 shows, Abba is the Aramaic word which Jesus used to address his Father in prayer, and it is probable that the prayer he taught the disciples began with this word [*Luke* 11:2]. Since this was the familiar title used by Jewish children to address their earthly father, its application by Jesus to God was revolutionary in its implications, suggesting the intimacy of a Father-child relationship not found in Judaism (Kittel, *TDNT*, vol. I, p. 5). When we realize that the spiritual experience of *every* believer is summed up in this *one* word, we are not surprised that it was preserved in transliteration by Greek-speaking Christians for the permanent enrichment of the church universal.

V16: The Spirit himself beareth witness with our spirit, that we are children of God:

This shows that there is a double testimony to our adoption. The first is the witness borne *by our spirit* as we are prompted by the Holy Spirit to cry, Abba, Father; the second is the witness borne by the Holy Spirit *to our spirit* to assure us that we are indeed children of God. As John Murray points out, This is a witness to our spirit so that we are not to understand it in terms of a direct revelation to the effect, 'Thou art a child of God'. It is rather an inward certitude which is made particularly clear in sealing to our hearts the promises that belong to us as the heirs of God and in generating in us the assurance of the Father's adopting love.

Paul gives absolutely no hint that he is here speaking of a higher experience of assurance which might be unknown to some of his readers. Indeed his words cannot be understood of a coming of the Spirit subsequent to conversion, as the *parallel passage* in Galatians clearly shows: 'To prove that you are sons, God has sent into our hearts the Spirit of his Son, crying, "Abba! Father!" You are therefore no longer a slave but a son, and if a son, then also by God's own act an heir' [*Gal* 4:6, 7 NEB].

The Galatians ceased to be slaves when they received the filial spirit of sons in their conversion [cf 3:1: 'did you receive the Spirit by keeping the law or by believing the gospel message?' NEB]. And it is not without significance that Paul confidently makes this appeal to their *experience* of the Spirit as the proof of the genuineness of their faith in Christ [cf *vv* 9, 14]. Perhaps if modern evangelism were less obsessed with conversion without feeling – 'Do not doubt your salvation even though you do not *feel* any different' – there would be less emphasis upon post-conversion experiences!

*V*17: **and if children, then heirs; heirs of God, and joint-heirs with Christ; if so be that we suffer with him, that we may be also glorified with him.**

and if children, then heirs; Those who are children must also be heirs. By their adoption believers are entitled to an eternal inheritance. 'As the birthright of a child confers a title to the property of its father, and so distinguishes such property from what the child may acquire by industry and labour, so also is the case with adoption. Here we see the difference between the law and the gospel. The law treats men as mercenaries, and says, Do, and live; the gospel treats them as children, and says, Live, and do.' (Haldane)

heirs of God, and joint-heirs with Christ; The possession of the Holy Spirit is the earnest or deposit which assures believers that they will receive the promised inheritance [*Eph* 1:14; cf *v* 23]. This divine gift enables them to embrace the stupendous thought that they are heirs of God and fellow-heirs with Christ. In its broadest manifestation the inheritance is the kingdom of God, but the sum of its bliss will be the eternal enjoyment of God himself [*Ps* 16:5f, 73:25, 26; *Lam* 3:24]. As the natural Son of the Father Christ is the proper heir; believers being sons by adoption are only heirs in virtue of their union with him. Christ has already entered into the glory which was won for his people by his obedience unto death, and this exaltation is the pledge that they shall follow him there.

if so be that we suffer with him, that we may be also glorified with him. But just as the cross preceded the crown in the experience of Christ, so his people must first suffer with him before they can be glorified with him. Their identification with Christ inevitably involves believers in suffering for his name's sake, and in this sense they suffer with him [*John* 15:18; *Phil* 1:29; 1 *Pet* 4:13]. These sufferings are both internal and external, and they result from taking their stand with Christ against the world, the flesh, and the devil. And though such sufferings contribute nothing towards the cost of their salvation which was wholly borne by him [*Is* 53:5], they are a necessary part of the refining process that prepares them for glory [1 *Pet* 1:6, 7].

*V*18: **For I reckon that the sufferings of this present time are not worthy to be compared with the glory which shall be revealed to us-ward.**

The reference to future glory leads the apostle to enlarge upon this expectation. He brings forward a threefold testimony to confirm suffering believers in their hope: 1. Creation itself groans for deliverance, *vv* 19–22; 2. Christians groan for glory, *vv* 23–25; 3. The Spirit himself groans with them in their longing, *vv* 26–27.

In the light of faith Paul reckons that the sufferings of the present age are not worthy to be compared with the glory of the age to come. His calculation is comprehensive in its scope. It covers every kind of suffering we may experience in this age of distress as well as that which is endured for Christ's sake [*v* 17]. 'We need comfort and assurance not only when we suffer for Christ but also and often much more when we endure other suffering.' (Lenski) The glory to be revealed already exists in the person of the glorified Christ, but it shall then reach unto us. It 'is to be bestowed upon us, so that we become the actual partakers; it is not a glory of which we are to be mere spectators.' (John Murray)

*V*19: **For the earnest expectation of the creation waiteth for the revealing of the sons of God.**

As W. J. Grier explains, 'All nature, now groaning under the curse pronounced at the Fall, awaits a deliverance and renovation corresponding to the deliverance of the redeemed.' (*The Momentous Event*, p. 65) [*Gen* 3:17; *Matt* 19:28; *Acts* 3:21; *2 Pet* 3:13; *Rev* 21:1] In thus attributing to inanimate creation a longing that properly belongs to rational creatures, Paul vividly shows that the restoration of the material world is intimately bound up with the fulfilment of God's redemptive purpose.

for the revealing of the sons of God. 'Their status as sons of God with all privileges attached, such as freedom and heirship, existed before, but had not been openly demonstrated. Not their celestial body, but their supreme sonship was in hiding. It is this *status* that will be revealed, and this revelation will be accomplished, by laying upon them the glory, the medium for whose manifestation, to be sure, is the body of the resurrection.' (Geerhardus Vos, *The Pauline Eschatology*, p. 198)

*V*20: **For the creation was subjected to vanity, not of its own will, but by reason of him who subjected it, in hope**

When God cursed the ground for man's sake, the whole creation was subjected to vanity through no fault of its own. The sin of Adam involved the created order in a judgment which condemned it to the futility and frustration of falling short of its original purpose. But as God's sentence upon sin did not cut off man from the hope of redemption, creation was made a sharer in his hope as well as his punishment.

'When the curse is completely removed from man, as it will be when the sons of God are revealed, it will pass from creation also; and for this creation sighs. It was made subject to vanity on the footing of this hope; the hope is latent, so to speak, in the constitution of nature, and comes out, in its sighing, to a sympathetic ear.' (Denney)

V21: **that the creation itself also shall be delivered from the bondage of corruption into the liberty of the glory of the children of God.**

The content of this hope is that creation shall at length be delivered from its slavery to corruption to share in the liberty of the glory that belongs to the children of God. 'Corruption' explains 'vanity' by showing that the failure of creation to reach its goal is due to the principle of decay and death which ends everything. But failure is not God's final word for creation. 'It is, and always shall be, the world which God Almighty has created, which He, in spite of all the sins of angels and of men, has in its broad dimensions upheld and maintained, and which at the time of the end He will so bring out to a perfect form of life, that it will perfectly correspond to His purpose of creation, and which, in spite of the sins of angels and of men shall make his original plan – now no more susceptible of corruption – shine forth resplendently in fulness and richness of form.' (Abraham Kuyper, *The Revelation of St John*, p. 344)

V22: **For we know that the whole creation groaneth and travaileth in pain together until now.**

'For' confirms this miserable state by showing that the whole creation is groaning together in what Philippi calls 'a grand symphony of sighs'. Nevertheless, these groans are not seen as the death-throes of creation, but as the birth-pangs that point to its restoration. 'Because the creatures are subject to corruption, not through their natural desire, but by God's appointment, and also because they have a hope of being freed hereafter from corruption, it follows that they groan like a woman in labour until they have been delivered. This is a most appropriate comparison to inform us that the groaning of which he speaks will not be in vain or without effect. It will finally bring forth a joyful and happy fruit.' (Calvin)

*V*23: **And not only so, but ourselves also, who have the firstfruits of the Spirit, even we ourselves groan within ourselves, waiting for our adoption, to wit, the redemption of our body.**

This 'groaning for glory' is consciously shared by the Christian who longs for the consummation of his salvation in the 'redemption of the body' [2 *Cor* 5:2]. This full and final deliverance from all the consequences of sin is here called the 'adoption' because the resurrection will constitute the supreme manifestation of the sonship. The possession of the 'firstfruits of the Spirit' not only points to the certainty of the final harvest, but also arouses within the Christian 'a painful sense of hunger', since present 'partial enjoyment' has only 'whetted the appetite for the true food in its abundance'. The same idea is present in the description of the Spirit as the 'earnest' or 'pledge' of future glory [2 *Cor* 1:22, 5:5; *Eph* 1:14]. 'The present possession of the Spirit is regarded in the light of an anticipation. The Spirit's proper sphere is the future aeon (age); from thence he projects himself into the present, and becomes a prophecy of himself in his eschatological (or final) operations.' (Vos, *op. cit.*, pp. 40, 165)

*V*24: **For in hope were we saved: but hope that is seen is not hope: for who hopeth for that which he seeth?**

For in hope were we saved: Salvation as a present reality of the believer's experience cannot be an object of hope, 'for who hopeth for that which he seeth?' 'In hope' therefore refers to the 'redemption of the body' mentioned in the previous verse. The context makes it clear that the Christian hope does not terminate in the heavenly bliss of the soul in the intermediate state, but eagerly anticipates the final fulfilment of the promise of the resurrection of the body unto life eternal.

V25: But if we hope for that which we see not, then do we with patience wait for it.

The patient endurance of present trials is a fruit of hope, for as Calvin remarks, 'all that the gospel promises concerning the glory of the resurrection vanishes away, unless we spend our present life in bearing with patience the cross and tribulations'. [1 *Thess* 1:3] 'Impatience spells dispute and dissatisfaction with God's design ... Expectancy and hope must not cross the bounds of history; they must wait for *the end*, "the liberty of the glory of the children of God".' (John Murray) [Cf 2 *Cor* 4:18, 5:7]

V26: And in like manner the Spirit also helpeth our infirmity: for we know not how to pray as we ought; but the Spirit himself maketh intercession for us with groanings which cannot be uttered;

Although the believer is even now a child of God, his present state is characterized by weakness and infirmity. This verse provides the comforting assurance that the exigencies of this situation are met by the ministry which the Holy Spirit exercises within the hearts of believers. The Christian is not crushed under an abounding sense of his own infirmity, because the Holy Spirit graciously shares with him in the bearing of this burden.

for we know not how to pray as we ought; Inability in prayer is not only an illustration of the weakness of the believer but also an explanation of it. He neither knows what to pray for, nor how to present his petitions as he ought. Hence the necessity for the illumination and the inspiration of the Spirit, who is the true author of prevailing prayer.

but the Spirit himself maketh intercession for us with groanings which cannot be uttered; The children of God are represented by two advocates. Their glorified Redeemer ever lives to make intercession for them in heaven, and the Holy Spirit condescends to plead for them from within their own hearts [*John* 14:16, 26, 15:26, 16:7; *Heb* 7:25; 1 *John* 2:1]. This is 'not an intercession through us as mere conduits, unengaged in the intercession ourselves; it is an intercession made by the Spirit as our helper and not as our substitute . . . The Spirit intercedes for us then by working in us right desires for each time of need; and by deepening these desires into unutterable groans. They are our desires, and our groans. But not apart from the Spirit. They are his; wrought in us by him.' (B. B. Warfield, 'The Spirit's Help in our Praying' in *Faith and Life*, pp. 199–200)

*V*27: **and he that searcheth the hearts knoweth what is the mind of the Spirit, because he maketh intercession for the saints according to the will of God.**

Since this groaning is nothing less than the expression of 'the mind of the Spirit', it has not only a meaning, but also that meaning is perfectly discerned by God, the searcher of hearts [*Ps* 139:1, 23; *Jer* 17:10]. It further follows that this intercession of the Spirit must be in perfect harmony with 'the will of God'. The strong encouragement which this passage offers to believers is that when God searches their hearts he finds in the groanings of the Spirit a perfect reflection of his own loving purpose for them. 'Both the intercession of Christ and the intercession of the Spirit are represented in the New Testament as made on behalf of those who are in Christ – saints, the Church, not mankind in general.' (Denney) [*John* 17:9]

*V*28: **And we know that to them that love God all things work together for good, even to them that are called according to his purpose.**

This verse is the climax of the chapter. 'We know' is not the language of tentative conjecture, but of experimental certainty. Paul is very far from saying that everything is for the best in the best of all possible worlds, for this sublime assurance is limited by a double qualification. It is only the children of God who can claim this promise. Nothing will be found to work for the final good of the wicked, but all things must work together for the ultimate blessing of those who love God and are called according to his purpose [see for example: Gen 50:20; Acts 8:4; Phil 1:12].

'If all things work together for good, there is nothing within the compass of being that is not, in one way or other, advantageous to the children of God. All the dispensations of Providence, whether prosperous or adverse, all occurrences and events – all things, whatsoever they be – work for their good. They do not work thus of themselves: It is God that turns all things to the good of his children. The afflictions of believers, in a peculiar manner, contribute to this end [Ps 119:67, 71].

'Even the sins of believers work for their good, not from the nature of sin, but by the goodness and power of him who brings light out of darkness. That it is turned to good, is the work of God, and not ours [cf Luke 22:31-34]. We ought no more to conclude that on this account we may sin, than that wicked men do what is right when they persecute the people of God, because persecutions are overruled by him for good. That all things work together for good to them who love God, establishes the doctrine of the perseverance of the saints; for if all things work together for their good, what or where is that which God will permit to lead them into condemnation?' (Haldane)

Those who thus love God are 'the called'; and they are called because they were first chosen. Charles Hodge points out that 'called' is 'never, in the epistles of the New Testament, applied to those who are the recipients of the mere external invitation of the gospel. It always means *effectually called*, i.e., it is always applied to those who are really brought to accept the blessings to which they are invited . . . This call is not according to the merits of men, but according to the divine purpose.' [*Rom* 9:11; *Eph* 1:11; 2 *Tim* 1:9] In *Romans* 8:28–30 Paul describes 'an unbreakable chain of events proceeding from God's eternal purpose in foreknowledge and predestination to the glorification of the people of God. It is impossible to remove calling from this setting. The called are called according to purpose; the purpose is antecedent to the calling.' (John Murray, *Redemption Accomplished and Applied*, pp. 156–157)

*V*29: **For whom he foreknew, he also foreordained to be conformed to the image of his Son, that he might be the firstborn among many brethren:**

For whom he foreknew, This word may not be reduced to mean the mere foresight of faith by God; it is virtually the equivalent of foreloved [cf *Ps* 1:6, 144:3; *Jer* 1:5; *Amos* 3:2; *Hos* 13:5; *Matt* 7:23; 1 *Cor* 8:3; *Gal* 4:9]. 'God has always possessed perfect knowledge of all creatures and of all events. There has never been a time when anything past, present, or future was not fully known to Him. But it is not His knowledge of future events (of what people would do, etc.) which is referred to in *Rom* 8:29, 30, for Paul clearly states that those whom He *foreknew* He predestined, He called, and He justified. Since all men are *not* predestined, called, and justified, it follows that all men were *not foreknown* by God in the sense spoken of in verse 29 . . . Although God knew *about* all men before the world began, He did not *know* all men in the sense that the Bible sometimes uses the word "know", i.e., with intimate personal awareness and love. It is in this latter sense that God fore*knew* those whom He predestined, called, and justified.' (Steele and Thomas, *Romans – An Interpretive Outline*, pp. 132, 134)

he also foreordained to be conformed to the image of his Son, As 'whom he foreknew' draws our attention to the distinguishing love of God, so 'he also foreordained' informs us of the high and holy destiny for which the elect are appointed by God. Since this destination is their conformity to the image of their incarnate and glorified Redeemer, it is nothing less than their conformity to the image of the eternal Son of God [cf 2 *Cor* 3:18; *Eph* 1:4, 5; *Phil* 3:21]. Therefore a true understanding of what is involved in election can never lead to careless security in sin [2 *Pet* 1:1–12].

that he might be the firstborn among many brethren:
This shows us that the divine decree has for its ultimate end the exaltation of Christ. 'The term "firstborn" reflects on the *priority* and the *supremacy* of Christ [cf *Col* 1:15, 18; *Heb* 1:6; *Rev* 1:5] . . . The fraternal relationship is subsumed under the ultimate end of the predestinating decree, and this means that the pre-eminence of Christ carries with it the eminence that belongs to the children of God. In other words, the unique dignity of the Son in his essential relation to the Father and in his messianic investiture enhances the marvel of the dignity bestowed upon the people of God. The Son is not ashamed to call them brethren [*Heb* 2:11].' (John Murray)

*V*30: **and whom he foreordained, them he also called: and whom he called, them he also justified: and whom he justified, them he also glorified.**

The eternal purpose of God for his children finds its historical expression in their calling and justification, and these acts are the earnest of their future glorification, the certainty of which is indicated here by the use of the past tense. No such assurance would be conveyed to believers if 'calling' depended upon the will of man, for no chain is stronger than its weakest link [*John* 1:13]. However, it must be noted that throughout the passage Paul speaks of salvation exclusively in terms of God's action. Those whom he foreloved are none other than those whom he glorified.

Thus God's foreknowledge, predestination, calling, justification, and glorification of his people form five links in an unbreakable chain of salvation. The invincibility of God's purpose is the guarantee that those whom he has quickened to new life in Christ shall not fall short of future glory, for that which has been forged upon the anvil of God's grace cannot be thwarted by the will of the creature. By means of this revelation made through the apostle, the Christian's vision transcends the frontiers of time. Eternal election is the spring of grace and eternal glory is its consummation. Present trials are only seen in their true proportions when they are viewed within the context of these eternal vistas of grace.

Paul does not mention the believer's present experience of sanctification 'because the difference between sanctification and glory is one of degree only, not one of kind. Sanctification is progressive conformity to the image of Christ here and now [cf 2 *Cor* 3:18; *Col* 3:10]; glory is perfect conformity to the image of Christ there and then. Sanctification is glory begun; glory is sanctification completed.' (F. F. Bruce)

*V*31: **What then shall we say to these things? If God is for us, who is against us?**

The argument concluded, Paul turns to a triumphant application of the teaching. The note of victory is immediately struck in the challenging question, 'What then shall we say to these things?' It covers all the apostle has taught in the epistle. And it serves to introduce four rhetorical questions whose purpose is to assure all who are 'in Christ' of their impregnable security so that they might enjoy an invincible confidence in God [*vv* 31, 33, 34, 35]. Each question really answers itself, but Paul is not content to leave it at that. He uses these questions as pegs on which to hang this glorious paean of praise to God's sovereign grace. 'If God is for us, who is against us?' 'If' implies no doubt, but states a condition of reality. Since God *is* for us, then all our adversaries are of no account, for who can frustrate his saving purpose? Indeed, the fact that God is for us was supremely demonstrated in the sacrifice of his Son on our behalf [*v* 32].

V32: **He that spared not his own Son, but delivered him up for us all, how shall he not also with him freely give us all things?**

He that spared not his own Son, Paul's language here appears to be taken from the Greek version of *Gen* 22:12. The willingness of Abraham to offer up Isaac provides only a faint analogy of the Father's ultimate self-sacrifice in refusing to spare his own Son. 'He would have spared his Son had he wished to execute upon us the punishment we had incurred. He would have spared his Son, and removed the cup of suffering from him, had he not purposed to confer upon us all conceivable good. But, in love to us, he spared not his own Son. He removed not the cup from him, that it might never be presented to us. This scripture connects the Christian's safety under divine protection with the fact that God spared not his own Son, – a phrase which implies that he spared not the Surety, that he might rescue us.' (George Smeaton, *The Apostles' Doctrine of the Atonement*, p. 181)

but delivered him up for us all, 'Spared not' is negative; 'delivered up' is positive. It was the Father who delivered up his Son to the damnation and dereliction of that death which sin merited [*Mark* 15:34]. It was the Father who delivered up his Son to all the powers of darkness and the hands of wicked men, so that he might endure and exhaust the sentence of doom on behalf of those for whom he vicariously bore it [*Luke* 22:53; *Acts* 2:23]. 'Who delivered up Jesus to die? Not Judas, for money; not Pilate, for fear; not the Jews, for envy; but the Father, for love!' (Octavius Winslow)

Hence Calvary was the fulfilment of Zechariah's prophecy, 'Awake, O sword, against my shepherd, and against the man that is my fellow, saith the Lord of hosts' [*Zech* 13:7; *Matt* 26:31]. This is not the sword of judicial power as in *Rom* 13:4, but the sword of divine justice. For behind the farce of his earthly trial, there was the reality of his arraignment as the appointed sin-bearer of a sinful people before the heavenly tribunal [*Is* 53:4-7]. 'The sheep had deserved the blow, but the shepherd bares his own bosom to the sword, and is wounded for the sins of his people, and bears those sins in his own body on the tree.' (T. V. Moore)

As Poole comments, 'for us all' refers to 'such persons as he had before mentioned, such as God foreknew, predestinated, called, etc., which is not all men in general, but a set number of persons in particular: it is an expression both of latitude and restriction; of latitude, in the word *all*; of restriction, in the word *us*.'

how shall he not also with him freely give us all things?
As Lenski says, 'The argument is not merely from the greater to the less but a statement of the impossibility of not completing what God began at so tremendous a cost to himself.' For it is inconceivable that God should thus give his Son up to death, even the death of the cross, and then withhold the lesser gifts of grace which his people will need to finish their pilgrimage of faith in triumph.

*V*33: **Who shall lay anything to the charge of God's elect? It is God that justifieth;**

Those who press charges against believers are doomed to disappointment, for they fight against God's decree. It is impossible to curse, still less to condemn, those whom God has determined to bless [*Num* 23:19, 20]. Paul's intention in tracing every blessing to its ultimate source in God's sovereign choice, is to lay the only foundation for a genuine sense of Christian assurance, even as he demolishes all possibility of pride in the creature. If imaginary merit could never constrain God's love, neither could real demerit extinguish it. All the glory and all the praise belong to God alone. Election is never taught in Scripture as a speculative dogma, but as a practical reality of Christian experience. Those who know that they have been 'loved with everlasting love' will not surrender this precious truth simply because it arouses the antipathy of carnal minds.

It is God that justifieth; The answer shows that God cannot fail to justify those whom he has chosen to be the free recipients of his loving kindness. The term 'justify' is significant, for it indicates that God's love is never exercised at the expense of God's law. 'If justice is not satisfied, there can be no justification, no peace of conscience, no security either for salvation or for the moral government of God. The Bible knows nothing of mere pardon. There can be no pardon except on the ground of satisfaction of justice. It is by declaring a man just, (that is, that justice in relation to him is satisfied), that he is freed from the penalty of the law, and restored to the favour of God.' (Hodge) [*Is* 50:8, 9]

*V*34: **who is he that condemneth? It is Christ Jesus that died, yea rather, that was raised from the dead, who is at the right hand of God, who also maketh intercession for us.**

The confidence that it is God who justifies prompts this further challenge. The answer shows that Christ's finished work and his present heavenly ministry of intercession guarantee the security of his people, who are thereby assured that nothing shall be able to separate them from the love of Christ [*v* 35].

It is Christ Jesus that died, Paul simply states the fact of Christ's death, for he has fully explained its purpose earlier in the epistle [3:21–26, 4:25, 5:8–11, 6:4–10, 8.3, 4]. 'The terseness at this point draws attention to the stupendous significance of the death of Christ in the series of redemptive facts instanced in this verse. That Christ Jesus should have died is in itself so arresting a fact that the simple statement summons us to reflection on the implications.' (John Murray)

yea rather, that was raised from the dead, The efficacy of the death resides in the reality of the resurrection, for a dead Saviour is a contradiction in terms. The testator lives again to become his own executor, thus personally ensuring that all the beneficiaries of the will actually receive the benefits of his death [*Heb* 9:16, 17].

who is at the right hand of God, The glorious exaltation of the Mediator to the place of supreme authority and power in heaven is itself an assurance that his people shall follow him there [*John* 14:2, 3]. Since the heavens have now received the bodily presence of the Lord 'until the times of restoration of all things', it therefore follows that there can be no corporeal manifestation in the Lord's Supper, whatever priestly pretensions are made to the contrary [*Acts* 3:21].

who also maketh intercession for us. 'His session denotes his *power* to save us; his intercession, his *will* to do it.' (Bengel) Calvin warns against the danger of measuring this intercession by carnal judgment, 'for we must not think of him as humbly supplicating the Father on bended knee and with outstretched hands'. It must rather be understood as his claim that 'the efficacy of his death should be made good to the uttermost' after the style adopted in his great high priestly prayer, 'Father, *I will* that they also whom thou hast given me be with me where I am.' (David Brown) [*John* 17:24; *Heb* 7:24, 25]

*V*35: **Who shall separate us from the love of Christ? shall tribulation, or ang ish, or persecution, or famine, or nakedness, or peril, or sword?**
*V*36: **Even as it is written,**
> **For thy sake we are killed all the day long;**
> **We were accounted as sheep for the slaughter.**

In the final question 'the love of Christ' refers to Christ's love for his people, and not their love to him, because no assurance could be derived from the latter [cf *v* 37]. Here Paul returns to the thought of 'the sufferings of this present time' [*v* 18]. The world always sees these afflictions as the proof that Christ has removed his favour from us, whereas in fact they serve to bring us into even closer fellowship with him [*Phil* 3:10].

As Denney points out, 'For thy sake' is the crux of the quotation which comes from *Ps* 44:22. 'This is what the Psalmist could not understand. That men should suffer for sin, for infidelity to God, was intelligible enough; but he and his countrymen were suffering because of their faithfulness, and the psalm is his daring expostulation with God. But the apostle understood it. To suffer for Christ's sake was to enter into the fellowship of Christ's sufferings, and that is the very situation in which the love of Christ is most real, near, and sure to the soul.' [cf 5:3]

*V*37: **Nay, in all these things we are more than conquerors through him that loved us.**

In view of the accumulated evils which are faced and overcome by the Christian warrior, 'conquer' is far to weak a word for Paul to use. Only the word in its heightened form can do justice to this conquest which is snatched out of seeming defeat. Nay, in all these afflictions which come upon us for the sake of the name we confess, we are *more than* conquerors! Overwhelming victory is ours because we are given the strength to endure 'through him who did love us' [cf *Col* 2:15]. For he who loved us unto the death of the cross, loves us still and we stand fast in our faith through his matchless grace!

*V*38: **For I am persuaded, that neither death, nor life, nor angels, nor principalities, nor things present, nor things to come, nor powers,**

*V*39: **nor height, nor depth, nor any other creature, shall be able to separate us from the love of God, which is in Christ Jesus our Lord.**

In the magnificent conclusion Paul affirms his God-given persuasion that nothing can ever sever the Christian from the love of God [*Jude* 24, 25]. Men have been wrongly persuaded of many things, but the apostle states the abiding reality of Christian experience.

neither death nor life, As we must either live or die, these cover every eventuality that can befall us. If our last enemy death cannot separate us because Christ has vanquished it and robbed it of its sting [1 *Cor* 15:55f], then we are assured that nothing which precedes that final crisis will be any more successful [*Matt* 10:29, 30].

nor angels, nor principalities, The evil angels and hostile principalities [*Eph* 6:12], who would be glad to separate us from Christ, have been stripped of their power to effect their malevolent design by Christ's great victory on the cross [*Col* 2:14].

nor things present, nor things to come, As therefore Christ has made all history his own, the Christian must neither yield to the temptation to despair in present affliction, nor entertain any fearful foreboding of what the future might hold for him [*v* 28].

nor powers, If taken together with angels and principalities as in the AV, 'powers' would likewise refer to these cosmic forces of evil. But its separation in the best texts lends weight to John Murray's suggestion that 'no mighty work or miracle [cf especially 2 *Thess* 2:9] can be effective in separating from Christ'.

nor height, nor depth, These were technical terms in astrology, and if Paul had this meaning in mind, the reference would be to the movements of the planets which were thought to control the destinies of mortals. 'But fate, whether real or imaginary, has no power over those whose lives are "hid with Christ in God" [*Col* 3:3].' (F. F. Bruce)

nor any other creature, Paul doubtless adds this to include any other aspect of created reality he has omitted to mention.

He thus leaves no loophole for any contradiction of the sublime confidence that is expressed in his concluding words. *Nothing* 'shall be able to separate us from the love of God, which is in Christ Jesus our Lord!' Denney finely says, 'The love of Christ is God's love, manifested to us in him; and it is only in him that a divine love *is* manifested which can inspire the triumphant assurance of this verse.' So ends one of the most glorious chapters in the whole of Scripture. It should surely prompt our praise: *Hallelujah, for the Lord God Omnipotent reigneth!*

CHAPTER NINE

Paul now moves to the pressing problem of Israel's present unbelief, which he proceeds to show is 'neither total nor final'. (Hodge) The present rejection of the gospel by the majority of his kinsmen after the flesh is not to be interpreted as an abrogation of the divine promises, nor does it indicate any abdication of divine power. Whatever present appearances may say to the contrary, Paul will not permit any compromise on the question of God's sovereignty, for capitulation at this point marks the abandonment of belief in the living God. Chapters 9–11 are in no sense a parenthesis, but must be understood as the natural culmination of the apostle's doctrinal teaching in this epistle, for he is jealous to maintain and vindicate the purpose of God in history, and this remains a matter of paramount importance in the church today.

*V*1: **I say the truth in Christ, I lie not, my conscience bearing witness with me in the Holy Ghost,**
*V*2: **that I have great sorrow and unceasing pain in my heart.**

Although he was hated bitterly by his own people, Paul's conversion had only intensified his natural affection for them, and he regards their continuing unbelief with unceasing anguish. He confirms this revelation of his inward feelings with a most solemn oath. Paul is not only united by faith to Christ who is himself the truth, but he is also indwelt by the

Holy Spirit who endorses the testimony of his conscience. Therefore his readers may rest assured that his confession is without a vestige of dissimulation. His grief for Israel is not feigned, it is the constant burden of his heart.

*V*₃: **For I could wish that I myself were anathema from Christ for my brethren's sake, my kinsmen according to the flesh:**

So deep is his feeling for his brethren 'according to the flesh' that Paul could wish himself accursed for their sake. 'The expression is evidently hypothetical and conditional, "I could wish, were the thing allowable, possible, or proper".' (Hodge) [cf *Exod* 32:32] 'In this we may discern a characteristic of a Christian. He who has no sorrow for the perishing state of sinners, and especially of his kindred, is not a Christian. No man can be a Christian who is unconcerned for the salvation of others.' (Haldane)

*V*₄: **who are Israelites; whose is the adoption, and the glory, and the covenants, and the giving of the law, and the service of God, and the promises;**
*V*₅: **whose are the fathers, and of whom is Christ as concerning the flesh, who is over all, God blessed for ever. Amen.**

This impressive enumeration of the religious privileges of the Jews serves to emphasize the tragedy of their repudiation of Christ, the fulfiller of all the promises made to them. The title 'Israelites' marks their descent from Jacob whose name was changed to 'Israel' in 'honour of his prevailing faith which would not let God go until God had blessed him'. (Lenski) [*Gen* 32:28] 'The adoption' refers to their theocratic election by which they were separated from the heathen nations to become God's peculiar people [*Exod* 4:22, 19:5; *Hos* 11:1]. 'The glory' was the visible sign of God's presence with them; it was seen in the pillar of cloud that guided them through the wilderness, and in the cloud of glory that rested on the tabernacle and upon the mercy seat [*Exod* 29:43, 40:34; *Lev* 16:2]. 'The covenants' is plural because God's covenant was progressively revealed and confirmed to the patriarchs, and publicly ratified at Sinai. It was here that God signally favoured them by 'the giving of the law', thus leaving all other nations to walk in the vanity of their mind. And as their worship was also instituted by God, 'the service of God' was with them the worship of the true God in the true way. But what gave all these privileges their *saving content* were 'the promises' that related to the Messiah, and it was *through faith* in these promises that the saints of the old dispensation laid hold of eternal life [cf *Heb* 11].

In verse 5 the phrase 'whose are the fathers' no doubt refers to Abraham, Isaac, and Jacob, the fathers of faith of whom they might be proud [*Exod* 3:6; *Luke* 20:37]. But Israel's greatest glory consists in Christ's consenting to be their kinsman 'as concerning the *flesh*', even he 'who is over all, *God* blessed for ever. Amen.' It is not piety that has prompted the Unitarians and their fellow travellers to contend that this is a doxology to God (cf RV margin, RSV, NEB), but the anxiety to avoid Paul's plain ascription of the title 'God' to Christ. Oscar Cullmann has shown that it is not a true independent doxology (these always begin with 'Blessed', cf 2 *Cor* 1:3; *Eph* 1:3), but a doxological apposition; and that the reference to Christ's flesh requires a continuation which goes beyond flesh, after the fashion of the analogous formula in *Rom* 1:3, 4. (*The Christology of the New Testament*, p. 313) Moreover, the idea that this is a doxology to God is ruled out by the context. For as Lenski says, 'What makes the grief of Paul so poignant is the fact that God should have favoured Israel so highly. To say the least, if Paul were to insert a doxology to God at this point, it would be out of place, the incongruity would be evident.' It is, however, highly appropriate for Paul to show that the Christ the Jews rejected and crucified is the One 'who is over all, God blessed for ever' – a statement to which we are also glad to add our own emphatic *AMEN*!

V6: But it is not as though the word of God hath come to nought. For they are not all Israel, that are of Israel:

'The reason why the rejection of the Jews involved no failure on the part of the divine promise, is, that the promise was not addressed to the mere natural descendants of Abraham. "For they are not all Israel which are of Israel," i.e., all the natural descendants of the patriarch are not the true people of God, to whom alone the promises properly belong.' (Hodge) [*Is* 55:10, 11]

V7: neither, because they are Abraham's seed, are they all children: but, In Isaac shall thy seed be called.

This shows that natural descent from Abraham is no guarantee of spiritual kinship with Abraham. Ishmael was also Abraham's child, but he did not belong to the line of faith which God established in Isaac. The true seed of Abraham all embrace the promise of God, so that it is useless to claim Isaac's inheritance without sharing Isaac's faith in the promise. As Abraham was compelled by God to disown Ishmael, the child who was conceived in unbelief [*Gen* 16:2, 21:12], so none but those who share his justifying faith in the promise shall be acknowledged by God as his seed [4:16–25; *Gal* 4:28]. As the Puritan John Flavel put it, 'If Abraham's faith be not in your hearts, it will be no advantage that Abraham's blood runs in your veins.'

V8: That is, it is not the children of the flesh that are children of God; but the children of the promise are reckoned for a seed.

It is because 'that which is born of the flesh is flesh' that a fleshly pedigree, far from ensuring salvation, actually excludes it [*John* 3:1–10]. God has never recognized the children of the flesh as his own, but ever and only the children of the promise, who are brought forth from the tomb of their unbelief by the regenerating power of the promise [1 *Pet* 1:23; *James* 1:18]. Thus the true children of Abraham are those 'who are born

after the manner of Isaac, by the word and promise of God.'
(Poole)

*V*9: **For this is a word of promise, According to this season will I come, and Sarah shall have a son.**

As the accent here falls upon the *creative power* of God's promise [cf 4:17], so what follows serves to define its *elective purpose* [vv 10–13]. God gave the promise of a son to Abraham and Sarah when they were beyond all hope of an heir. That promise did not fall short of its appointed fulfilment, because it was accompanied by the power to make it good. 'Is any thing too hard for the Lord?' was the rebuke Sarah received from the Lord for the laughter of unbelief with which she first greeted this announcement of the divine purpose [*Gen* 18:10, 14]. Hence Isaac was literally the child of promise, for it was evident that he owed his existence to nothing but the power of God's word.

*V*10: **And not only so; but Rebecca also having conceived by one, even by our father Isaac –**

As it might be argued that there was good reason for God to choose Isaac in preference to the resentful son of a slave, this is added to prove the unconditional nature of God's sovereign choice. For there was no such disparity between Esau and Jacob, 'either in birth or in works: they had both one and the same mother; Rebecca conceived with them at one and the same time, and that by no other person than our father Isaac; and yet the one of these is chosen, and the other refused. This now was an undeniable proof, that the promise belongs not to all the children of Abraham, or of Isaac, according to the flesh; all the seed of neither are the children of the promise.' (Poole)

*V*11: **for the children being not yet born, neither having done anything good or bad, that the purpose of God**

according to election might stand, not of works, but of him that calleth,

God made known his will concerning the children before their birth in order to show that his choice was not based on works, for his preference was expressed long before there could be any manifestation of their character. 'As for original sin, they were both alike tainted therewith.' (Poole) [*Eph* 2:3]

not of works, but of him that calleth, 'This doctrine is alone consistent with Christian experience. "Why was I made to hear thy voice?" No Christian answers this question by saying, Because I was better than others.' (Hodge) [cf comment on 8:28; 1 *Tim* 1:9]

*V*12: **it was said unto her, The elder shall serve the younger.**

Those who believe that the election spoken of in this passage is national and not personal are quick to point out that Jacob was never personally served by Esau. However, it cannot be gainsaid that in a spiritual sense Esau did in fact 'serve the younger', for he forfeited his birthright, and therefore 'in reference to the highest interests, Esau was placed below Jacob, as much as Ishmael was below Isaac. This is the real spirit of the passage.' (Hodge) [*Gen* 25:23]

*V*13: **Even as it is written, Jacob I loved, but Esau I hated.**

It cannot be denied that in this quotation from Malachi 1:2-3 the prophet has in view the nations of Israel and Edom, but it must not be assumed that their respective destinies can be considered in isolation from that difference which God first made between their respective heads. As the election of Jacob is the proof of God's love, so the rejection of Esau is the evidence of God's hatred. The two aorists look back to the acts which caused these twins to differ. Both were hateful on account of Adam's sin, so that it is in fact easier to explain

God's hatred of Esau than his love for Jacob. For as Warfield well says, 'When all deserve death it is a marvel of pure grace that any receive life; and who shall gainsay the right of him who shows this miraculous mercy, to have mercy on whom he will, and whom he will to harden?' Certainly Jacob deserved this mercy no more than Esau. But God sovereignly chose Jacob in Christ, whereas he just as sovereignly passed by Esau. Hence God hated Esau for no other reason but his sin – for God hates nothing but sin – and this holy hatred of sin may not be defined in terms of a loving less, as some commentators try to do. 'Nothing, then, is said of Esau here that might not be said of every man who shall finally perish.' (Haldane)

V14: **What shall we say then? Is there unrighteousness with God? God forbid.**

As usual Paul proposes an objection to his teaching in order emphatically to repudiate it. It is the very height of madness for men to charge God with injustice because he elects some and rejects others [*Gen* 18:25; *Job* 33:13].

V15: **For he saith to Moses, I will have mercy on whom I have mercy, and I will have compassion on whom I have compassion.**

Paul justifies his strong denial by an appeal to Scripture [*Exod* 33:19]. As all deserve nothing but wrath, none can claim mercy as a right. Hence God is not unjust when he leaves some to reap the due reward of their deeds. For though he is bound to punish sin, he is under no obligation whatever to exercise mercy. Since, then mercy is not a debt which God owes to man, he is free to dispense it on *whomsoever* he pleases. Such distinguishing mercy is *pure* mercy, because it is not called forth by any mitigating factors in those to whom it is extended. Men therefore have no just ground for complaint if God gives some more than they earned [cf 6:23], 'Is it not lawful for me to do what I will with mine own?' [*Matt* 20:15]

[163]

V16: So then it is not of him that willeth, nor of him that runneth, but of God that hath mercy.

From this it follows that 'God's election is not of Jacob's, or of any other man's, willing or running; i.e. it is not from his good desires or deeds, his good inclinations or actions, or from the foresight thereof; but it is of God's mere mercy and good pleasure. This text wounds Pelagianism under the fifth rib.' (Poole)

V17: For the scripture saith unto Pharaoh, For this very purpose did I raise thee up, that I might show in thee my power, and that my name might be published abroad in all the earth.

The choice of some unto eternal life inevitably implies the rejection of others, and this is confirmed by the example of Pharaoh [*Exod* 9:16]. The verse states that God brought this implacable adversary on to the stage of history for the express purpose of providing the world with an unforgettable demonstration of the fate that awaits all those who set themselves up to oppose the fulfilment of his promise of grace and mercy.

'It was not the not yet existent Scripture that made this announcement to Pharaoh, but God himself through the mouth of his prophet Moses. These acts could be attributed to "Scripture" only as the result of such a habitual identification, in the mind of the writer, of the text of Scripture with God as speaking, that it became natural to use the term "Scripture says", when what was really intended was "God, as recorded in Scripture, said".' (B. B. Warfield, *The Inspiration and Authority of the Bible*, pp. 299–300)

V18: So then he hath mercy on whom he will, and whom he will he hardeneth.

The apostle now affirms the general principle which is to be drawn from this particular example. Since God is sovereign in the exercise of his mercy, the case of Pharaoh illustrates his determination to pass by others, whom he leaves to perish in their sins for the manifestation of his justice (cf Canons of Dort, 1:15). This doctrine of reprobation is the counterpart of the doctrine of election, for the election of some inevitably implies the reprobation of others [cf *Matt* 11:25, 26; 1 *Pet* 2:8; *Jude* 4]. 'In fact, every passage of Scripture which teaches that any will be finally lost, teaches at the same time, by necessary implication, if the doctrine of election be true, that they were eternally reprobated or left out of the number of the elect. The two doctrines stand or fall together.' (J. H. Thornwell, *The Collected Writings*, Vol. 2, p. 144)

and whom he will he hardeneth. Paul 'as explicitly affirms the sovereignty of reprobation as of election, – if these twin ideas are, indeed, separable even in thought: if he represents God as sovereignly loving Jacob, he represents Him equally as sovereignly hating Esau; if he declares that He has mercy on whom He will, he equally declares that He hardens whom He will.' (B. B. Warfield, *Predestination*)

V19: **Thou wilt say then unto me, Why doth he still find fault? For who withstandeth his will?**

Paul anticipates a plausible objection of the carnal mind. If God hardens whom he will, why does he still find fault? If God is sovereign, then man can no longer be held responsible for the result.

For who withstandeth his will? i.e. His decretive will, and the answer implied in the question is, None. However, with regard to the preceptive will of God, man can and does withstand it, and for this he is justly held responsible by God. 'It was the preceptive will of God that the Jews should not crucify the Lord Jesus Christ. They acted in this manner contrary to God's command, and were therefore guilty; still, it was the decretive will that the Saviour should be crucified, for the Jews and Roman soldiers did only what "his hand and his counsel determined before to be done." The preceptive will of God is the rule of duty to us; the decretive will, the plan of operations, to himself. The distinction is plainly just, natural and scriptural. The preceptive will of God is sometimes called his *revealed* will, and his decretive called his *secret* will . . . The preceptive will is the sole rule of duty to man, as its name shows; and fearful guilt is always incurred when the commands of God are disregarded or despised. It is not my business to inquire whether God has a secret decree – that I shall or shall not, in point of fact, comply with his injunctions; it is enough that I am bound to do so, and am justly held punishable if I do not obey. Whatever rule of operations he may prescribe to himself, the one which he has given to me is plain and intelligible, and his unrevealed purposes will afford me no shelter if I neglect or disregard it.' (Thornwell, *op. cit.*, pp. 163–165) [*Deut* 29:29]

In a most helpful discussion of the very difficult question, 'God and evil,' Gordon Clark has this to say on the subject of human responsibility: 'Although the betrayal of Christ was foreordained from eternity as a means of effecting the atonement, it was Judas, not God, who betrayed Christ. The secondary causes in history are not eliminated by divine causality, but rather they are made certain. And the acts of these secondary causes, whether they be righteous acts or sinful acts, are to be immediately referred to the agents; and it is these agents who are responsible.' (*Religion, Reason and Revelation*, p. 239)

*V*20: Nay but, O man, who art thou that repliest against God? Shall the thing formed say to him that formed it, Why didst thou make me thus?

Here all who are tempted to echo this sinful suggestion are vigorously taken to task by the apostle. His first question rebukes the reckless impiety of the man who replies against God, while the second logically refutes the creature's self-assumed right to complain against his Creator. For it is indisputable that 'God has the Creator's right to do what he will with those whom he has himself moulded and fashioned.' (Sanday and Headlam) [*Is* 45:9]

V21: Or hath not the potter a right over the clay, from the same lump to make one part a vessel unto honour, and another unto dishonour?

Paul employs the familiar Old Testament figure of the potter and the clay to illustrate the authority of God over his creatures [cf *Is* 29:15, 16, 64:8, 9; *Jer* 18:1-6]. He argues from the less to the greater, for if a potter has power over his clay, to form it as he pleases, then God has much more power over his creatures, to form or order them as he chooses. God's authority over his creature is greater than that of a potter over his clay. The potter made not his clay; but both clay and potter are made by God (Poole).

from the same lump Both types of vessel are fashioned from the same lump, which represents human nature ruined by the fall. As Warfield says, 'The body out of which believers are chosen by God's unsearchable grace is the mass of justly condemned sinners, so the destruction to which those that are passed by are left is the righteous recompense of their guilt. Thus the discrimination between men in the matter of eternal destiny is distinctly set forth as taking place in the interests of mercy and for the sake of salvation: from the fate which justly hangs over all, God is represented as in his infinite compassion rescuing those chosen to this end in his inscrutable counsels of mercy to the praise of the glory of his grace; while those that are left in their sins perish most deservedly, as the justice of God demands.' (*Predestination*)

V22: What if God, willing to show his wrath, and to make his power known, endured with much longsuffering vessels of wrath fitted unto destruction:

As the future manifestation of God's wrath will perfectly

reveal his righteous character, it is therefore the most flagrant folly to mistake his present longsuffering for an unholy indifference to sin [cf v 17; Eccles 8:11]. Although it is perfectly true that the non-elect fit themselves for destruction by their own wickedness, it must not be too hastily assumed that this is the apostle's meaning in this place. The verse 'does not say the vessels of wrath *fitted themselves*, nor does it say they are *fit for* destruction; instead, it declares they are "fitted *to* destruction", and the context shows plainly it is *God* who thus "fits" them – objectively by his eternal decrees.' (Arthur Pink, *The Sovereignty of God*, p. 120) [cf vv 20, 21][1]

*V*23: **and that he might make known the riches of his glory upon vessels of mercy, which he afore prepared unto glory,**

'The elect differ from the reprobate only in the fact of their deliverance from the same gulf of destruction. This, moreover, is by no merit of their own, but by the free goodness of God. It must, therefore, be true that the infinite mercy of God towards the elect will gain our increasing praise, when we see how wretched are all those who do not escape his wrath.' (Calvin)

*V*24: **even us, whom he also called, not from the Jews only, but also from the Gentiles?**

If the rejection of ethnic Israel is demonstrated by their unbelief, then the calling of the Gentiles indicates their inclusion within the scope of the divine promise. Since those who are the subjects of God's promise are also called by God, this gift of faith provides a proof of election. 'None of the Jews or Gentiles were vessels of mercy, except those whom he had effectually called to himself. This verse incontestably proves,

---

1. As Gerhard Delling insists, '*fitted* unto destruction' here means '*foreordained* for destruction', and not merely '*ready* or *ripe* for destruction' as B. Weiss and H. A. W. Meyer suggest without philological justification (*TDNT*, Vol. I, p. 476).

contrary to the erroneous glosses of many, that the apostle is here speaking of the election of individuals, and not of nations.' (Haldane)

*V*25: **As he saith also in Hosea,**
I will call that my people, which was not my people;
And her beloved, that was not beloved.

The conversion of the Gentiles from heathendom exhibits on a far grander scale the same principle which was set forth in Hosea's message of mercy to apostate Israel [*Hos* 2:23 which is applied to the church in 1 *Pet* 2:10].

*V*26: **And it shall be, that in the place where it was said unto them, Ye are not my people,**
There shall they be called sons of the living God.

God's promise to restore a rejected people is here applied by Paul to the calling of the Gentiles. In this case, the phrase 'in the place where' is best taken as referring to 'every place, where the people had been regarded as aliens, they should be called the children of God'. (Hodge) For the believing Gentiles are now recognized by God in the very place where previously they had been regarded as 'aliens from the commonwealth of Israel' [*Eph* 2:12]. Consequently under the new covenant no place is more sacred than any other, for a change of heart makes a change of locality as unnecessary as it renders pilgrimages irrelevant [*John* 4:20–24].

*V*27: **And Isaiah crieth concerning Israel, If the number of the children of Israel be as the sand of the sea, it is the remnant that shall be saved:**
*V*28: **for the Lord will execute his word upon the earth, finishing it and cutting it short.**

As the apostle quoted Hosea [*vv* 25, 26] to prove the election of a part of the Gentiles, so he now cites Isaiah to prove the reprobation of a part of the Jews [*Is* 10:22, 23]. Calvin comments, 'His description of Isaiah as *exclaiming*, and not speaking, is deliberately intended to arouse greater attention. The words of the prophet are plainly designed to prevent the Jews from boasting excessively in the flesh. It is a terrible thing to learn that only a small number out of an incalculable multitude shall obtain salvation.'

cutting it short. 'If only a remnant of the Jewish Church, God's own people, were saved, how careful and solicitous should all professors of religion be, that their faith and hope be well founded.' (Hodge)

*V*29: **And, as Isaiah hath said before,**
Except the Lord of Sabaoth had left us a seed,
We had become as Sodom, and had been made
like unto Gomorrah.

This citation of *Is* 1:9 is in agreement with the prophet's previous statement [*vv* 27, 28]. For unless the Lord of Hosts had left us a seed, Israel would have been long since visited with the same annihilating judgment that fell upon Sodom and Gomorrah. 'That only a remnant is saved points up the severity and extent of the judgment executed. That a remnant is saved is the evidence of the Lord's favour and the guarantee that his covenant promise has not failed.' (John Murray)

*V*30: **What shall we say then? That the Gentiles, who**
followed not after righteousness, attained to righteousness even the righteousness which is of faith:
*V*31: **but Israel, following after a law of righteousness,**
did not arrive at that law.

What then are we to conclude from this discussion? We are faced with the paradoxical result that Gentiles who did not pursue righteousness, attained it; while Israel, pursuing a law of righteousness, did not attain to that law. This was because unrighteous Gentiles were glad to embrace 'the righteousness of faith' [3:22ff], whereas Israel's pride in their possession of a law, which prescribed but could not bestow righteousness, was at the root of their vain attempts to catch up with its impossible demands. It is not the function of the law to justify, but to bring sinners under the conviction of their utter failure to reach its standard of perfection [3:20].

'Error is often a greater obstacle to the salvation of men than carelessness or vice. Christ said that publicans and harlots would enter the kingdom of God before the Pharisees. In like manner the thoughtless and sensual Gentiles were more susceptible of impression from the gospel, and were more frequently converted to Christ, than the Jews, who were wedded to erroneous views of the plan of salvation . . . Let no man think error in doctrine a slight practical evil. No road to perdition has ever been more thronged than that of false doctrine. Error is a shield over the conscience, and a bandage over the eyes.' (Hodge)

V32: **Wherefore? Because they sought it not by faith, but as it were by works. They stumbled at the stone of stumbling;**

Such an unexpected result obviously calls for an explanation. As Denney says, 'Everything in religion depends on the nature of the start. You may start *from faith*, from an utter abandonment to God, and an entire dependence on him, and in this case a righteousness is possible which you will recognize as *God's righteousness*, God's own gift and work in you; or you may start *from works*, which really means in independence of God, and try to work out, without coming under obligation to God, a righteousness of your own, for which you may subsequently claim his approval, and in this case, like the Jews, all your efforts will be baffled. Your starting-point is unreal, impossible.'

Thus it was because the Jews were infatuated by this imaginary self-righteousness that they refused the real faith-righteousness which was offered to them in the gospel. A gratuitous salvation is always an offence to those who desire to earn it by their own efforts; hence the Christ, whom believers regard as the chief corner stone, became to them the stone of stumbling [1 *Pet* 2:6–8]. The offence of the cross, 'at which they stumbled, is not simply the fact that it *is* a cross, whereas they expected a Messianic throne; the cross offended them because, as interpreted by Paul, it summoned them to begin their religious life, from the very beginning, at the foot of the Crucified, and with the sense upon their hearts of an infinite debt to him, which no "works" could ever repay.' (Denney)

*V*33: **even as it is written,**
   Behold, I lay in Zion a stone of stumbling and a
   rock of offence:
   And he that believeth on him shall not be put to
   shame.

In this verse Paul combines two passages from *Isaiah* 8:14 and 28:16. Poole remarks, 'Jesus Christ is properly a corner-stone, elect and precious; but accidentally and eventually a stumbling-stone, *Luke* 2:34.' Consequently an encounter with the One who is the great Divider of mankind cannot be avoided. Those who do not find him to be their rock of refuge will be ruined by stumbling on the stumbling-stone [*John* 16:9]. As it is the summation of all wickedness to find in Christ nothing but a rock of offence, so believers are assured that all who put their trust in him shall never be ashamed or confounded.

CHAPTER TEN

V1: **Brethren, my heart's desire and my supplication to God is for them, that they may be saved.**

Brethren, This affectionate address to those who are Paul's brethren in the Lord is intended to focus their attention upon his earnest desire for the salvation of those who are only his kinsmen according to the flesh. He is not discussing Israel's unbelief with any sense of academic detachment, for he longs that they might be brought to faith in Christ. And no doubt remembering his former blindness, he prays that the Lord might remove the veil of unbelief from their heart [2 *Cor* 3:14-16]. The comments of John Murray on this verse deserve the closest consideration for they are of the utmost importance in preserving the balance of truth: 'In the preceding chapter the emphasis is upon the sovereign and determinative will of God in the differentiation that exists among men. God has mercy on whom he wills, and whom he wills he hardens. Some are vessels for wrath, others for mercy. And ultimate destiny is envisioned in destruction and glory. But this differentiation is God's action and prerogative, not man's. And, because so, our attitude to men is not to be governed by God's secret counsel concerning them. It is this lesson and the distinction involved that are so eloquently inscribed on the apostle's passion for the salvation of his kinsmen. We violate the order of human thought and trespass the boundary between God's prerogative and man's when the truth of God's

[173]

sovereign counsel constrains despair or abandonment of concern for the eternal interests of men.'

V2: For I bear them witness that they have a zeal for God, but not according to knowledge.

Zeal is always misdirected when it is misinformed. In his speech before Agrippa, Paul confessed, 'I verily thought with myself, that I ought to do many things contrary to the name of Jesus of Nazareth' [*Acts* 26:9–11]. In thus condemning his former course the apostle has for ever laid bare the categorical imperative which governs every unregenerate heart. This is only to be expected, for all who are not ruled by Christ do that which is right in their own eyes, but zeal can never make it right to do those things which are contrary to that Name which is above every name. And where there is no submission to the will of Christ, there can be no knowledge of the mind of Christ [*Acts* 9:6, 7]. Hence nothing is known as it should be known, for every truth coheres in him who is the truth ('What is truth? said jesting Pilate; and would not stay for an answer' – Bacon). Today the measure of man's guilt before God is demonstrated by his determination to discover self-existent 'truths'. The quest for knowledge apart from Christ is the supreme evidence of arrogant unbelief, for it directly opposes God's plan to sum up all things in Christ. There are no neutral 'facts' in a Theistic universe!

V3: For being ignorant of God's righteousness, and seeking to establish their own, they did not subject themselves to the righteousness of God.

If the Jews had not known of God's righteousness, their ignorance would have been excusable. But this was a willing ignorance which refused the instruction of God's word in favour of *their own* inventions. They preferred, as Poole observes, 'a home-made righteousness' of their own spinning, for 'they will not go abroad for that which they think they have, or may have, at home. They will not be beholden to another for that which they suppose they have in themselves. They have righteousness enough of their own working; and therefore they reject and withdraw themselves from that which is of God's appointing.'

This is not simply a Jewish mistake; it is the cardinal delusion in the religion of the natural man. He always seeks to justify himself, and may succeed before men, but he remains a stranger to God's justification [*Luke* 16:15, 18:9-14]. 'All legal endeavour is hostility to evangelical requirement. He who would work out a personal righteousness rejects Christ's righteousness. The "worker" excludest the "believer" [4:4, 5].' (Shedd)

V4: For Christ is the end of the law unto righteousness to every one that believeth.

Since God gave his law to a people redeemed by grace, they did not imagine that his favour could be earned by their obedience, even though the continued enjoyment of blessing was suspended upon it. It should be remembered that Paul's polemic was directed against that false interpretation of the law which had erased the whole concept of grace from the Old Testament. According to the Judaizers salvation was gained by a meritorious obedience to the law. Such was Paul's former course, and his kinsmen are still blinded by the same error [*Phil* 3:9]. Unbelievers expect to attain righteousness by the works of the law, but this relationship to the law has been terminated by Christ for all believers, who therefore no longer regard it as the instrument of their justification. 'There is *no* believer, *Gentile or Jew*, for whom law, *Mosaic or other*, retains validity or significance as a way to *righteousness*, after the revelation of the righteousness of God in Christ.' (Denney)

V5: For Moses writeth that the man that doeth the righteousness which is of the law shall live thereby.

The principle enunciated in *Lev* 18:5 became a sentence of

condemnation when it was artificially isolated from the context of grace in which it was originally set. Hence the relevance of its testimony against those who sought after righteousness by the deeds of the law. Paul quotes it again in *Gal* 3:12.

*V*6: **But the righteousness which is of faith saith thus, Say not in thy heart, Who shall ascend into heaven? (that is, to bring Christ down:)**

Paul finds an admirable description of the 'righteousness of faith' in *Deut* 30:11–14. In his farewell discourse Moses warns the people against giving way to a spirit of unbelief, for God has drawn near to them in the covenant of grace, and everything which pertains to their temporal and eternal good has been clearly revealed to them. If the light afforded by the old dispensation then made unbelief inexcusable, what shall be said of those who remain in darkness now that the Light of the world has been fully manifested? Thus the appropriateness of the apostle's application is evident. Paul interprets the first question as a denial of the reality of the Incarnation. It is quite beyond man's power to scale the heights of heaven either by legalistic endeavour or by speculative philosophy, and there is now no necessity to make the attempt, for 'the Word became flesh and tabernacled among us' [*John* 1:14 ASV margin]. The sheer perversity of unbelief is shown by the many who prefer to undertake an impossible Odyssey rather than put their trust in an accessible Christ.

*V*7: **or, Who shall descend into the abyss? (that is, to bring Christ up from the dead.)**

It is equally futile to attempt a descent into the abyss or grave to discover the truth. The reality of life after death is not to be proved by the unlawful attempts of the Spiritists to communicate with the souls of the departed [*Deut* 18:9–12; *Is* 8:19, 20]. One came back from the realm of the dead in all the splendour of his resurrection life as the first-fruits of them that slept [1 *Cor* 15:20]. Death holds no terrors for the Christian, for the keys of death have been committed to him who broke its dominion over mankind through his glorious victory over all the powers of darkness [1 *Cor* 15:55-57; *Eph* 4:9; *Rev* 1:18].

*V*8: **But what saith it? The word is nigh thee, in thy mouth, and in thy heart: that is, the word of faith, which we preach:**

In this quotation of *Deut* 30:14 Paul identifies the word spoken of by Moses with the 'word of faith, which we preach'. As the word was the means by which grace was ministered to the hearts of God's people in the period of promise, so the preached word of the gospel now conveys the justifying righteousness of Christ to all who receive it by faith and thus take it into their mouths and hearts. But as then many of the Jews only received the law outwardly, not taking the gospel promise it contained into their hearts; so now the majority had rejected the gift of righteousness that was openly offered to them in the preaching of the gospel.

*V*9: **because if thou shalt confess with thy mouth Jesus as Lord, and shalt believe in thy heart that God raised him from the dead, thou shalt be saved:**

In this description of the essence of saving faith Paul places confession before belief to correspond with the order followed in *Deut* 30:14 [*v* 8], and then inverts them in the next verse to show the order of experience.

because if thou shalt confess with thy mouth Jesus as Lord, This word of the gospel saves 'because' it has Christ himself for its content. The complications of later theological development are often adversely compared with the apparent simplicity of the earliest Christian confession of faith, 'Jesus is Lord'. However, the significance of this credal formula is not to be judged by the conciseness of its expression, for the supernatural character of its content demands nothing less than a supernatural faith to embrace it [1 *Cor* 12:3]. In this identification of the historical Jesus with his subsequent exaltation to supreme lordship and universal dominion, all the facts of the gospel are presupposed [cf *Phil* 2:5–11].

This was the consistent emphasis of the apostolic proclamation, and no preaching which fails to do justice to Christ's present sovereignty is faithful to the authoritative pattern laid down in the New Testament. Open confession of his name before men is an indispensable condition for all authentic discipleship. 'Those who are ashamed or afraid to acknowledge Christ before men, cannot expect to be saved. The want of courage to confess, is decisive evidence of the want of heart to believe.' (Hodge) [*Matt* 10:32; *Luke* 12:8; 1 *John* 4:15].

and shalt believe in thy heart that God raised him from the dead, thou shalt be saved: The part is put for the whole, for to believe that 'God has raised Christ from the dead, involves the belief that Christ is all that he claimed to be, and that he has accomplished all that he came to perform.' (Hodge) [1:4, 4:24, 25] The term 'heart' stands for the whole man in the unity of his selfhood. Man is more than an artificial agglomeration of thought, feeling, and will. The modern notion which equates the 'heart' with the emotions is not sanctioned by the use of this word in Scripture.

Haldane draws attention to Paul's sustained use of the second person. 'If *thou* shalt confess with *thy* mouth, and shalt believe in *thine* heart, *thou* shalt be saved. He speaks of every one, so that all may examine themselves, for to every one believing and confessing, salvation is promised; thus teaching each one to apply the promise of salvation to himself by faith and confession.'

V10: for with the heart man believeth unto righteousness; and with the mouth confession is made unto salvation.

Paul again underlines the fact that there is no salvation without confession and faith, but here they are exhibited in their true order: 'faith being the root, confession the branch, Matt 12:34; 2 Cor 4:13.' (Shedd) The Jews knew very well that it was necessary to attain righteousness in order to be saved, but in seeking to attain it by the works of the law they simply sentenced themselves to failure and rejection. For nothing but heart-faith can receive the righteousness which ensures salvation, and such faith is glad to confess its indebtedness to Christ for this priceless boon.

V11: For the scripture saith, Whosoever believeth on him shall not be put to shame.

Paul again invokes the testimony of Is 28:16 to confirm his doctrine [9:33], but here substitutes 'whosoever' for 'he that believeth' as he wishes to stress the universality of the gospel offer of salvation. This good news must be preached to all men, because the promise is that 'whosoever' puts his trust in Christ shall never be put to shame. Hence a man's natural birth neither qualifies nor hinders him from receiving the righteousness which is of faith.

V12: For there is no distinction between Jew and Greek: for the same Lord is Lord of all, and is rich unto all that call upon him:
V13: for, Whosoever shall call upon the name of the Lord shall be saved.

Paul has already stated that there is no distinction in regard to guilt [3:22]; now he affirms that there is no distinction in regard to grace! The Jews believed otherwise and maintained that there was a distinction which was entirely in their favour, one that required that a Gentile become a Jew before he could be saved [cf Acts 15:1–31]. But instead of compelling a Greek to become like a legalistic Jew, the Jew must drop his legalism and become like a believing Greek (Lenski). There are not two gospels, one for Jews and another for Gentiles, because both are under the same condemnation and so both have the same need. There is therefore but *one* gospel which promises that the same Lord, who is Lord of *all*, is abounding in wealth toward *all* who call upon him. The immediate context makes it clear that 'Lord' is to be referred to the exalted Christ, and this is confirmed by the use of this expression elsewhere in the New Testament [cf *vv* 9, 12, 13: See *Acts* 7:59, 60, 9:14, 21, 10:36, 22:16; 1 *Cor* 1:2; *Phil* 2:11; 2 *Tim* 2:22].

The words of verse 13 are taken from *Joel* 2:32, which is also quoted by Peter in his sermon on the day of Pentecost [*Acts* 2:21]. David Brown remarks, 'This is but one of many Old Testament passages of which *Jehovah* is the subject, and which in the New Testament are applied to *Christ* – an irrefragable proof of his proper divinity.' And as there is salvation in no other Name [*Acts* 4:12], all who refuse to call upon that Name thereby exclude themselves from his kingdom of grace and glory.

*V*14: **How then shall they call on him in whom they have not believed? and how shall they believe in him whom they have not heard? and how shall they hear without a preacher?**

*V*15: **and how shall they preach, except they be sent? even as it is written, How beautiful are the feet of them that bring glad tidings of good things!**

Paul has proved that salvation depends on calling on Christ, but Israel refuses to recognize him as Lord. How is this mystery to be explained? Paul runs through the chain that leads to faith and confession: 1. There can be no calling on him in whom one does not believe; 2. there can be no believing in him of whom one has not heard; 3. there can be no hearing without a preacher; 4. there will be no preachers unless God sends them (Nygren). What, then, is the reason for Israel's failure to confess Christ as Lord? Beginning with the last point, he works backwards and shows from Scripture that Israel cannot plead ignorance as an excuse for their unbelief.

For God has certainly sent forth the heralds of salvation to preach the good news to Israel [Is 52:7]. The prophet pictures the joy with which the exiles receive the news of their release from the Babylonian captivity, but the approach of the messengers who run with the news of a far richer deliverance is not welcomed by Israel. Unhappily, their dust-covered feet are not 'beautiful' to them!

*V*16: **But they did not all hearken to the glad tidings. For Isaiah saith, Lord, who hath believed our report?**

This poignant understatement heightens the tragedy of Israel's refusal to give heed to the glad tidings they undoubtedly heard 'Not all' but nearly all repudiated the gospel, and so failed to receive the righteousness which was offered to them in the Word [*v* 3]. It is very significant that the prophet's lament, which is echoed by Paul, appears at the head of the clearest prediction of Christ's sufferings in the whole of Scripture [Is 53:1]. 'The very heart of the gospel Israel would not believe, neither then nor thereafter, not even after the Messiah had already come.' (Lenski)

*V*17: **So belief cometh of hearing, and hearing by the word of Christ.**

The result of this reasoning is now presented in summary form: 'So faith comes from what is heard, and what is heard comes by the preaching of Christ.' (RSV) If Israel had not heard this preaching of Christ there would have been an excuse for their unbelief. Hence Paul immediately goes on to show that such is not the case.

*V*18: **But I say, Did they not hear? Yea, verily,**
      Their sound went out into all the earth,
      And their words unto the ends of the world.

The plea of ignorance is decisively dismissed in the words of Ps 19:4. For the message has been so widely diffused among the Diaspora (the Jews dispersed among the Gentiles) that

Paul can appropriately describe its universal proclamation in terms of the general witness of creation to its Creator. 'There is not a synagogue which has not been filled with it; not a Jew in the world who can justly plead ignorance on the subject.' (Godet)

*V*19: **But I say, Did Israel not know? First Moses saith,**
     I will provoke you to jealousy with that which
     is no nation,
          With a nation void of understanding will I
     anger you.

Thus Israel has heard the message through which faith comes, and yet has not trusted in him of whom it speaks [*v* 14]. To bring out the reason for this, Paul adds another question: Can it be that Israel did not *understand* the gospel? He has a two-fold answer ready to hand from both the law and the prophets. First, there is Moses' testimony against Israel's forthcoming apostasy for which they would be rejected by God in favour of a 'no nation' [*Deut* 32:21]. As a people who are insensible of God's mercies will provoke him to jealous anger by their idolatry, so he in turn will arouse the same feelings in them by blessing a senseless people with his salvation. Paul sees this prophecy has been fulfilled in the calling of the 'foolish' Gentiles who had both heard and understood the gospel, to the jealous fury of the Jews who above all people *ought* to have understood it [cf *Acts* 17:5, 13].

*V*20: **And Isaiah is very bold, and saith,**
     I was found of them that sought me not;
     I became manifest unto them that asked not of me.

Finally, in applying the testimony of Isaiah to the calling of the Gentiles Paul draws attention to the boldness of the prophet, for the Jews vainly imagined that they alone enjoyed the monopoly of God's grace and favour [*Is* 65:1].

*V*21: **But as to Israel he saith,**
All the day long did I spread out my hands unto a
disobedient and gainsaying people.

In *Isaiah* 65:2 the prophet eloquently contrasts God's patient entreaties and continued loving-kindness with Israel's stubborn refusal to yield to the overtures of his mercy. 'The arms outstretched all the day long are the symbol of that incessant pleading love which Israel through all its history has consistently despised. It is not want of knowledge, then, nor want of intelligence, but wilful and stubborn disobedience, that explains the exclusion of Israel (meanwhile) from the Kingdom of Christ and all its blessings.' (Denney)

CHAPTER ELEVEN

*V*1: **I say then, Did God cast off his people? God forbid. For I also am an Israelite, of the seed of Abraham, of the tribe of Benjamin.**

It is in view of Israel's continuing unbelief that Paul now asks, 'Did God cast off his people?' Although the form of the question demands a negative reply, he emphatically rejects the suggestion with his usual expression of abhorrence. Because even now there is a believing remnant to which Paul is proud to belong, for though he was specially called to minister to the Gentiles, he does not permit his readers to forget that he is himself an 'Israelite'. 'Paul was a Jew by descent from Abraham, and not merely a proselyte; and he was of one of the most favoured tribes. Judah and Benjamin, especially after the exile, were the chief representatives of the theocratical people.' (Hodge)

*V*2a: **God did not cast off his people which he foreknew.**

It is evident that 'his people which he foreknew' refers to *the nation* of Israel and not to the elect from among the Jews, because it would be inconceivable that God should cast off *his elect*. (Alford) On the subject of God's foreknowledge Warfield says: 'According to the Old Testament conception, God foreknows only because he has pre-determined, and it is therefore also that he brings it to pass; his foreknowledge, in other words, is at bottom a knowledge of his own will, and his works of providence are merely the execution of his all-embracing plan.' (*Predestination*)

V2b: **Or know ye not what the scripture saith of Elijah? how he pleadeth with God against Israel,**
V3: **Lord, they have killed thy prophets, they have digged down thine altars: and I am left alone, and they seek my life.**
V4: **But what saith the answer of God unto him? I have left for myself seven thousand men, who have not bowed the knee to Baal.**

The quotation is apposite to Paul's purpose, for Elijah's angry prayer against Israel in a time of general apostasy received a surprising rejoinder [1 *Kings* 19:10, 14, 18]. 'Notwithstanding the apostasy of Israel as a whole, yet there was a remnant, though only a remnant, whom God had kept for himself and preserved from the idolatry of Baal's worship. This example is adduced to prove that God had not cast off Israel as his chosen and beloved people. The import, therefore, is that the salvation of a small remnant from the total mass is sufficient proof that the people as a nation had not been cast off.' (John Murray)

V5: **Even so then at this present time also there is a remnant according to the election of grace.**

It should be remembered that the first converts to Christianity were Jews, and though the great mass of Israel rejected the gospel, the existence of an elect remnant proved that God's plan had not miscarried. Times of religious declension make it evident that the believing remnant 'is a remnant according to the election of grace' [cf 1 *Cor* 4:7].

V6: **But if it is by grace, it is no more of works: otherwise grace is no more grace.**

David Brown remarks, 'The general position here laid down is fundamental, and of unspeakable importance. It may be thus expressed: There are but two possible sources of salvation – men's works and God's grace; and these are so essentially distinct and opposite, that salvation cannot be of any combination or mixture of both; it must be wholly either of the one or of the other.' [*Eph* 2:8, 9]

***V7*: What then? That which Israel seeketh for, that he obtained not; but the election obtained it, and the rest were hardened:**

At present then, Israel as a nation has not obtained the righteousness it sought, 'because they sought it not by faith, but as it were by works' [9:32]. That they entertained such a false hope was the result of a self-hardening which was judicially confirmed by God [*v* 8]. However, some Jews have attained to the righteousness of faith, because these had been elected unto eternal life [*v* 5]. Paul uses the abstract noun 'the election' to place the emphasis upon the sovereignty of God's choice. 'When men are saved they are saved by the sovereign grace of God, and when they perish, it is by the appointment of God, *Jude* 4, through their own fault.' (Haldane)

***V8*: according as it is written, God gave them a spirit of stupor, eyes that they should not see, and ears that they should not hear, unto this very day.**

The language here is taken from *Is* 29:10 and *Deut* 29:4 and it is probably not improper to detect in it an echo of the thought of *Is* 6:9. 'The design of such citations frequently is to show that what was fulfilled partially in former times, was more perfectly accomplished at a subsequent period. The Jews had often before been hardened, but at no former period were the people so blinded, hardened, and reprobate, as when they rejected the Son of God, and put him to an open shame. It had often been predicted that such should be their state when the Messiah came. The punitive character of the evils here threatened, cannot escape the reader's notice. This blindness and hardness were not mere calamities, nor were they simply the natural effects of the sins of the people. They were punitive inflictions. They are so denounced. God says, I will give you eyes that see not. It is a dreadful thing to fall into the hands of the living God. The strokes of his justice blind, bewilder, and harden the soul.' (Hodge)

*V*9: **And David saith,**
   Let their table be made a snare, and a trap,
   And a stumblingblock, and a recompense unto
   them:
*V*10: **Let their eyes be darkened, that they may not see,**
   And bow thou down their back always.

These words are from *Psalm* 69:22, 23. J. A. Alexander comments, 'The imprecations in this verse and those following it are revolting only when considered as the expression of malignant selfishness. If uttered by God, they shock no reader's sensibilites, nor should they, when considered as the language of an ideal person, representing the whole class of righteous sufferers, and particularly Him who, though he prayed for his murderers while dying [*Luke* 23:34], had before applied the words of this very passage to the unbelieving Jews [*Matt* 23:38], as Paul did afterwards [*Rom* 11:9, 10]. The general doctrine of providential retribution, far from being confined to the Old Testament, is distinctly taught in many of our Saviour's parables. See *Matt* 21:41, 22:7, 24:51.' (*Commentary on Psalms*, p. 295)

*V*11: **I say then, Did they stumble that they might fall? God forbid: but by their fall salvation is come unto the Gentiles, to provoke them to jealousy.**
*V*12: **Now if their fall is the riches of the world, and their loss the riches of the Gentiles; how much more their fulness?**

This question introduces a new section in which the apostle shows that the fall of Israel *as a nation* is not final. The present preservation of an elect remnant is the earnest of their future

restoration. Meanwhile even their fall is not without its bene-
ficent consequences for the world at large. Paul argues that if
the 'stumbling' of Israel has brought salvation to the Gentiles,
then their 'fulness' must bring untold blessing to mankind
[v 15]. Moreover, the realization that the covenant favour of
God has been extended to the Gentiles is designed to provoke
Israel earnestly to seek after an interest in the same salvation.
'The Jews, even those who were professors of Christianity,
were, in the first place, very slow to allow the gospel to be
preached to the Gentiles; and in the second, they appear
almost uniformly to have desired to clog the gospel with the
ceremonial observances of the law. This was one of the
greatest hindrances to the progress of the cause of Christ
during the apostolic age, and would, in all human proba-
bility, have been a thousandfold greater, had the Jews, as a
nation, embraced the Christian faith. On both these accounts,
the rejection of the Jews was incidentally a means of facilitat-
ing the progress of the gospel. Besides this, the punishment
which befell them on account of their unbelief, involving the
destruction of their nation and power, of course prevented
their being able to forbid the general preaching of the gospel,
which they earnestly desired to do.' (Hodge) [*Acts* 13:46]

*V*13 : **But I speak to you that are Gentiles. Inasmuch then
as I am an apostle of Gentiles, I glorify my ministry;**
*V*14: **if by any means I may provoke to jealousy them
that are my flesh, and may save some of them.**

Paul does not regard his ministry to the Gentiles as a work
which is hostile to Jewish interests, but as one whose constant
tendency is to promote the spiritual good of his kinsmen. The
strength of his feeling for them may be gauged by the description given in *v* 14, 'them that are my flesh'. He hopes that
when they see the blessings brought to the Gentiles through
his labours 'some of them' will be saved. What is here implied
will be explicitly stated presently, namely, that the love and
compassion which their great apostle exercised towards the

unbelieving Jews is an example which should be followed by all Gentile believers. The shameful failure of the church to heed the plain teaching of Paul on this matter is without doubt one of the greatest blots upon its history. The address adopted in verse 13 gives the impression that the church in Rome was largely a Gentile community [cf 1:13].

V15: **For if the casting away of them is the reconciling of the world, what shall the receiving of them be, but life from the dead?**

The Gentiles need not fear that the future conversion of Israel will impoverish them. On the contrary, it will bring unimaginable blessing to the world. From the first God designed to bless mankind through the seed of Abraham [*Gen* 28:14]. Now if the fall of the Jews has resulted in the 'reconciling of the world' what shall their restoration be, 'but life from the dead?' David Brown comments: 'The meaning seems to be that the reception of the whole family of Israel, scattered as they are among all nations under heaven, and the most inveterate enemies of the Lord Jesus, will be such a stupendous manifestation of the power of God upon the spirits of men, and of his glorious presence with the heralds of the cross, as will not only kindle devout astonishment far and wide, but so change the dominant mode of thinking and feeling on all spiritual things as to seem like a *resurrection from the dead*.'

V16: **And if the firstfruit is holy, so is the lump: and if the root is holy, so are the branches.**

Israel's consecration to God is now illustrated by two metaphors. As the offering of the first part of the dough consecrated the whole lump, so the dedication of the root to God ensures the 'holiness' of the branches [*Num* 15:17-21]. Hodge is careful to point out that in this verse the word 'holy' does not mean 'morally pure', but is used to describe the special separation of the Jews from the rest of the world for the service of God. The application of both figures to the consecration of the patriarchs appears to be confirmed by verse 28. The final restoration of Israel is therefore guaranteed by the distinguishing love of God for Abraham, Isaac, and Jacob.

V17: **But if some of the branches were broken off, and thou, being a wild olive, wast grafted in among them, and didst become partaker with them of the root of the fatness of the olive tree;**

V18: **glory not over the branches: but if thou gloriest, it is not thou that bearest the root, but the root thee.**

Since the Gentiles have been made profitable only by a supernatural act of divine grace, they have no occasion to boast against those natural branches which have been broken off through unbelief. They have contributed nothing, and received everything. All their spiritual vitality is derived *from the root* of the cultivated olive tree, 'for salvation is of the Jews' [*John* 4:22]. As the purpose of all grafting is to impart new life and vigour *to the root*, it is plain that Paul is here pointing a spiritual analogy, which has no exact parallel in the natural realm [cf *v* 24: 'contrary to nature'].

V19: **Thou wilt say then, Branches were broken off, that I might be grafted in.**

Contempt for those who have fallen through unbelief, and a sense of pride in the present possession of gospel privileges are both reflected in this imaginary Gentile objection. To describe such an attitude is the best argument against its adoption. 'I' is given emphatic expression by the word *egō* which, as John Murray observes, underlines the 'egoism and vainglory of this boasting'.

V20: **Well; by their unbelief they were broken off, and thou standest by thy faith. Be not highminded, but fear:**

It should be noted that Paul does not represent fear as an emotion which is incompatible with the exercise of faith, for those who truly trust God also have learned wholly to distrust themselves. Self-confidence and confidence in God are polar opposites. On more than one occasion the apostle puts forward the fear of failure as a proper stimulant to Christian endeavour [1 Cor 2:3; Eph 6:5; Phil 2:12. Cf Heb 4:1; 1 Pet 1:17]. 'Seest thou thy brother shipwrecked! look well to thy tackling.' (Trapp) [1 Cor 10:12].

V21: **for if God spared not the natural branches, neither will he spare thee.**

Those who commit the same fault may expect to share the same fate. There is no respect of persons with God. If Israel's natural privileges afforded no protection against God's righteous judgment, then the Gentiles must know what surely awaits them if they do not continue in God's goodness [v 22].

V22: **Behold then the goodness and severity of God: toward them that fell, severity; but toward thee, God's goodness, if thou continue in his goodness: otherwise thou also shalt be cut off.**

This is an invitation to contemplate God in the character in which he has been pleased to reveal himself. It is the goodness of God which justifies his existence in the eyes of most men, for they are unwilling to admit that the Deity has any higher purpose than the advancement of their own good. On the other hand, the severity of God is a most distasteful concept to autonomous man, because it is at once a denial of man's independence and an unequivocal assertion of God's sovereignty. 'Men generally form in their imagination the character of God according to their own inclination. It is the duty of the Christian to take God's character as it is given by himself. His goodness is no evidence that he will not punish the guilty; and the most dreadful punishment of the guilty is consistent with the existence of supreme goodness in the divine character.' (Haldane)

The exhortations to persevere in the faith, which are found

[191]

throughout the New Testament, are not inconsistent with the promise of divine preservation unto life eternal. Rather it is by giving heed to such admonitions that Christians are brought to glory. 'God graciously causes a man to persevere in willing. That is the whole truth . . . the true doctrine is *not* that salvation is certain if we have once believed, but that *perseverance in holiness* is certain if we have truly believed.' (A. A. Hodge, *The Confession of Faith*, pp. 234–235) [*Acts* 13:43]

*V*23: **And they also, if they continue not in their unbelief, shall be grafted in: for God is able to graft them in again.**

This verse marks a smooth transition from warning to hope, for if unbelief separates, it is equally true that faith is the bond of union. Paul has said that if the Gentiles lose their faith, they shall be broken off. Conversely, if Israel does not remain unbelieving they shall be grafted in again. Since such an event is not likely to occur after the 'natural' order of events, it is here expressly attributed to the power of God. And it is a representation which is entirely consonant with the supernatural character of faith. Faith is not self-originated; it is the gift of God. It is his prerogative to remove the veil of unbelief from the heart, and to bestow the capacity to respond to the gospel.

*V*24: **For if thou wast cut out of that which is by nature a wild olive tree, and wast grafted contrary to nature into a good olive tree; how much more shall these, which are the natural branches, be grafted into their own olive tree?**

Now if such foreign branches have been so unexpectedly incorporated into the good olive tree, how much more likely is the restoration of the natural branches to what is after all their own olive tree? The emphasis rests upon the fitness of such a restoration. There is no derogation of the power which would be required to accomplish it.

contrary to nature 'Therefore nature contributes nothing toward the work of conversion.' (Trapp) [*Eph* 2:3]

V25: **For I would not, brethren, have you ignorant of this mystery, lest ye be wise in your own conceits, that a hardening in part hath befallen Israel, until the fulness of the Gentiles be come in;**

For I would not, brethren, have you ignorant of this mystery, Spiritual ignorance is dispelled only by divine revelation. This characteristic form of address is designed to secure the readers' close attention to the important statement which is to follow it [cf 1:13; 1 *Cor* 10:1, 12:1; 2 *Cor* 1:8; 1 *Thess* 4:13]. This is not a mystery 'in the pagan sense of an esoteric doctrine known only to the initiated, but in the Christian sense of a doctrine that requires a divine revelation in order to be known. Compare *Rom* 16:25; 1 *Cor* 2:7-10, 15:51; *Eph* 3:4, 5.' (Shedd)

lest ye be wise in your own conceits, 'Ignorance of the Scriptures is the cause of high-mindedness in Christians.' (Haldane)

that a hardening in part hath befallen Israel, until the fulness of the Gentiles be come in; This amounts to a divine disclosure of what could not have been naturally anticipated. There is to be a spiritual restoration of Israel as a nation, but this will not take place 'until the fulness of the Gentiles be come in'. The gathering into the kingdom of the majority of the *elect* Gentiles will mark the terminus of Israel's unbelief. This expectation is not inconsistent with Paul's prediction of the widespread apostasy which will occur in connection with the revelation of the Man of Sin, for as Geerhardus Vos is careful to point out, 'the coming in of the Gentiles does not preclude the falling away again from the

Gentiles of considerable groups'. (*The Pauline Eschatology*, p. 133) [cf 2 *Thess* 2:3]

Although the central thrust of the apostle is unmistakable, the manner of its accomplishment remains obscure, and no doubt this is intentional. As Hodge wisely observes, 'Prophecy is not proleptic history. It is not designed to give us the knowledge of the future which history gives us of the past. Great events are foretold; but the mode of their occurrence, their details, and their consequences, can only be learned by the event. It is in the retrospect that the foreshadowing of the future is seen to be miraculous and divine.'

*V*26: **and so all Israel shall be saved: even as it is written,**
There shall come out of Zion the Deliverer;
He shall turn away ungodliness from Jacob:
*V*27: **And this is my covenant unto them,**
When I shall take away their sins.

The context makes it certain that 'Israel' must refer to the nation of Israel, but the word 'all' gives no warrant for believing that every individual Jew is to be saved. It simply means the nation as an elect body. Paul quotes from *Is* 59:20 and *Jer* 31:33 to prove that he is propounding no novelty, but is only bringing to more explicit expression what has been long foretold in Scripture. It is in harmony with the miraculous nature of the event predicted that the accent in these prophecies 'falls upon what God will do.' (John Murray)

*V*28: **As touching the gospel, they are enemies for your sake: but as touching the election, they are beloved for the fathers' sake.**

With regard to the gospel the Jews are now enemies through their temporary unbelief, though this alienation has been the means of bringing the Gentiles into the sphere of blessing. However, this present enmity cannot impair their election of God, for the people of Israel 'are beloved for the fathers' sake'. God's attitude to the nation of Israel may not be gauged by their present rejection, but is to be viewed in the light of the promises made to the patriarchs. Thus Israel's exclusion is not final, and their eventual restoration is guaranteed.

V29: **For the gifts and the calling of God are not repented of.**

'These words, considered simply and abstractedly, afford this truth; that the special gifts of God, his election, justification, adoption, and in particular, effectual calling, are irrevocable. God never repents of giving, nor we of receiving them. It is otherwise with common gifts and graces, 1 *Sam* 15:11. But if you consider these words relatively, as you respect what went before, the sense seems to be this; that "the gifts and calling of God," whereby he was pleased to adopt the posterity of Abraham, and to engage himself by covenant to them, are inviolable, and are such as shall never be reversed or repented of.' (Poole)

V30: **For as ye in time past were disobedient to God, but now have obtained mercy by their disobedience,**
V31: **even so have these also now been disobedient, that by the mercy shown to you they also may now obtain mercy.**

As the disobedient Gentiles have obtained mercy through the disobedience of Israel, even so Israel shall find mercy through the Gentiles' experience of God's mercy. If God has brought good out of that which is in itself evil, what may he not bring out of that which is good?

V32: **For God hath shut up all unto disobedience, that he might have mercy upon all.**

Defenders of the doctrine of election are sometimes accused of dwelling too much upon the severities of chapter 9 without taking due account of the closing stages of Paul's argument. But Warfield has well said, 'We do not escape from the doctrine of predestination of the ninth chapter in fleeing to the eleventh.' And of this verse, he remarked: 'On the face of it there could not readily be framed a more explicit assertion of the divine control and the divine initiative than this; it is only another declaration that he has mercy on whom he will have mercy, and after the manner and in the order that he will.' (*Predestination*)

As there can be no exercise of mercy where there is no disobedience, God has shut up both Jew and Gentile in this common prison in order that his mercy might be bestowed upon both without distinction. 'The apostle is not here dealing with individuals, but with those great divisions of mankind, Jew and Gentile. And what he here says is, that God's purpose was to shut up each of these divisions of men to the experience, first, of an unhumbled, condemned state, without Christ, and then to the experience of his mercy in Christ.' (David Brown)

$V33$: O the depth of the riches both of the wisdom and the knowledge of God! how unsearchable are his judgments, and his ways past tracing out!

This survey of the divine purpose in history has evoked in Paul a profound feeling of awe and adoration. When finite understanding encounters Infinite Wisdom the only proper response is one of unqualified wonder and worship. John Murray makes the important point that this doxology was not prompted by what was unknowable in God, but by the incomprehensibility of that which God has revealed! It is a revelation which it is completely beyond our capacity to fathom, and therefore we must cry with the apostle, 'O the depth!' 'It is not the reaction of painful bewilderment but the response of adoring amazement, redolent of joy and praise. When our faith and understanding peer to the horizons of revelation, it is then our hearts and minds are overwhelmed with the incomprehensible mystery of God's works and ways.' (John Murray)

V34: **For who hath known the mind of the Lord? or who hath been his counsellor?**

V35: **or who hath first given to him, and it shall be recompensed unto him again?**

These quotations from the Old Testament are taken from *Isaiah* 40:13 and *Job* 41:11. 'As it is the tendency and result of all correct views of Christian doctrine to produce the feelings expressed by the apostle at the close of this chapter, those views cannot be scriptural which have a contrary tendency; or which lead us to ascribe, in any form, our salvation to our own merit or power.' (Hodge)

V36: **For of him, and through him, and unto him, are all things. To him be the glory for ever. Amen**

'Here we have the grand truth which lies at the foundation of all religion. All things are *of God*, for he is the Author of all; his will is the origin of all existence. All things are *through him*, for all things are created by him as the grand agent. All things are likewise *to him*, for all things tend to his glory as their final end.' (Haldane)

CHAPTER TWELVE

V1: **I beseech you therefore, brethren, by the mercies of God, to present your bodies a living sacrifice, holy, acceptable to God, which is your spiritual service.**

I beseech you therefore, brethren, by the mercies of God. This eloquent appeal proves that acceptable obedience is always the grateful response of redeemed hearts to the multiplied mercies of God. That Paul should choose to entreat rather than command underlines the voluntary nature of the response which a real experience of these compassions should constrain. Paul knows that if his readers have truly understood his exposition of the doctrines of grace, this knowledge will be clearly exhibited in a holy walk. Christian doctrine is never taught to provide a species of intellectual enlightenment but to promote practical obedience. For if theology is *grace*, then ethics is *gratitude* (F. F. Bruce).

to present your bodies, Christianity sanctions no unnatural dichotomy between the spirit and the body, and the realism of the apostle is very evident in this requirement. A sanctification which does not extend to the body is essentially spurious [1 *Thess* 5:23, 24]. The same body through which sin once found its concrete expression must now be presented to God as the vehicle of righteousness [6:19].

a living sacrifice, holy, acceptable to God, It is the great reality of Christ's sacrifice which 'has swept all dead victims

[198]

from off the altar of God.' (David Brown) Thus it is the body
as raised to new life in Christ which is to be presented to God
[6:13]. Such living sacrifices are holy and acceptable to God
solely through the efficacy of Christ's redemptive travail.
Believers find their acceptance with God through his beloved
Son in whom he is well pleased. 'The sacrifice of the mass not
being appointed by God, and actually subversive of the sacrifice of the cross, instead of being agreeable to God, must be
odious in his sight.' (Haldane)

which is your reasonable service. (AV) This dedication of
the body to the service of God is to be informed and directed
by the mind, for it is here described as 'your rational worship.'
The superiority of the new covenant is shown in the replace-
ment of the ritual offering of a dead body by the rational consecration of the living body. 'The lesson to be derived from
the term "rational" is that we are not "Spiritual" in the biblical
sense except as the use of our bodies is characterized by conscious, intelligent, consecrated devotion to the service of
God.' (John Murray)

*V*2: **And be not fashioned according to this world: but
be ye transformed by the renewing of your mind, that
ye may prove what is the good and acceptable and perfect will of God.**
' "Do not fall in," says the apostle, "with the fleeting fashions
of this world, nor be yourselves fashioned to them, but
undergo a deep abiding change by the renewing of your
mind, such as the Spirit of God alone can work in you" [cf
2 *Cor* 3:18].' (Trench) The inward transformation of the mind
is the only effective preservative against outward conformity
with the spirit of this present age.
    Since Christians properly belong to the 'high mountain-
land above' they must refuse to descend to the level of those
whose minds are blinded by the god of this world and

whose outlook is consequently circumscribed by that which is
temporal [2 *Cor* 4:4, 18].

**that ye may prove what is the will of God, even the
thing which is good and acceptable and perfect.** (ASV
margin) The purpose of this renewal of the mind is that
Christians may be able to test and approve in practice what is
the will of God. The three adjectives serve to show that God's
will defines the morally good, prescribes what is well pleasing
to him, and provides a standard which is ethically complete
[*Matt* 5:48]. 'No one discovers the line of action which from
possessing these characteristics can be identified as the will of
God unless he is transformed from his native affinity to the
world by the renewing of his mind by the Holy Spirit.'
(Denney)

*V*3: **For I say, through the grace that was given to me,
to every man that is among you, not to think of himself
more highly than he ought to think; but so to think as to
think soberly, according as God hath dealt to each man
a measure of faith.**

Paul begins this exhortation to humility by reminding his
readers that every gift, including that of apostleship, is the
bestowal of God's grace which therefore excludes all boasting.
Christians are neither to over-value nor to under-estimate their
talents but must seek to assess them realistically, 'according as
God hath dealt to each man a measure of faith.'

Paul's play on words is well brought out by David Brown:
'not to be high-minded above what he ought to be minded,
but so to be minded as to be sober-minded.' [*Phil* 2:3, 5]

*V*4: **For even as we have many members in one body,
and all the members have not the same office:**
*V*5: **so we, who are many, are one body in Christ, and
severally members one of another.**

This familiar Pauline figure perfectly conveys the idea of

diversity in unity; there are many members but only one body [1 *Cor* 10:17, 12:27]. It is necessary to recognize the true value of these spiritual endowments and the proper sphere in which they are to be exercised, for the gifts which are peculiar to each member only promote the well-being and harmony of the whole body when they are practised in a spirit of genuine humility. Those who do not hold to the Head can have no fellowship with the members; hence a desire for pre-eminence spells death to all spiritual usefulness [*Col* 2:19, 3 *John* 9]. Meekness is the mint-mark of all true followers of the Lamb.

*V*6: **And having gifts differing according to the grace that was given to us, whether prophecy, let us prophesy according to the proportion of our faith;**
*V*7: **or ministry, let us give ourselves to our ministry; or he that teacheth, to his teaching;**
*V*8: **or he that exhorteth, to his exhorting: he that giveth, let him do it with liberality; he that ruleth, with diligence; he that showeth mercy, with cheerfulness.**

No particular order is followed here, for this is not a list of offices, but a series of examples which show how various gifts are to be exercised within the body of Christ. 'It is quite obvious that the apostle is not distinguishing offices, but gifts. Every gift does not require a different office. Many of the gifts required no office at all.' (Haldane)

Paul's definite instruction to those with the gift of prophecy, 'to prophesy in agreement with the faith' (Arndt-Gingrich), indicates their subordination to apostolic authority [1 *Cor* 14:37]. They must not exceed their brief, nor fall short of its commission. This principle holds good whether 'prophecy' refers to those miraculous gifts which flourished in the Early Church or whether, as Calvin prefers, 'he is referring simply to ordinary gifts which remain perpetually in the Church.' In either case, no revelation or exposition is valid which departs from the infallible norm established by the apostolate. Every human utterance is subject to, and must be tested by the supreme authority of Scripture, which is the inspired record of 'the faith which was once for all delivered unto the saints' [*Jude* 3].

Ministry, teaching, and exhortation are to be faithfully practised by those who are thus gifted. 'Ministry' may refer either to the ministry of the word or to the office of a deacon. 'Teaching is addressed to the understanding; exhortation, to the conscience and feelings.' (Hodge) These must always go together, for if teaching gives exhortation its content, exhortation gives teaching its force. Giving is to be graced by liberality. Those who have freely received must freely give without ulterior design for gain, or ostentatious desire for fame. Those entrusted with responsibility in the government of the church are to be diligent, and not negligent, in the performance of their duties. Finally, the ministry of mercy is to be distinguished by a cheerful spirit. Kindly acts must be seen to stem from a loving concern for the sufferer, for 'if he observes gloominess on the face of those who help him, he will take it as an affront.' (Calvin)

*V*9: **Let love be without hypocrisy. Abhor that which is evil; cleave to that which is good.**
*V*10: **In love of the brethren be tenderly affectioned one to another; in honour preferring one another;**

From 'gifts' Paul now passes to 'love' [cf *vv* 3–8 with 1 *Cor* 12; *vv* 9–21 with 1 *Cor* 13]. Although Christians are bound to acknowledge the supremacy of love, they must not allow their profession of it to run ahead of their real feelings for others, for those who do are guilty of hypocrisy [2 *Cor* 6:6; 1 *Pet* 1:22]. A new concept of love needed a new word to describe it, and *agapē* 'is a word born within the bosom of revealed religion.' (Trench) 'Christian love, whether exercised toward the brethren, or toward men generally, is not an impulse from the feelings, it does not always run with the natural inclinations, nor does it spend itself only upon those for whom some affinity is discovered.' (Vine) and this is because Christian love is ever patterned upon an experience of the self-giving love of God, a love which has no regard for the worthiness of its objects [cf 5:8].

The Christian's attitude towards good and evil must be violently partisan. He cannot look upon evil with benevolent neutrality, nor can he regard it as something which is 'less good.' His rejection of it must be unqualified and total [*Ps* 119:104; *Amos* 5:15; *Jude* 23]. On the other hand, he must steadfastly 'cleave to that which is good.' This does not indicate a slight preference for the good, it means 'be glued to it.' The same word is used to signify the permanence of the marriage relation [*Matt* 19:5].

'In honour preferring one another' is the method recommended by Paul for the maintenance of a spirit of brotherly love (*v* 10). 'As there is nothing more opposed to brotherly concord than the contempt which arises from pride, while each esteems others less and exalts himself, so modesty, by which each comes to honour others, best nourishes love.' (Calvin) [*Phil* 2:3]

*V*11: **in diligence not slothful; fervent in spirit; serving the Lord;**

The progression of thought in this trio of exhortations is well noted by Lenski. First, Christians must be marked by a diligence in devotion that does not lag behind. This negative effectively enjoins the prompt performance of present duty. Secondly, this zeal is to be maintained by ensuring that their spiritual temperature remains on the boil [*Acts* 18:25]. 'A man's spirit must move him to diligence; when enough steam is generated in the boiler, the engine speeds over the rails.' (Lenski) Thirdly, this energy is to be expended in serving the Lord. 'Many are diligent enough, some have fanatical zeal; many glow and literally boil over in their spirit; but so much of the busy effort and the steam back of it is not at all work for the Lord.' (Lenski) 'Serving the Lord' really means working

[203]

as a slave in his service, taking orders only from him and obeying them implicitly.

*V*12: **rejoicing in hope; patient in tribulation; continuing stedfastly in prayer;**

The summons to be 'patient in tribulation' is significantly sandwiched between the call to rejoice in hope and to continue instant in prayer. The Christian does not sink under present trials, because he is buoyed up by the hope of future glory and the divine strength which is imparted to him through prayer. Those who are without God in the world are necessarily destitute of hope, for hope belongs only to those who know God [*Eph* 2:12]. Believers therefore ought to enjoy the assurance of their salvation and eagerly anticipate its consummation, but exhortation is required if they are to live up to the level of their spiritual privileges in Christ Jesus [*Heb* 6:11; 1 *Pet* 1:8]. 'The measure of perseverance in the midst of tribulation is the measure of our diligence in prayer. Prayer is the means ordained of God for the supply of grace sufficient for every exigency and particularly against the faint-heartedness to which affliction tempts us.' (John Murray)

*V*13: **communicationg to the necessities of the saints; given to hospitality.**

These are two ways in which the brotherly love enjoined in verses 9, 10 is to be given practical expression. The poverty and persecution which made these injunctions especially relevant in the Early Church also gave the opportunity for an impressive demonstration of the true meaning of Christian fellowship [*Heb* 13:2; 1 *John* 3:17].

*V*14: **Bless them that persecute you; bless, and curse not.**

This Pauline echo of the Lord's teaching was also faithfully reproduced in his own life, for those who bear Christ's image are partakers of his sufferings and must meet them in the same spirit [*Matt* 5:44; *Luke* 6:28, 23:34; *John* 15:20; 1 *Cor* 4:12, 13].

The inflexible determination of the natural man to persecute the righteous affords the most striking proof of his total depravity [*Gal* 4:29]. The young man Saul first learned the difference between the achievements of law-righteousness and the triumph of grace through Stephen's memorable obedience to this 'impossible' demand. It should be noted that the command freely to forgive the persecutor and to call down blessings upon his head does not involve the Christian in the obligation to approve actions which are morally wrong. Christians cannot approve the *character* of their persecutors, even though they are required to love their *persons*. Thus Stephen cried, 'Lord, lay not *this sin* to their charge' [*Acts* 7:60]. 'When Jesus Christ commands us to love our enemies, it is with the love of benevolence and compassion . . . This love of benevolence for the person of a bad man ought to be, in the Christian, the finite reflection of what it is in God, limited only by the higher attribute of righteousness.' (R. L. Dabney, *Discussions*, Vol. I, p. 717) This distinction by no means lessens the difficulty of such an obedience, but it does show that this obedience is not inconsistent with the demands of righteousness.

V15: **Rejoice with them that rejoice; weep with them that weep.**

As divided joy is doubled, so divided sorrow is halved (Lenski). It is because Christians are members of one body that they must share in the joys and sympathize with the sorrows of their fellow-members [1 *Cor* 12:26]. 'Respecting this injunction, Chrysostom remarks that it is easier to weep with those that weep, than to rejoice with those that rejoice; because nature itself prompts the former, but envy stands in the way of the latter.' (Shedd)

V16: **Be of the same mind one toward another. Set not your mind on high things, but condescend to things that are lowly. Be not wise in your own conceits.**

Differences in gifts and capacities among Christians offer no excuse for any differentiation within the Christian fellowship [*Phil* 2:2, 4:1]. Christians are here warned against the ambition and conceit which would turn these differences, which are ordained of God, into occasions of strife, envy, or vain-glory. The fellowship of believers is to be distinguished by that love which 'seeketh not its own' but rather seeks the good of others [1 *Cor* 13:5]. 'Be not wise in your own conceits' is taken from *Prov* 3:7. To state this danger is to exhibit its folly. 'Just as there is to be no social aristocracy in the Church, so there is to be no intellectual autocrat.' (John Murray)

*V*17: **Render to no man evil for evil. Take thought for things honourable in the sight of all men.**

'Public reparation is when the magistrate, according to the justice and mercy of the divine law, sentences an evil person who has injured his fellow. Private revenge is when those who are not magistrates take matters into their own hands and retaliate against those who have wronged them. The former is clearly permitted, for an apostle declared the magistrate is "the minister of God" for executing judgment upon evil-doers; the same apostle as expressly forbids retaliation: "Recompense to no man evil for evil." ' (Arthur Pink, *The Sermon on the Mount*, p. 116)

Take care to preserve an honourable testimony in the sight of all. (Bruce) This is a quotation of the Greek version of *Prov* 3:4. Christians are to avoid disgracing their profession by maintaining a standard of conduct which will commend itself to the consciences of their unbelieving neighbours. That the conscience of the natural man is sufficiently enlightened to acknowledge such a standard is also the condemnation of his own failure to conform to it [2 *Cor* 8:21; *Phil* 4:8; 1 *Pet* 3:16].

*V*18: **If it be possible, as much as in you lieth, be at peace with all men.**

This exhortation to live peaceably with all men is introduced by a double limitation. 'If it be possible' implies that it will not always be possible. When truth is the price of peace, then peace is bought at too dear a rate. 'We are never to seek to maintain peace, either with the world or with Christians, by the sacrifice of any part of divine truth. A Christian must be willing to be unpopular, that he may be useful and faithful. To whatever obloquy or opposition it may expose him, he ought earnestly to contend for the faith which was once delivered unto the saints.' (Haldane) However, as the second qualification indicates, a relish for discord is no part of Christian virtue and the Christian, so far as it depends on him, must make every effort to preserve and promote peace with his fellowmen [*Heb* 12:14].

*V*19: **Avenge not yourselves, beloved, but give place unto the wrath of God: for it is written, Vengeance belongeth unto me; I will recompense, saith the Lord.**

'Beloved' mirrors Paul's awareness of the difficulty of this requirement. Christians are not to avenge themselves, but are to leave room for the wrath of God. For it is his right to punish wrong-doers whom he has promised to repay in full measure [*Deut* 32:35]. 'The idea is not that instead of executing vengeance ourselves we are to abandon the offender to the more tremendous vengeance of God; but this – that God, not injured men or those who believe themselves such, is the maintainer of moral order in the world, and that the righting of wrong is to be committed to him.' (Denney)

*V*20: **But if thine enemy hunger, feed him; if he thirst, give him to drink: for in so doing thou shalt heap coals of fire upon his head.**
*V*21: **Be not overcome of evil, but overcome evil with good.**

But the Christian must not only refuse to avenge himself, he is also to repay enmity with every form of kindness. Verse

20 is a quotation of *Prov* 25:21, 22, which is to be taken in a good sense. As Derek Kidner remarks, 'The "coals of fire" represent the pangs which are far better felt now as shame than later as punishment.' Evil is not vanquished by retaliation, but it may be conquered by kindness. 'The true victory over evil consists in transforming a hostile relation into one of love by the magnanimity of the benefits bestowed. Thereby it is that good has the last word, that evil itself serves it as an instrument: such is the masterpiece of love.' (Godet)

CHAPTER THIRTEEN

*V*1: **Let every soul be in subjection to the higher powers: for there is no power but of God; and the powers that be are ordained of God.**

The first seven verses of this chapter define the Christian's duty to the state. Paul begins by showing that the state lawfully claims the obedience of 'every soul' because the power it wields is of God. There can be no exercise of power apart from God [*Is* 10:5–7, 45:1; *Dan* 5:26]. The admission of this truth establishes the important principle that the authority of the state is a delegated, and not an absolute authority. It is only the recognition of this principle which prevents the state from usurping supreme power over the souls of men. Thus when the demands of the state are in conflict with the law of God, the resistance to them becomes a positive duty for the Christian [1 *Kings* 21:3; *Dan* 3:18, 6:12; *Mark* 12:17; *Acts* 4:19, 5:29; *Heb* 11:23].

History has shown that when Theism comes to its rights, human liberty is assured, while the natural tendency of Atheism is ever towards totalitarianism. However, at the time this letter was written the systematic persecution of Christians by the state had not yet begun, and therefore this inference is not drawn by the apostle, but when Caesar later demanded the things which belonged to God Christians could not doubt that he had exceeded his just claims upon their obedience.

'Some have supposed that the right or legitimate authority of human government has its foundation ultimately in "the consent of the governed", "the will of the majority," or in some imaginary "social compact" entered into by the forefathers of the race at the origin of social life. It is self-evident, however, that the divine will is the source of all government; and the obligation to obey that will, resting upon all moral agents, the ultimate ground of all obligation to obey human governments.' (A. A. Hodge, *The Confession of Faith*, p. 293)

*V*2: **Therefore he that resisteth the power, withstandeth the ordinance of God: and they that withstand shall receive to themselves judgment.**

'When Paul insists that every soul should be subject to the powers that be, he is evidently removing from the individual judgment any question as to a *de jure* as opposed to a *de facto* government . . . The powers that be, i.e., the actually existing powers are ordained of God.' (Gordon Clark, *A Christian View of Men and Things*, p. 140) Therefore those who resist the civil government resist the ordinance of God and consequently incur the judgment of God, who will punish this disobedience. Yet this passage does not provide rulers with a *carte blanche* authority to exercise unlimited powers. These powers are limited by the nature of the authority which is committed to the civil magistrate. It was Paul's object to establish the simple principle 'that magistrates are to be obeyed. The extent of this obedience is to be determined from the nature of the case. They are to be obeyed as magistrates, in the exercise of their lawful authority. When Paul commands wives to obey their husbands, they are required to obey them as husbands, not as masters, nor as kings; children are to obey their parents as parents, not as sovereigns; and so in every other case.' (Hodge) Thus the crown rights of the Redeemer lie well beyond the sphere of the state's sovereignty.

*V*3: **For rulers are not a terror to the good work, but to**

[210]

the evil. And wouldest thou have no fear of the power? do that which is good, and thou shalt have praise from the same:

Unrestrained freedom results in anarchy, for then every man does that which is 'right in his own eyes' [*Judges* 21:25]. The state is ordained by God to meet the exigencies of the situation created by sin. The fabric of society is preserved from total corruption by the authority of the magistrate. 'It is with the *deed* that the magistrate is concerned. Paul speaks of the good and evil *work*. It is not the prerogative of the ruler to deal with all sin but only with sin registered in the action which violates the order that the magistrate is appointed to maintain and promote.' (John Murray) [1 *Pet* 3:13]

Charles Hodge draws the following conclusions from verses 3-7. 'The design of civil government is not to promote the advantages of the rulers, but of the ruled. They are ordained and invested with authority, to be a terror to evil doers, and a praise to them that do well. They are the ministers of God for this end, and are appointed for "this very thing". On this ground our obligation to obedience rests, and the obligation ceases when this design is systematically, constantly, and notoriously disregarded. Where unfaithfulness on the part of the government exists, or where the form of it is incompatible with the design of its institution, the governed must have a right to remedy the evil. But they cannot have the moral right to remedy one evil, by the production of a greater. And, therefore, as there are few greater evils than instability and uncertainty in governments, the cases in which revolutions are justifiable must be exceedingly rare.'

*V*4: **for he is a minister of God to thee for good. But if thou do that which is evil, be afraid; for he beareth not the sword in vain: for he is a minister of God, an avenger for wrath to him that doeth evil.**

Christians should regard the preservation of law and order as an incalculable good, for the impartial administration of justice protects and promotes the highest interests of religion.

But if . . . The state is described as 'the minister of God' because 'it is charged with a function which has been explicitly forbidden to the Christian [12:17a, 19].' (F. F. Bruce) It is to be 'an avenger for wrath to him that doeth evil,' and this infliction is regarded by Paul as an expression of the wrath of God.

In order effectively to discharge this duty the state is armed with the sword. In these degenerate days when the poison of humanism has directed sympathy to the criminal instead of the victim, it ought to be particularly noted that the apostle describes the restraints imposed by the law in terms of retributive vengeance. As John Murray says, 'Nothing shows the moral bankruptcy of a people or of a generation more than disregard for the sanctity of human life. And it is this same atrophy of moral fibre that appears in the plea for the abolition of the death penalty. It is the sanctity of life that validates the death penalty for the crime of murder.' (*Principles of Conduct*, p. 122) [*Gen* 9:6]

The state is also armed with the sword in order to defend its frontiers and the lives of its citizens against the aggressor. Gordon Clark aptly remarks, 'Christ said, "Render unto Caesar the things that are Caesar's." Of course, the immediate reference was taxes, but Christ knew that Caesar had an army. He did not refuse to pay taxes to Rome on the ground that some of the tribute would be used to support that army.' (*What do Presbyterians Believe?* p. 208) Pacifism receives no encouragement from the New Testament. It is true that harlots are commanded to go and 'sin no more,' but soldiers are not asked to resign from the army! [cf *Luke* 3:14]

*V*5: **Wherefore ye must needs be in subjection, not only because of the wrath, but also for conscience' sake.**

It is because the civil government is ordained by God that the

Christian must obey its demands as a matter of conscience, and not simply to escape threatened punishment. Hence when the supremacy of God is recognized, every subordinate relationship is transformed and the performance of every duty is ennobled [*Eph* 6:1–9; 1 *Pet* 2:13, 14].

*V*6: **For for this cause ye pay tribute also; for they are ministers of God's service, attending continually upon this very thing.**

This verse is to be understood as an explanatory statement rather than a command. Even if the rulers do not consciously fulfil the role assigned to them by God, they are nevertheless God's servants, and therefore Christians should not scruple to pay the taxes necessary to maintain the government God has appointed to office. 'This very thing' refers to the collection of these taxes by God's 'ministers', – *leitourgos*, a term which in the New Testament, is almost invariably used to describe religious service [15:16]. Furthermore, these lawful dues are collected to defray public expenditure and not to satisfy private greed, a point which is well taken by Calvin. 'It is right, however, that they should remember that all that they receive from the people is public property, and not a means of satisfying private lust and luxury. We see the uses for which Paul appoints the tributes which are paid, viz. that heads of state may be furnished with assistance for the defence of their subjects.'

*V*7: **Render to all their dues: tribute to whom tribute is due; custom to whom custom; fear to whom fear; honour to whom honour.**

This sums up what Paul has to say on the duty of Christians towards the state. They are to pay their rulers their lawful dues, in direct taxes and in the taxes levied on goods, also rendering to them the reverence and honour that is due to their office.

But as the *temporal* state is not the *eternal* kingdom, 'the duty of obedience to secular authorities is a temporary one, for the present period of "night" [v 12]; in that "day" which is "at hand" a new order of government will be introduced, when "the saints shall judge the world." [1 Cor 6:2] The state is to "wither away" (on this Paul and Karl Marx agree); "the city of God remaineth." ' (F. F. Bruce)

*V*8: **Owe no man anything, save to love one another: for he that loveth his neighbour hath fulfilled the law.**

Owe no man anything, The verbs which begin verses 7 and 8 are both in the imperative mood. The Christian is not only to render obedience to the state, but also faithfully to discharge his obligations to society. First and foremost, he must shun the stigma of unpaid debts, for transparent honesty is to characterize all his transactions with his fellow-men. The conscientious observance of this very practical axiom is the essential prelude to all effective witness-bearing [Ps 37:21].

save to love one another: The Christian's love for his neighbour is but the visible reflection of his love for God. It is his consistent obedience to the second great commandment which affords the most convincing proof of his unqualified commitment to the first [Mark 12:30, 31]. Although the unregenerate commonly interpret 'love' in terms of acquisitive desire, the recipients of free grace have learned a better definition, for they know that it is 'more blessed to give than to receive' [Acts 20:35]. While Christian love enriches every human relationship, the love which seeks its own leads only to impoverishment.

for he that loveth his neighbour hath fulfilled the law. The modern disjunction between law and love is quite foreign to Paul's thought, for Christian love is not exercised in a void but in accordance with revealed commandment. Law gives love its content; love gives law its fulfilment. 'We may speak, if we will, of the law of love. But, if so, what we must have in view is the commandment to love or the law

[214]

which love fulfils. We may not speak of the law of love if we meant that love is itself the law. Love cannot be equated with the law nor can law be defined in terms of love . . . Law prescribes the action, but love it is that constrains or impels to the action involved.' (John Murray, *Principles of Conduct*, pp. 22, 24)

*V*9: **For this, Thou shalt not commit adultery, Thou shalt not kill, Thou shalt not steal, Thou shalt not covet, and if there by any other commandment, it is summed upon in this word, namely, Thou shalt love thy neighbour as thyself.**

Paul now gives four examples from the second table of the law to illustrate the way in which this love is to be manifested. This appeal to the Decalogue exhibits the abiding validity of the moral law and proves that there is no abrogation of it under the new covenant. The negative form of these commandments is eloquent of the havoc which sin has wrought, and points to the absolute necessity of deliverance from its enslaving power. The whole of the second table is summed up in the command, 'Thou shalt love thy neighbour *as thyself'* [*Lev* 19:18]. Here legitimate self-love is made the searching standard by which love for others is to be measured [*Eph* 5:29]. But no such limitation is placed upon the love which the first commandment demands. 'The love of God is supreme and incomparable. We are never asked to love God as we love ourselves or our neighbour as we love God. To God our whole being in all relationships must be captive in love, devotion, and service. To conceive of such captivity to our own selves or to any creature would be the essence of ungodliness.' (John Murray) [*Mark* 12:30, 31]

*V*10: **Love worketh no ill to his neighbour: love therefore is the fulfilment of the law.**

Love worketh no ill to his neighbour: Nothing less than

positive love for others can prompt such an abstention from all ill-doing.

love therefore is the fulfilment of the law. 'If we may use the metaphor, love fills to the brim the cup which the law puts into our hands. Love is the first drop; it is the last drop; and it is all the drops in between. From start to finish it is love that fulfils the law. When love is all-pervasive and inclusive, then the fulfilment of the law is completed.' (John Murray, *Principles of Conduct*, p. 23)

*V*11: **And this, knowing the season, that already it is time for you to awake out of sleep: for now is salvation nearer to us than when we first believed.**

Knowing 'the season' (the critical nature of the time in which they are living: the period that precedes the end) must spur Christians to live as they ought! This consciousness of moving towards the final goal invests time with a special significance for believers, and provides them with a powerful stimulus to regulate their conduct in the light of that hope [cf *Heb* 10:24f].

Hence Paul says that it is already time for his readers in Rome to awake out of sleep; not as though they were completely asleep, but that they should shake off all sleepiness and face the present situation with the urgency it demands [cf 1 *Thess* 5:6–8]. For the consummation of our salvation is now nearer than when we first believed the gospel! He thus encourages the imminent expectation of Christ's return, while avoiding any specific reference to the *chronological* nearness of that event [*Acts* 1:7; 2 *Pet* 3:8].

*V*12: **The night is far spent, and the day is at hand: let us therefore cast off the works of darkness, and let us put on the armour of light.**

The knowledge that 'the day is at hand' is here presented as the grand incentive to Christian obedience. It is natural for those who are of the night to commit 'the works of darkness,' but those upon whom the Sun of righteousness has arisen must discard the former lusts of their ignorance and don 'the armour of light' [cf *Eph* 6:11–18; 1 *Thess* 5:8].

*V*13: **Let us walk becomingly, as in the day; not in revelling and drunkenness, not in chambering and wantonness, not in strife and jealousy.**

'The day' has not yet dawned [*v* 12], but because believers belong to it they are to behave as if it had. So though the night still surrounds them, they must shun the deeds which evil men love to practise under its cloak, and are to walk with as much decorum as men do in the full light of day. As then daylight and decency go together, all intemperance, impurity, and discord must be renounced.

*V*14: **But put ye on the Lord Jesus Christ, and make not provision for the flesh, to fulfil the lusts thereof.**

As Hodge says, 'All Christian duty is included in putting on the Lord Jesus; in being like him, having that similarity of temper and conduct which results from being intimately united to him by the Holy Spirit.' [*Gal* 3:27] This union forbids the indulgence of all sinful propensities. Salvation is *from* sin, and *to* holiness.

CHAPTER FOURTEEN

*V*1: **But him that is weak in faith receive ye, yet not for decision of scruples.**

Here for the first time in the epistle Paul turns to deal with a particular problem on which the Christians in Rome needed clear guidance. This was the relation between the 'weak' and the 'strong' in regard to their respective attitudes towards 'things indifferent'. That this was not a matter of indifference to the apostle is indicated by the length of his masterly discussion which extends to 15:13.

But him that is weak in faith i.e. 'not "him that is weak in the truth believed," but "him whose faith wants that firmness and breadth which would raise him above small scruples."' (David Brown) Agreement with the cardinal truths of the gospel is assumed, for without this there is no basis for Christian fellowship at all. It is evident that the 'weakness' envisaged here was not associated with any departure from the faith, and this accounts for the irenical tone adopted by the apostle, whereas the motive which prompted the ascetic observances which are so unsparingly condemned in the Galatian and Colossian epistles was a subversion of the gospel itself.

receive ye, Those who have a clearer conception of Christian liberty are to welcome without reserve those who have not yet been emancipated from conscientious scruples concerning food and the observance of special days. John Murray points out that the 'weak' brother is described as a total abstainer from certain kinds of food, and that there is therefore no case for applying Paul's teaching in this place to the intemperate. The 'weakness' of those who go to excess 'is inquity and with those who are guilty of this sin Paul deals in entirely different terms. Drunkards, for example, will not inherit the kingdom of God [1 *Cor* 6:10] and Paul enjoins that if any one called a brother is a drunkard with such an one believers are not to keep company or even eat [1 *Cor* 5:11]. How different is *Romans* 14:1: "Him that is weak in faith receive ye." ' (John Murray, 'The Weak Brother,' Appendix E, *Commentary*, Vol. II, p. 260)

yet not for decision of scruples. The 'weak' brother was not to be received for the deciding of doubts or scruples, i.e. 'not for the purpose of arguing him out of them, which indeed usually does the reverse; whereas to receive him to full brotherly confidence and cordial interchange of Christian affection is the most effectual way of drawing them off.' (David Brown)

*V*2: One man hath faith to eat all things: but he that is weak eateth herbs.

Perhaps it is the fear of eating meat which has been previously dedicated to idols which prompts the 'weak' believer to restrict himself to a vegetarian diet, but the Christian who is fully instructed realizes that all food laws have been abolished under the gospel. There is no virtue or value in going without meat on Fridays, and it is certainly not sinful to drink tea and coffee!

*V*3: Let not him that eateth set at nought him that eateth not; and let not him that eateth not judge him that eateth: for God hath received him.

Paul warns both the 'strong' and the 'weak' against giving

[219]

way to the particular temptation to which each was especially prone, in order to prevent their difference from providing sin with an opportunity to introduce a division within the Christian fellowship. The 'strong' must not despise the 'weak' for refusing to eat, and the 'weak' must not judge the 'strong' for using his liberty in eating.

for God hath received him. That God is specifically stated to have received 'him that eateth' must be taken to imply the divine approval of his action, and thus marks the impropriety of his condemnation by him who is 'weak'. 'Though the weak are accepted with God through the righteousness of Christ, this weakness is not acceptable to him. It is an error, and cannot be pleasing to God. And accordingly the strong, and not the weak, are here said to be accepted.' (Haldane)

*V*4: **Who art thou that judgest the servant of another? to his own lord he standeth or falleth. Yea, he shall be made to stand; for the Lord hath power to make him stand.**

This reproof is directed to the 'weak' who condemned the 'strong' for their liberty in eating all things. By assuming the right to judge another's servant they exceeded their prerogative and were therefore to blame. Such judgments are irrelevant and impertinent, because it is obvious that the opinions of others can neither impair nor improve the standing of a servant before his own master [1 *Cor* 4:3ff].

Yea, he shall be made to stand . . . This makes it clear that even the 'strong' do not stand in their own strength. The power to stand is imparted to every believer by Christ himself, apart from whom all would inevitably and irrevocably fall. It is the Lord Christ who grants persevering strength, and who also maintains the present standing of his servants despite the unjust censures of those who are completely unqualified to judge them.

[220]

*V*5: **One man esteemeth one day above another: another esteemeth every day alike. Let each man be fully assured in his own mind.**

It is evident that this verse has no bearing on the weekly observance of the Lord's day since this was not regarded in the Early Church as a matter of human opinion, but of divine obligation. The meaning is rather that those who were 'weak' would still think that they ought to observe the feast days of the old economy, while the 'strong' would realize that all such distinctions now belonged to the past. 'Let each man be assured in his own mind' shows that an enforced conformity has no place in the fulfilment of the Christian ethic which demands the unfettered freedom of the individual conscience before God.

*V*6: **He that regardeth the day, regardeth it unto the Lord: and he that eateth, eateth unto the Lord, for he giveth God thanks; and he that eateth not, unto the Lord he eateth not, and giveth God thanks.**

'The true criterion of Christian character is found in the governing purpose of the life. He that lives unto the Lord, i.e., he who makes the will of Christ the rule of his conduct, and the glory of Christ his constant object, is a true Christian, although from weakness or ignorance he may sometimes mistake the rule of duty, and consider certain things obligatory which Christ has never commanded.' (Hodge)

*V*7: **For none of us liveth to himself, and none dieth to himself.**
*V*8: **For whether we live, we live unto the Lord; or whether we die, we die unto the Lord: whether we live therefore, or die, we are the Lord's.**

What Paul is saying in verse 7 is made clear in verse 8. His thought is not that our actions affect others, but that whatever we do is done in relation to the Lord. Since our whole life and even our death gathers its meaning from our union with him, how can we think of making an exception in regard to such non-essentials as the food one eats or does not eat? Paul refuses to indulge in moral casuistry. He does not make a definite ruling which would satisfy legalists. Instead he lifts the whole discussion to the highest level, so that each may determine these matters in the light of this fundamental relationship. He brings in our death in order to put these small questions into their proper perspective. 'When they are placed in the light of our end, so many things shrivel into the trivialities they really are.' (Lenski)

V9: For to this end Christ died and lived again, that he might be Lord of both the dead and the living.

Paul's previous statement, 'we are the Lord's,' is now explained. Believers belong to Christ because they have been bought with a price [1 Cor 6:20]. Christ died and rose again in order to secure the lordship which he exercises over his people. It is a lordship which therefore belongs to the sphere of redemptive accomplishment. As the triumphant Mediator he has been invested with absolute sovereignty over both the dead and the living. Since all believers live in virtue of the resurrection-life of Christ, it also follows that the death of the body cannot dissolve this vital union with their Redeemer, for 'it would be absurd to suppose that he reigns over them as mere insensible matter.' (Haldane) [Matt 22:32] Poole says, 'As God, he hath a universal dominion over all; but as Mediator, he hath a more special dominion over all the Father gave to him: this dominion he purchased at his death, and he had the full exercise of it when he rose again, Matt 28:18; Phil 2:9, 10.'

V10: But thou, why dost thou judge thy brother? or thou again, why dost thou set at nought thy brother? for we shall all stand before the judgment-seat of God.

These questions, addressed respectively to the 'weak' and the 'strong,' are vibrant with rebuke. The repetition of the word 'brother' not only indicates the equality of their standing but is also a timely reminder that their relationship should be distinguished by that mutual love which delights to cover a multitude of faults. Paul here prefers to speak of 'the judgment-seat of God' in order to prepare for the quotation of *Is* 45:23 in the following verse, and the inference to be drawn from it in *v* 12 ('to God'). But 2 *Cor* 5:10 shows that 'the judgment-seat of God' is also 'the judgment-seat of Christ,' which means that all believers shall be judged by God in Christ [cf 2:16; *Acts* 17:31]. Therefore instead of anticipating that solemn assize by their presumptuous mutual criticism, the 'weak' and the 'strong' should rather take the present opportunity to correct their conduct towards one another before it is too late to make amends.

*V*11: **For it is written,**
    As I live, saith the Lord, to me every knee shall bow,
    And every tongue shall confess to God.

'The passage, as it stands in the prophet, has no immediate reference to any "day of judgment," but is a prediction of the ultimate subjugation to the true God (in Christ) of every soul of man; but this of course implies that they shall bow to the award of God upon their character and actions.' (David Brown) [*Is* 45:23 which is again quoted by Paul in *Phil* 2:10, 11]

*V*12: **So then each one of us shall give account of himself to God.**

'As, therefore, God is the supreme judge, and we are to render our account to him, we should await his decision, and not presume to act the part of judge over our brethren.' (Hodge)

*V*13: **Let us not therefore judge one another any more: but judge ye this rather, that no man put a stumbling block in his brother's way, or an occasion of falling.**

The following verses make it evident that the 'strong' are now addressed. Paul insists that the greater liberty of conscience which they enjoy must be limited by the superior demands of love, for freedom which is exercised without regard to the scruples of those who are 'weak' places a stumbling block in their path. The conduct of the 'strong' is not to provide the 'weak' brother with 'an occasion of falling.' Cain's indignant disclaimer, 'Am I my brother's keeper?' thus demands an affirmative response from those who own a stronger bond than natural brotherhood. There is a play on the word 'judge' in this verse, which Hodge renders as, 'Do not *judge* one another, but *determine* to avoid giving offence.'

V14: **I know, and am persuaded in the Lord Jesus, that nothing is unclean of itself: save that to him who accounteth anything to be unclean, to him it is unclean.**

The first part of the verse is concessive. The 'strong' are right in their belief that moral evil cannot reside in things [*Tit* 1:15]. The typical service rendered by the ceremonial law was no longer required when the Antitype himself appeared. Christ fittingly abolished its restrictions by showing that the true source of all defilement was found within man, and therefore nothing from without could make him unclean [*Mark* 7:1–23]. It is not to be supposed, however, that Paul has gleaned this knowledge with difficulty through hearing the teaching of Jesus at second-hand, for the familiar formula, '*in* the Lord Jesus,' points to an unshakeable conviction which is enjoyed in virtue of his vital union with Christ. But all men are not in possession of the great liberating truth, and the man who believes 'anything to be unclean, to him it is unclean' [1 *Cor* 8:4, 7]. 'Persons in ignorance ought to be instructed, but they ought never to be encouraged to do what they themselves judge to be contrary to the will of God.' (Haldane)

V15: **For if because of meat thy brother is grieved, thou**

walkest no longer in love. Destroy not with thy meat him for whom Christ died.

Christ's dying love for the 'weak' brother is here strongly contrasted with that loveless abuse of liberty which would tempt him to sin against his conscience. This arresting language is not intended to suggest that any man could actually rob Christ of the fruit of his passion, but it is designed to remind strong believers of their very real responsibility towards their weaker brethren [1 *Cor* 8:11]. David Brown remarks, 'The word "meat" is purposely selected as something contemptible, in contrast with the tremendous risk run for its sake . . . Whatever tends to make any one violate his conscience tends to the destruction of his soul; and he who helps, whether wittingly or no, to bring about the one is guilty of aiding to accomplish the other.'

*V*16: **Let not then your good be evil spoken of:**

'Do not so use your liberty, which is good and valuable, as to make it the occasion of evil, and so liable to censure.' (Hodge) In practice Christian liberty is limited by the higher claims of Christian love, for love teaches us that this freedom must never be exercised to the spiritual detriment of another [*vv* 20 21; 1 *Cor* 10:23, 24].

*V*17: **for the kingdom of God is not eating and drinking, but righteousness and peace and joy in the Holy Spirit.**

In the interests of their weaker brethren the 'strong' may indeed abstain from certain foods without loss, because the kingdom of God does not consist in carnal things like meat and drink, but in the enjoyment of those blessings of which the Holy Spirit is the author. Righteousness, peace, and joy are therefore to be regarded as the subjective experience of the objective salvation which was fully expounded in the doctrinal section of the epistle. In other words, they must first be received as blessings from above before they can be manifested as virtues among men. 'That the religious import ought to be put in the forefront is shown by *joy in the Holy Spirit* which is a grace, not a virtue. In comparison with these great spiritual blessings, what Christian could trouble the Church about eating and drinking? For their sake, no self-denial is too great.' (Denney)

V18: For he that herein serveth Christ is well-pleasing to God, and approved of men.

He who in this way serves Christ (i.e. by putting first things first: spiritual blessings before food and drink), is well-pleasing to God and approved by the consciences of his fellow-men. For Christians must always conduct themselves in a manner which should constrain the admiration of the unbelieving, and so deprive them of any occasion for just criticism. Paul's habit of passing almost imperceptibly from God to Christ, and vice versa, is all the more striking because it provides an incidental disclosure of his attitude towards Christ. The Deity of the Saviour was the fundamental axiom of Paul's thought, and the very heart of his religious experience.

V19: So then let us follow after things which make for peace, and things whereby we may edify one another.

This exhortation to the 'strong' is based upon the whole of the preceding argument [*vv* 19-22]. Those who are members of the body of Christ must constantly seek to promote peace within that body, and play their full part in the mutual edification of their fellow-members [1 *Cor* 10:23].

V20: Overthrow not for meat's sake the work of God. All things indeed are clean; howbeit it is evil for that man who eateth with offence.

The lack of any connective makes this command all the more impressive [cf *v* 15b]. Let not the 'strong' find themselves

[226]

pulling down God's work just for the sake of meat! 'The apostle sees in whatever tends to violate a brother's conscience the *incipient* destruction of God's work (for every converted man is such) – on the same principle as "he that hateth his brother is a murderer" [1 *John* 3:15].' (David Brown)

Paul again acknowledges that all food is clean [*v* 14], but he points out that not all eating is without offence. 'The strong are to consider these two facts: eating despite giving dangerous offence – refraining from eating to avoid offence. A strong Christian will have little difficulty in making a choice between the two. Who would want to place a stumbling block into the path of anyone?' (Lenski)

*V*21: It is good not to eat flesh, nor to drink wine, nor to do anything whereby they brother stumbleth.

In a useful note on Christian liberty Steele and Thomas write: 'It must be emphasized that by its very nature *Christian liberty is limited to things not sinful in themselves*. There is danger of confusion at this point, for Paul, in Romans 14:21, uses wine as an *example* of the type of thing which should be given up IF its use offends others. The danger of confusion lies in the fact that many Christians today think that drinking wine is a sin in itself. Some think that the Bible forbids its use even in moderation; others mistakenly identify drinking wine with drunkenness and thus wrongly conclude that because the latter is a sin so is the former. But inasmuch as Paul uses wine as an example of the kind of thing that a Christian is *free to use, unless it offends others*, it is evident that its use is not itself a violation of God's law and therefore is not a sin. Note carefully that Romans 14:21 *does not read*: "it is right not to eat meat or *get drunk* or do anything that makes your brother stumble." The reason is evident; *getting drunk is a sin* whether it offends a brother or not, whereas *drinking wine is not wrong unless* it results in drunkenness or causes others to stumble. "So, whether you eat or drink, or whatever you do, do all to the glory of God. Give no offence to Jews or to Greeks or to the church of God" [1 *Cor* 10:31, 32].' (*Romans – An Interpretive Outline*, pp. 117-118)

*V*22: **The faith which thou hast, have thou to thyself before God. Happy is he that judgeth not himself in that which he approveth.**

Paul first insists that the 'strong' are not to indulge in the unloving exercise of their liberty to the spiritual detriment of others. So though the conviction they rightly hold may not be waived to confirm the wrong ideas of the 'weak', they are forbidden to flourish it in a way which causes their brethren to stumble.

In the second part of the verse Paul lays down the principle by which Christians are to be guided in 'things indifferent.' In all cases where believers are without a plain commandment to follow, they are to obey the dictates of their own conscience. This principle is first stated positively for the 'strong' [*v* 22b], and then negatively for the 'weak' [*v* 23a]. Thus the 'faith' of the 'strong' is to be 'a firm and intelligent conviction before God that one is doing what is right, the antithesis of feeling self-condemned in what one permits oneself to do.' (F. F. Bruce)

*V*23: **But he that doubteth is condemned if he eat, because he eateth not of faith; and whatsoever is not of faith is sin.**

On the other hand, the 'weak' believer who emulates the liberty of the 'strong' without sharing their convictions, stands condemned not only by his own conscience but also by God. Therefore the 'strong' must not tempt the 'weak' to violate their consciences by expecting them to act as if they also had no scruples about eating.

Hence Paul concludes that 'whatsoever is not of faith is sin.' This means that 'whatsoever is not done with a conviction that it is agreeable to the will of God, is sinful in the doer,

although it should be right in itself. This is the generalization of the preceding doctrine. It applies not merely to meats, but to everything. If any person be convinced that a thing is contrary to God's law, and yet practises it, he is guilty before God, although it should be found that the thing was lawful.'
(Haldane)

CHAPTER FIFTEEN

*V*1: Now we that are strong ought to bear the infirmities of the weak, and not to please ourselves.

*V*2: Let each one of us please his neighbour for that which is good, unto edifying.

In this chapter the same subject of Christian forbearance is continued. Paul identifies himself with the 'strong' and says we are under an obligation to use our strength in bearing the infirmities of the 'weak'. For even a lawful liberty is not to be enjoyed at the expense of a weak brother. Wilful *self-pleasing* must not be allowed to masquerade under the disguise of Christian principle. Nor as verse 2 indicates, is such self-pleasing to be sacrificed in the interests of *men-pleasing*, which would be inconsistent with fidelity to Christ [*Gal* 1:10; *Eph* 6:6]. The aim is the spiritual advantage of the neighbour, his building up in the faith.

*V*3: For Christ also pleased not himself; but, as it is written, The reproaches of them that reproached thee fell upon me.

In this verse Paul reminds his readers that those who bear Christ's name must also follow Christ's example. The assertion that Christ did not please himself is corroborated by an appeal to *Ps* 69:9, which shows that Christ attracted the reproaches of men by his unswerving fidelity to the Father's will. 'Men, even the most wicked, approve of morality and acts of kindness to the human race. They hate Christ and Christians only because of their holding forth the character of God, which they dislike.' (Haldane) This reflection upon the cost of Christ's obedience affords an astonishing contrast with the slight sacrifice the 'strong' are here exhorted to make in the interests of the 'weak.' 'This Psalm is so frequently quoted and applied to Christ in the New Testament, that it must be considered as directly prophetical. Compare *John* 2:17, 15:25, 19:28; *Acts* 1:20.' (Hodge)

V4: For whatsoever things were written aforetime were written for our learning, that through patience and through comfort of the scriptures we might have hope.

The important principle now adduced explains the apostle's frequent appeals to the Old Testament in confirmation of his doctrine. It is the preservation of the Word of God in permanent form which constitutes proof of its abiding purpose and therefore of its contemporary relevance. Since nothing which God has revealed and recorded is superfluous, no part of that testimony can be neglected without spiritual loss [1 *Cor* 10:6, 10; 2 *Tim* 3:16, 17]. The instruction imparted by the scriptures not only sustains believers under their present trials but also informs and inspires their hope for the future [8:23–25].

V5: Now the God of patience and of comfort grant you to be of the same mind one with another according to Christ Jesus:
V6: that with one accord ye may with one mouth glorify the God and Father of our Lord Jesus Christ.

This beautiful prayer sums up what Paul desires for both the 'strong' and the 'weak'. He first directs them to God as the author of that patience and comfort which is ministered to their hearts through his Word of truth [*v* 4; cf *John* 17:7].

grant you to be of the same mind one with another

according to Christ Jesus: His request is that they may be given that unity of mind and purpose which is according to the divine norm established for them by Christ Jesus, their exalted Redeemer and covenant Head. This serves to remind us that unanimity on the horizontal level can be secured only as each believer realizes the implications of his vertical relationship with Christ. Fellowship depends upon what Christ Jesus has done for his people and what he is for them as the consequence of that work. Fellowship is therefore that corporate experience which results from an individual participation in him who 'is made unto us wisdom, and righteousness, and sanctification, and redemption.' [1 Cor 1:30].

that with one accord As Heidland observes, 'with one accord' is a term which is used in the New Testament to emphasize the inner unanimity of the community. For though there were many personal and material tensions in the first congregations, these tensions were continually transcended as the church addressed itself to the glorifying of the one Lord. Hence constant worship is the key to continuing unanimity. [Acts 2:46]. (TDNT, Vol. V, p. 186)

ye may with one mouth glorify the God and Father of our Lord Jesus Christ. Where there is such oneness of mind there is also this oneness of mouth. Unity of belief leads to unity in praise; the order is significant because the latter can never be attained without the former! In the gospel God is glorified by the worship that acknowledges him in the character in which he has been pleased to reveal himself to us, i.e. as 'the God and Father of our Lord Jesus Christ.' This majestic designation is in fact a compressed confession of faith [cf 2 Cor 1:3, 11:3; Eph 1:3; 1 Pet 1:3]. For to say this is to express our belief in the reality of the Incarnation (God is 'the God' of Christ *as man*); the eternal Deity of the Son (God is 'the Father' of Christ *as God*); and the efficacy of his redeeming work ('*our* Lord Jesus Christ').

*V*7: **Wherefore receive ye one another, even as Christ also received you, to the glory of God.**

This verse serves a dual function. It concludes the apostle's discussion of the problem of the 'strong' and the 'weak' [14:1–15:6], and it prepares the way for his wider application of the same principle to relations between Jewish and Gentile believers [*vv* 8–13]. When Christ has received all believers without distinction, then clearly they must not allow unimportant differences to cause divisions within the Church. Therefore we must receive one another, even as Christ received us to the glory of God's faithfulness and mercy [*vv* 8, 9]. As God is glorified by Christ's reception of us, so he is to be glorified by that mutual fellowship which transcends all individual and accidental diversities. For what does not matter to Christ should not matter to us!

*V*8: **For I say that Christ hath been made a minister of the circumcision for the truth of God, that he might confirm the promises given unto the fathers,**

Paul now proceeds to explain how the mixed congregation of Jews and Gentiles in Rome glorifies God. For God's veracity is vindicated in the conversion of Jews, and his mercy is magnified in the salvation of Gentiles [*v* 9]. For the sake of God's truth Christ has become a minister of the circumcision in order to fulfil the promises which God gave to the patriarchs. Moreover, it is Christ who continues to exercise this ministry in the present proclamation of the apostolic gospel throughout the world, and Paul sees a convincing proof of God's faithfulness in the many Jews who have already hailed Christ as the Messiah who suffered and triumphed for them.

*V*9: **and that the Gentiles might glorify God for his mercy; as it is written,**
> **Therefore will I give praise unto thee among the Gentiles,**
> **And sing unto thy name.**

Paul now proves that the inclusion of the Gentiles within the scope of God's mercy was no afterthought, by introducing a chain of testimonies from the Old Testament [*vv* 9-12]. The first of these is from *Ps* 18:49 in which David resolves to celebrate his victories over the Gentiles by confessing the Name of God in their midst. He thus saw his military conquest of the surrounding nations as an opportunity to dispel their heathen darkness by bringing them into a knowledge of the one true and living God.

*V*10: **And again he saith,**
    Rejoice, ye Gentiles, with his people.

The second quotation is from *Deut* 32:43 according to the LXX or Septuagint (Greek version of OT). The invitation it extends to the Gentiles to share in Israel's rejoicing in what Jehovah has done for them is really an inducement to join them in the sharing of these covenant blessings.

*V*11: **And again,**
    Praise the Lord, all ye Gentiles;
    And let all the people praise him.

Although the third testimony is taken from the shortest Psalm [*Ps* 117:1], the importance of a message may not be measured by its length! And this missionary summons to all Gentiles to praise the Lord manifests an astonishing insight into Israel's *role* as 'the mediator of saving truth' to the other nations on the face of the earth (H. C. Leupold). It is Messianic in the sense that it is prophetic of the spread of the gospel throughout the world [cf *John* 4:22].

*V*12: **And again, Isaiah saith,**
    There shall be the root of Jesse,
    And he that ariseth to rule over the Gentiles;
    On him shall the Gentiles hope.

The climax is reached in this quotation of Isaiah's prediction of Christ's lordship over the Gentiles [*Is* 11:10 LXX]. It is indeed astounding that a descendant of Jesse, David's father, a mere shoot of a defunct Jewish royal line should be elevated to this position of precedence so that the Gentiles would come to hope in him (Lenski). Even as Paul wrote these words he was conscious of their fulfilment in the multitudes throughout the empire who were flocking to Christ as he was lifted up before them in the preaching of the gospel.

*V*13: **Now the God of hope fill you with all joy and peace in believing, that ye may abound in hope, in the power of the Holy Spirit.**

Paul concludes his teaching on Christian forbearance, and the main body of the epistle, with a brief prayer for his readers in Rome. He commends them to God who, as the author of this gospel hope [*v* 12], is able to fill them with all joy and peace in believing, so that they abound in hope by the power of the Holy Spirit. And we are thereby taught that this objective hope is ours in subjective possession solely through the agency and power of the Holy Spirit.

*V*14: **And I myself also am persuaded of you, my brethren, that ye yourselves are full of goodness, filled with all knowledge, able also to admonish one another.**
*V*15: **But I write the more boldly unto you in some measure, as putting you again in remembrance, because of the grace that was given me of God,**

Before concluding the letter Paul wishes to make it clear that he has not written to the church at Rome because he thought that the believers there were either lacking in their Christian experience or deficient in their knowledge of divine truth. He tactfully points out that the design of his letter is not to introduce them to any new doctrine, but rather to remind them of the truth which they already possessed. The warmth of his address has not been inspired by any desire for self-aggrandizement, but stems from the grace of apostleship which had been given to him by God. It is therefore as the apostle to the Gentiles that he claims the right to minister to this predominantly Gentile congregation [v 16].

V16: that I should be a minister of Christ Jesus unto the Gentiles, ministering the gospel of God, that the offering up of the Gentiles might be made acceptable, being sanctified by the Holy Spirit.

to be a minister of Christ Jesus to the Gentiles in the priestly service of the gospel of God, so that the offering of the Gentiles may be acceptable, (RSV) 'There is in the Christian Church no real priesthood, and none but figurative sacrifices. Had it been otherwise, it is inconceivable that the 16th verse of this chapter should have been expressed as it is. Paul's only priesthood and sacrificial offerings lay, first, in ministering to them, as "the apostle of the Gentiles," not the sacrament, with the "Real Presence" of Christ in it, or the sacrifice of the mass, but "the Gospel of God," and then, when gathered under the wing of Christ, presenting them to God as a grateful offering, "being sanctified (not by sacrificial gifts, but) by the Holy Spirit".' (David Brown) [cf *Heb* 13:9-16]

being sanctified by the Holy Spirit. 'There were some, no doubt, who maintained that Paul's Gentile converts were "unclean", because they were not circumcised. To such cavillers Paul's reply is that his converts were "clean," because they were sanctified by the Holy Spirit who had come to dwell within them [cf *v* 19, "by the power of the Spirit of God"].' (F. F. Bruce)

V17: I have therefore my glorying in Christ Jesus in things pertaining to God.
V18: For I will not dare to speak of any things save those which Christ wrought through me, for the obedience of the Gentiles, by word and deed,

Having received such a divine commission Paul does not hesitate to glory in it, but this glorying is limited to those things which Christ has wrought through him [1 *Cor* 1:31; 2 *Cor* 10:17]. There is no need for him to claim the credit for another's work. He has abundant cause for rejoicing in the fruit of his own labours for Christ. The aim of Paul's ministry was to make the Gentiles obedient 'by word and deed,' for he well knew that the absence of such a grateful response meant that there had been no true experience of gospel grace. In opposing *legalism* the apostle made no concessions to *lawlessness*. He did not preach a cheap and easy 'believism,' because Christ will not admit to being the Saviour of those who refuse to follow him as Lord [2 *Thess* 1:8].

*V*19: **in the power of signs and wonders, in the power of the Holy Spirit; so that from Jerusalem, and round about even unto Illyricum, I have fully preached the gospel of Christ;**

It was by the remarkable assistance of the Spirit of God that Paul had fulfilled his apostolic commission within the boundaries mentioned in this verse [1 *Cor* 2:4]. Hodge points out that the expression 'fully preached' means 'to bring the gospel (i.e. the preaching of it) to an end, to accomplish it thoroughly; see *Col* 1:25. In this wide circuit had the apostle preached, founding churches, and advancing the Redeemer's kingdom with such evidence of the divine co-operation, as to leave no ground of doubt that he was a divinely appointed minister of Christ.'

*V*20: **yea, making it my aim so to preach the gospel, not where Christ was already named, that I might not build upon another man's foundation;**

The function of the apostolate was to establish churches in those areas where Christ was unknown, and Paul's missionary strategy was based upon this principle. The apostle therefore refused to build upon another man's foundation, because he had limited himself to this pioneer work in accordance with the distinctive commission he had received [1 *Cor* 3:10].

*V*21: but, as it is written,
They shall see, to whom no tidings of him came,
And they who have not heard shall understand.

Paul sees this preaching of the gospel in places where Christ's name was not known as a fulfilment of *Is* 52:15, which promises the Suffering Servant a world-wide dominion as the necessary sequel to his humiliation. So it happens that Gentiles now see what they had not before been told about the Messiah, and they who had not previously heard now understand in true faith.

*V*22: Wherefore also I was hindered these many times from coming to you:
*V*23: but now, having no more any place in these regions, and having these many years a longing to come unto you,
*V*24: whensoever I go unto Spain (for I hope to see you in my journey, and to be brought on my way thitherward by you, if first in some measure I shall have been satisfied with your company) –

The pressure of Paul's missionary work had so far prevented his eagerly anticipated visit to the church at Rome, but now that he had concluded his ministry around Illyricum, he is planning a journey to Spain. On his way there he hopes to have the opportunity to enjoy a season of fellowship and refreshment with the Christians in Rome. These verses make it evident that Paul would not permit his personal desire to visit Rome to interrupt his missionary programme. We do not know if Paul ever reached Spain, but when he came to Rome it was under very different circumstances from those contemplated when these words were written.

*V*25: but now, I say, I go unto Jerusalem, ministering unto the saints.

*V*26: **For it hath been the good pleasure of Macedonia and Achaia to make a certain contribution for the poor among the saints that are at Jerusalem.**

But before Paul can set sail for Spain he has one last service to accomplish. It is to deliver the contribution which the Gentile Christians have made for the relief of the hard-pressed community of Jewish believers in Jerusalem. Paul's insistence upon accompanying the Gentile delegates to Jerusalem shows how much importance he attached to this mission, for as F. F. Bruce explains, he regarded it as an act of worship which was to mark the climax of his Aegean ministry in 'the outward and visible sign of that "offering up of the Gentiles" which crowned his priestly service as apostle of Jesus Christ.'

*V*27: **Yea, it hath been their good pleasure; and their debtors they are. For if the Gentiles have been made partakers of their spiritual things, they owe it to them also to minister unto them in carnal things.**

Since the Gentiles owed their spiritual enrichment to the Jews, it was only natural that they should seek to repay this moral debt by ministering to the material necessities of their Jewish brethren in Christ. Nevertheless their contribution was quite voluntary. 'Charity is an obligation but it is not a tax.' (John Murray)

*V*28: **When therefore I have accomplished this, and have sealed to them this fruit, I will go on by you unto Spain.**

As soon as Paul has completed this mission of mercy he intends to fulfil his promise to visit the Roman Christians *en route* to Spain. 'And have sealed to them this fruit' indicates why he thought it necessary to deliver in person the gift which was the fruit of his ministry among the Gentiles. He clearly regarded this collection as the visible authentication of his mission to the Gentiles, and hoped that this fruit of the Spirit

[239]

would convince the Jewish believers in Jerusalem of the common bond which united them with their Gentile brethren in Christ [*Eph* 1:13].

*V*29: **And I know that, when I come unto you, I shall come in the fulness of the blessing of Christ.**

Paul's confidence that he would come to them 'in the fulness of the blessing of Christ' was amply justified by the event, even though he was to come to Rome as a prisoner. Christ brought him there in the most wonderful way 'in order to witness in Rome as he had witnessed in Jerusalem, which meant among *Jews* in Rome, and at once upon his arrival He opened the door to *the Roman Jews* for him [*Acts* 28:17-31].' (Lenski)

*V*30: **Now I beseech you, brethren, by our Lord Jesus Christ, and by the love of the Spirit, that ye strive together with me in your prayers to God for me;**

In conclusion Paul beseeches his brethren in Rome to strive together in prayer for him, as those who are doubly motivated by 'our Lord Jesus Christ' and by the love wrought in their hearts by 'the Spirit'. 'What Paul asks is that they should join him in striving with all their might – in wrestling as it were – against the hostile forces which would frustrate his apostolic work.' (Denney)

*V*31: **that I may be delivered from them that are disobedient in Judaea, and that my ministration which I have for Jerusalem may be acceptable to the saints;**
*V*32: **that I may come unto you in joy through the will of God, and together with you find rest.**
*V*33: **Now the God of peace be with you all. Amen.**

Paul asks them to pray that he might be delivered from the unbelieving Jews who hated him for seeking to convert them to the faith he had once persecuted, and that the collection might be acceptable to the believing Jews who might scorn a

CHAPTER 15, VERSES 31-33

gift from the Gentiles because of slanderous reports about the way in which he was receiving them into the church [cf *Acts* 21:17]. In verse 32 he looks hopefully beyond the hazards of his present undertaking to the joy of his meeting with the Christians in Rome. John Murray notes that 'the will of God' is here 'his decretive will realized through providence . . . It was not part of God's revealed will to Paul that he would go to Rome. Hence the reserve of submissiveness to what God determined his providence for Paul would prove to be.' The apostle concludes with the brief but comprehensive prayer that the God of peace would be with all his people in Rome.

CHAPTER SIXTEEN

**V1: I commend unto you Phoebe our sister, who is a
servant of the church that is at Cenchreae:**
**V2: that ye receive her in the Lord, worthily of the
saints, and that ye assist her in whatsoever matter she
may have need of you: for she herself also hath been a
helper of many, and of mine own self.**

Paul closes his letter by greeting all the believers in Rome. He
sends his personal greetings to the friends he had met elsewhere in the course of his labours, and he salutes the leaders
of the five groups in whose 'houses' the church met together
for worship [vv 5, 10, 11, 14, 15].

The most likely explanation of the apostle's commendation
of Phoebe is that she was the bearer of this letter. The Christians in Rome are asked to 'receive her in the Lord' and to help
her in whatever way they can, for she has been of great assistance to many, including Paul himself. From this it would
appear that Phoebe, like Lydia, was a woman whose wealth
and position enabled her to render such service to others.
Although the question cannot be decided with certainty, the
fact that she is introduced as 'a servant' *of the church* at Cenchreae lends support to the view that she served it in the
official capacity of 'deaconess' (ASV margin).

**V3: Salute Prisca and Aquila my fellow-workers in
Christ Jesus,**

V4: **who for my life laid down their own necks; unto whom not only I give thanks, but also all the churches of the Gentiles:**

Paul first greets his former hosts at Corinth, Prisca and Aquila, now living in Rome, and thankfully recalls an otherwise unrecorded occasion when they risked their lives on his behalf, an act of courage which has also earned the gratitude of all the Gentile churches, for 'his preservation redounded to the benefit of them all.' (Poole) [*Acts* 18:1–3]

V5: **and salute the church that is in their house. Salute Epaenetus my beloved, who is the firstfruits of Asia unto Christ.**

In the early days of Christianity there were no church buildings and so believers gathered for worship with a family whose house was suitable for this purpose. Usually there would be several such house-churches in a city, as there were also in Rome. Aquila and Priscilla were a couple whose house was always at the disposal of the Lord, whether they lived in Corinth or Rome [cf 1 *Cor* 16:19]. As Epaenetus was the first convert to Christ in the Roman province of Asia it was natural that Paul would feel a special bond of affection for him. The discovery of an Ephesian with this name on a Roman inscription is very interesting. (Denney)

V6: **Salute Mary, who bestowed much labour on you.**

Of the others Paul greets here nothing further is known, but perhaps Mary was one of the founder members of the church in Rome. It is possible that the apostle had learned of her outstanding service through Aquila and Priscilla. Denney notes that 'for you' is much better supported than 'for us' (AV), and says 'there is something finer in Paul's appreciation of services rendered to others than if they had been rendered to himself.'

V7: **Salute Andronicus and Junias, my kinsmen, and my**

fellow-prisoners, who are of note among the apostles, who also have been in Christ before me.

Andronicus and Junias are, like Paul, of Jewish descent, and evidently they were once his fellow-prisoners for the sake of the gospel. Apparently they are missionary-preachers of note in the church (using 'apostles' in its wider meaning as in *Acts* 14:14), and were believers before Paul who seems to envy them this priority in the faith. And truly if to be 'in Christ' is the 'most enviable human condition, the earlier the date of this blessed transition the greater the grace of it.' (David Brown)

*V*8: **Salute Ampliatus my beloved in the Lord.**

Ampliatus was a name common among Roman slaves. An inscription found on a tomb in the cemetery of Domitilla makes it probable 'that a person of this name was conspicuous in the earliest Roman church, and may have been the means of introducing Christianity to a great Roman house.' (Denney) This man is beloved of Paul as a brother 'in the Lord'.

*V*9: **Salute Urbanus our fellow-worker in Christ, and Stachys my beloved.**

Urbanus is also a slave name which means city-bred. The fact that Paul greets him as 'our' rather than as 'my' [*v* 3] 'fellow-worker' may suggest that all Christian workers had a common helper in him. (Denney) Stachys is a Greek name which means an 'ear of corn.'

*V*10: **Salute Apelles the approved in Christ. Salute them which are of the household of Aristobulus.**

'Approved' means that the faith of Apelles had been proved genuine by some conspicuous trial [*James* 1:12]. Paul salutes the Christian slaves [1 *Cor* 1:26–31] who belong to the household of Aristobulus, whom Lightfoot identified as the grandson of Herod the Great. It is probable that he had died before this letter was written, in which case his household, though continuing to bear his name, would have been transferred to the Imperial palace.

V11: Salute Herodion my kinsman. Salute them of the household of Narcissus, that are in the Lord.

'My kinsman' shows that Herodion was a Jew. His name suggests that he was a slave in the household of Aristobulus (v 10). Paul also here greets the Christian slaves who belonged to the household of Narcissus. This man was probably the influential freedman of Claudius. He committed suicide shortly before this letter was written. On his death his slaves would become the Emperor's property while continuing to bear the designation, 'those of Narcissus.' Lightfoot suggests that these were among the saints 'of Caesar's household' whom Paul mentions in *Phil* 4:22.

V12: Salute Tryphaena and Tryphosa, who labour in the Lord. Salute Persis the beloved, who laboured much in the Lord.

These women may have been twin sisters, but it is certain that they did not live up to their names. They were not too 'Dainty' or 'Delicate' to work for the Lord! Another woman, Persis the beloved, is here honoured for the hard work she has done for the Lord.

V13: Salute Rufus the chosen in the Lord, and his mother and mine.

As Mark probably wrote his gospel in Rome, it is almost certain that this Rufus was the son of Simon of Cyrene, who bore the cross for Jesus [*Mark* 15:21]. 'The chosen in the Lord' does not refer to his election, for that is true of every Christian; it means that he is a distinguished Christian (cf Denney: 'that choice Christian'). Paul also greets his mother as 'his mother *and mine*,' a tender touch that gratefully recalls an occasion when she had performed the part of a mother to him.

V14: Salute Asyncritus, Phlegon, Hermes, Patrobas, Hermas, and the brethren that are with them.

Although nothing is known of these five men, their names suggest that they were slaves, and it is likely that they were the members of a Christian fellowship within some nobleman's household.

V15: Salute Philologus and Julia, Nereus and his sister, and Olympas, and all the saints that are with them.

Philologus and Julia are evidently husband and wife, and it seems that a large group of believers met for worship in their home. Presumably Nereus and his sister (for whom A. F. Walls suggests the name Nereis) and Olympas (or Olympiodorus) were prominent members of that house-church. Thus Paul sends greetings to twenty-six Christians in Rome, of whom eight are women, and only five or six are Jews (Aquila and Prisca, Andronicus, Junias, Herodion, and possibly Mary).

V16: Salute one another with a holy kiss. All the churches of Christ salute you.

As Hodge remarks, 'It does not follow, because a custom prevailed in the early churches, and received the sanction of the apostles, that we are obliged to follow it. These customs often arose out of local circumstances and previous habits, or were merely conventional modes of expressing certain feelings, and were never intended to be made universally obligatory. As it was common in the East, (and is so, to a great extent, at present, not only here, but on the continent of Europe), to express affection and confidence by "the kiss of peace," Paul exhorts the Roman Christians to salute one another with a holy kiss; i.e. to manifest their Christian love to each other, according to the mode to which they were accustomed. The exercise and manifestation of the feeling, but not the mode of its expression, are obligatory on us. This is but one example; there are many other things connected with the manner of conducting public worship, and with the administration of baptism and the Lord's Supper, common in the apostolic churches, which have gone out of use. Christianity is a living principle, and was never intended to be confined to one unvarying set of forms.' As they salute one another in this way, Paul wishes them to know that all the churches with which he is associated join with him in sending a united greeting to their brethren in Rome.

*V*17: **Now I beseech you, brethren, mark them that are causing the divisions and occasions of stumbling, contrary to the doctrine which ye learned: and turn away from them.**

As Lenski points out, this admonition is an integral part of the whole letter. It is entirely natural that after having expounded the unified doctrine at length and extended these uniting salutations [*vv* 3–16], Paul should now warn them against giving heed to any contrary doctrine which would break their unity in the faith. 'Mark them' does not imply that false teachers are already at work in Rome [cf *v* 19]; it means 'look out for them,' be on your guard against those who cause divisions and occasions of stumbling by introducing their own ideas. The true doctrine is *one*; the divisions of error are *many*! Believers are to turn away from such men; they are to avoid them as they would the plague. This apostolic injunction is in striking contrast with the advice of certain present-day church leaders who urge us to have fellowship with them! To identify exactly those whom Paul had in mind is not so important [but see *Phil* 3:1ff]; what *is* vital is that we should avoid those who are fracturing the true unity of the church in their quest for a false unity.

*V*18: **For they that are such serve not our Lord Christ, but their own belly; and by their smooth and fair speech they beguile the hearts of the innocent.**

Here such false teachers are shown up for what they really are in order that innocent Christians may not be deceived by their flattering and deceitful speeches. For they do not serve our Lord Christ but their own belly [cf *Phil* 3:19]. It would seem that the allusion is to the Judaizers whose insistence upon the Gentile observance of Jewish food laws is unsparingly condemned as a service of the belly. And indeed all who peddle the corruptible doctrines of men [*Col* 2:22] in preference to the incorruptible gospel of God are mere belly-worshippers! Therefore let no Christian be deceived by their fair speeches which disguise the poison of deadly error [cf *Gen* 3:1-6; 2 *Cor* 11:3; *Eph* 4:14].

*V*19: **For your obedience is come abroad unto all men. I rejoice therefore over you: but I would have you wise unto that which is good, and simple unto that which is evil.**

In giving them this exhortation Paul is not suggesting that they have already succumbed to false doctrine; 'for *your* obedience is come abroad unto all men [1:8]. Over *you* therefore I rejoice.' The Roman church was free of doctrinal error and needed guidance only in connection with 'things indifferent' [*ch* 14]. Nevertheless, Paul would have them to be wise towards the good, which in this context must mean the doctrine they had learned [*v* 17], and 'simple' or 'unmixed' towards the evil teaching which is contrary to the truth [cf *Matt* 10:16]. 'That is what Paul "wants", and we know how he laboured for this. Today many frankly do *not* want this. Error does not stink in their nostrils; to them it has a holy smell. Although they offend and insult the true church they embrace open errorists, they are not as Paul says "unmixed", unadulterated with regard to the bad, but "mixed," adulterated, and often, sad to say, proud of the fact.' (Lenski)

*V*20: **And the God of peace shall bruise Satan under your feet shortly.**
   The grace of our Lord Jesus Christ be with you.

'We are to be wise and unmixed, but we depend upon God for the victory.' Hence they must look to the Author and Preserver of peace to maintain their peaceful unity in the doctrine they had learned [*v* 17]. For behind the work of errorists who cause divisions and death-traps stands Satan the father of lies [*Gen* 3:5], whom God will swiftly crush under their feet [*Gen* 3:15]. Paul here reveals the source of all falsehood so that no believer may be deceived as Satan's dupes go about their deadly work of destroying the souls of men. For the day will soon come when all who make and all who love lies shall be cast with Satan into the lake of fire for ever [*Rev* 20:10, 15, 21:8, 22:15]. Every Christian should therefore pray: 'Help me, O God, that I may never even unconsciously lend even my little finger to Satan for this work of spreading error!' (Lenski) The benediction fittingly concludes this important paragraph.

*V*21: **Timothy my fellow-worker saluteth you; and Lucius and Jason and Sosipater, my kinsmen.**

*V*22: **I Tertius, who write the epistle, salute you in the Lord.**

*V*23: **Gaius my host, and of the whole church, saluteth you. Erastus the treasurer of the city saluteth you, and Quartus the brother.**[1]

Paul's friends at Corinth now send their greetings to the Christians at Rome. Timothy heads the list, and is followed by the names of three Jewish believers. It is impossible to identify Lucius, but it is possible that the other two are mentioned in Acts, Jason in 17:5 and Sosipater in 20:4. Tertius who acted as the apostle's amanuensis was evidently also a Christian. Paul had himself baptized Gaius [1 *Cor* 1:14], who is noted for his hospitality, and he is probably to be identified with Titius Justus of *Acts* 18:7. It is significant that Paul should choose to associate the greeting of an otherwise unknown

1. Following the best texts the American Standard Version omits the repeated benediction of verse 24.

Christian, Quartus, with that of the distinguished treasurer of the city of Corinth, Erastus. The apostle knew nothing of a Christianity which recognized class distinctions! [Gal 3:28]

V25: **Now to him that is able to establish you according to my gospel and the preaching of Jesus Christ, according to the revelation of the mystery which hath been kept in silence through times eternal,**
V26: **but now is manifested, and by the scriptures of the prophets, according to the commandment of the eternal God, is made known unto all the nations unto obedience of faith;**
V27: **to the only wise God, through Jesus Christ, to whom be the glory for ever. Amen.**

Paul concludes his greatest epistle with a magnificent doxology which summarizes its leading themes [*vv* 25-27]. He commends the Christians in Rome to God who is able to establish them [1:11] in his gospel [2:16], that preached message whose subject is Jesus Christ [1:3, 4], which is the unveiling of the mystery kept secret for long ages but now disclosed [11:25; *Eph* 3:3ff; *Col* 1:26f].

The revelation of this age-old secret is made to the nations through 'the scriptures of the prophets.' Until Christ came their message had been confined to Israel, but Christ's fulfilment of the Old Testament hope made their words meaningful to the whole world [cf 1 *Pet* 1:10-12]. And this great change came about in accord with the command of the eternal God in the pursuance of his eternal purpose, namely, that the gospel should be proclaimed to all the nations to bring them to the obedience of faith [1:5].

The One who devised this great plan of salvation is 'the only wise God,' and it is in virtue of having this character that he is able to establish the Romans according to Paul's gospel. (Denney) It is therefore to him, through the mediation of Jesus Christ, that all glory is to be ascribed for ever. Amen.

Soli Deo Gloria

BIBLIOGRAPHY AND ACKNOWLEDGEMENTS

The author expresses his grateful thanks to the following authors and publishers who have kindly given permission to reproduce quotations from their copyright works.

Bruce, F. F., *Commentary on Romans* (Tyndale, 1963)

Bruce, F. F., *An Expanded Paraphrase on the Epistles of Paul* (Paternoster, 1965)

Calvin, John, *Commentary on Romans* (Oliver & Boyd, 1961) (translated by Ross Mackenzie)

Clark, Gordon, *Religion, Reason and Revelation* (Presbyterian & Reformed, 1961)

Kittel, Gerhard, and Friedrich, Gerhard, *Theological Dictionary of the New Testament* (translated by Geoffrey W. Bromiley) Vols. 1–9 (Eerdmans, 1964–1974)

Kuyper, Abraham, *The Revelation of St John* (Eerdmans, 1964)

Lenski, R. C. H., *The Interpretation of St Paul's Epistle to the Romans* (Augsburg, 1961)

Morris, Leon, *The Apostolic Preaching of the Cross* (Tyndale, 1965)

Murray, John, *The Epistle to the Romans* (Eerdmans, 1960, 1965) (NIC)

Murray, John, *Principles of Conduct* (Tyndale, 1957)

Murray, John, *The Imputation of Adam's Sin* (Eerdmans, 1959)

Steele, D. N. and Thomas, C. C., *Romans – An Interpretive Outline* (Presbyterian & Reformed, 1963)

Vine, W. E., *Expository Dictionary of New Testament Words* (Oliphants, 1958)

BIBLIOGRAPHY

Vos, Geerhardus, *The Pauline Eschatology* (Eerdmans, 1961)

Vos, J. G., *Surrender to Evolution: Inevitable or Inexcusable?* (Geneva Tracts)

In addition to these, the following books were consulted:

Alexander, Joseph Addison, *Commentary on the Psalms* (Zondervan, n.d.)

Alford, Henry, *The Greek Testament* (Rivingtons, 1859)

Arndt, W. F. and Gingrich, F. W., *A Greek–English Lexicon of the New Testament* (University of Chicago Press, 1957)

Barrett, C. K., *A Commentary on the Epistle to the Romans* (A & C Black, 1957)

Boettner, Loraine, *Roman Catholicism* (Banner of Truth 1966)

Brown, David, *Romans* (JFB) (Collins, 1874)

Bunyan, John, *The Holy War* (many editions)

Calvin, John, *The Institutes of the Christian Religion* (translated by Henry Beveridge) (James Clarke, 1957)

Clark, Gordon, *A Christian View of Men and Things* (Eerdmans, 1952)

Clark, Gordon, *What do Presbyterians Believe?* (Presbyterian & Reformed, 1965)

Cranfield, C. E. B., *Romans Vol. I, I–VIII* (New ICC) (T & T Clark, 1975)

Cullmann, Oscar, *The Christology of the New Testament* (SCM, 1963)

Dabney, R. L., *Discussions: Evangelical and Theological* (Banner of Truth, 1967)

Davidson, F. and Martin, Ralph P., *Commentary on Romans* (NBC) (Inter-Varsity Press, 1970)

Denney, James, *Commentary on St. Paul's Epistle to the Romans* (EGT) (Hodder & Stoughton, 1912)

Douglas, J. D. (Editor), *The New Bible Dictionary* (IVF, 1962)

Dunn, James D. G., *Jesus and the Spirit* (SCM, 1975)

Godet, F., *Commentary on St Paul's Epistle to the Romans* (T & T Clark, 1881)

Grier, W. J., *The Momentous Event* (Banner of Truth, 1970)

Haldane, Robert, *Commentary on Romans* (Banner of Truth, 1958)

Henry, Matthew, *Commentary on the Holy Bible* (various editions)

Hodge, A. A., *The Confession of Faith* (Banner of Truth, 1958)

Hodge, Charles, *Commentary on Romans* (Banner of Truth, 1972)

Kidner, Derek, *The Proverbs* (Tyndale, 1964)

Leupold, H. C., *Exposition of the Psalms* (Baker, 1961)

Lightfoot, J. B., *Notes on the Epistles of St Paul* (Zondervan, 1957)

Lloyd-Jones, D. M., *Romans: Atonement and Justification* (Banner of Truth, 1970)

Lloyd-Jones, D. M., *Romans: Assurance* (Banner of Truth, 1971)

Lloyd-Jones, D. M., *Romans: The New Man* (Banner of Truth, 1972)

Lloyd-Jones, D. M., *Romans: The Law: Its Functions and Limits* (Banner of Truth, 1973)

Lloyd-Jones, D. M., *Romans: The Sons of God* (Banner of Truth, 1974)

Lloyd-Jones, D. M., *Romans: Perseverance of the Saints* (Banner of Truth, 1975)

Machen, J. G., *The Origin of Paul's Religion* (Eerdmans, 1965)

Machen, J. G., *The Virgin Birth* (Presbyterian & Reformed, 1965)

Moore, T. V., *Commentary on Zechariah* (Banner of Truth, 1958)

Murray, John, *The Covenant of Grace* (Tyndale, 1956)

Murray, John, *Redemption Accomplished and Applied* (Banner of Truth, 1961)

Nygren, Anders, *Commentary on Romans* (Fortress Press, 1972)

Owen, John, *Works, Vol. 6* (Banner of Truth, 1966)

Philip, James, *The Epistle to the Romans* (Didasko Press, n.d.)

Pink, Arthur W., *Gleanings in Paul* (Moody Press, 1967)

Pink, Arthur, W., *The Sermon on the Mount* (Baker, 1959)

Pink, Arthur, W., *The Sovereignty of God* (Baker, 1965)

Poole, Matthew, *Commentary on the Holy Bible Vol. 3* (Banner of Truth, 1963)

Sanday, W. and Headlam, A. C., *A Critical and Exegetical Commentary on the Epistle to the Romans* (ICC) (T & T Clark, 1881)

Shedd, W. G. T., *A Critical and Doctrinal Commentary upon the Epistle of St Paul to the Romans* (Scribners, 1879)

Smeaton, George, *The Apostles' Doctrine of the Atonement* (Zondervan, 1957)

Thornwell, James Henley, *The Collected Writings, Vol. II* (Banner of Truth, 1974)

BIBLIOGRAPHY

Trapp, John, *Commentary on the New Testament* (Sovereign Grace Book Club, 1958)

Trench, R. C., *Synonyms of the New Testament* (James Clark, 1961)

Van Til, Cornelius, *The Defence of the Faith* (Presbyterian & Reformed, 1955)

Vos, Geerhardus, *Biblical Theology* (Banner of Truth, 1975)

Warfield, B. B., *Biblical and Theological Studies* (Presbyterian & Reformed, 1952)

Warfield, B. B., *The Inspiration and Authority of the Bible* (Marshall, Morgan & Scott, 1959)

Warfield, B. B., *Faith and Life* (Banner of Truth, 1974)

Whyte, Alexander, *A Commentary on the Shorter Catechism* (T & T Clark, 1961)